ATLA Monograph Series
edited by Dr. Kenneth E. Rowe

PERFECTIONIST PERSUASION:

The Holiness Movement and American Methodism, 1867-1936

by
CHARLES EDWIN JONES

ATLA Monograph Series, No. 5

The Scarecrow Press, Inc.
Metuchen, N. J.   1974

Library of Congress Cataloging in Publication Data

Jones, Charles Edwin, 1932-
     Perfectionist persuasion: the holiness movement and
American Methodism, 1867-1936.

     (ATLA monograph series, no. 5)
     Bibliography: p.
     1. Holiness churches--United States.   I.   Title.
II.   Series: American Theological Library Association.
ATLA monograph series no. 5.
BX7990. H6J66   287'. 6   74-13766
ISBN 0-8108-0747-5

to

MY PARENTS

EDITOR'S FOREWORD

Although most American and Canadian doctoral dissertations in religion are available to scholars on microfilm or expensive xerographic copies, their distribution and scholarly use are limited. A number of studies are submitted each year which deserve a better fate than to remain in the drawers of library microfilm cabinets.

The American Theological Library Association has undertaken responsibility for a modest dissertation publishing program in the field of religious studies. Our aim in this monograph series is to publish, in serviceable format and at reasonable cost, at least two dissertations of quality in the field of religious studies each year. Titles are selected by the Committee on Publications from titles nominated by graduate school deans or directors of graduate studies in religion.

We are pleased to publish Charles Jones' social profile of the national holiness movement within American Methodism, 1867-1936, as number five in our series. Charles Edwin Jones holds the Ph. D. degree from the University of Wisconsin. He has served in library and archival positions at Park College, Parkville, Missouri, the Nazarene Theological Seminary, Kansas City, Missouri, and the University of Michigan. Dr. Jones currently serves as cataloger for history at Brown University Library, Providence, Rhode Island.

Our special thanks go to Professor William G. McLoughlin of Brown University for preparing the fine introduction.

Kenneth E. Rowe, Editor

Drew University Library
Madison, New Jersey

v

TABLE OF CONTENTS

APPENDICES

LIST OF TABLES

LIST OF FIGURES

PREFACE

Most social commentary is in one way or another
biographical. The present work is no exception. Born into
a holiness home in Kansas City and graduated from a holiness college in Oklahoma, I have been fascinated with religious institutions and theology as long as I can remember.
Not until I was well along in adulthood, however, did I come
to recognize the relationship which sometimes exists between
religion and geographical movement.

Before that time I had always felt that my family's
religion placed us outside the mainstream of American life.
We were, I thought, part of a minority religious movement
of little historical or sociological significance. It came as
a shock, therefore, when I learned that the 1920's were the
high point of the long movement of country people to the
cities and that my parents, who had moved to Kansas City
during this decade, had participated in one of the major
social movements of the twentieth century. This was but
the beginning of a wave of insight into significant social participation: our residence in the streetcar suburbs; my
father's role in organizing a union during World War II;
our minority religion itself. I came to see that holiness
religion had aided my family and other like-minded country
folk in adjustment to urban life in much the same way that
religion had assisted various foreign immigrant groups in
accommodating to the New World.

An Introductory Note

Born in the new industrial centers of eighteenth-
century England, Methodism had its most notable impact in
America on the frontier. Methodism accommodated to its
new environment, deserting the formal worship Wesley pre-
ferred for the emotionalism of the frontier revival. So successful were Methodist preachers in making converts in new
areas that a rural aura came to pervade the American group's
activities generally. As rural Methodists moved into the
East Coast cities and prospered, they sought summer refuge

xiii

from the temptations and heat of the city by establishing
camp meetings on the seashore and in other nearby locations
where they might relax in a religious, morally guarded
atmosphere.

Material prosperity brought with it fear of losing the
essential Wesleyan faith and by mid-century a sizeable
group of Eastern Methodists had launched a campaign toward
their original goal, the perfect Christian life.   They believed that the essence of Christian perfection (or holiness)
was attainable sometime after conversion in the experience
of entire sanctification.   In the years following the Civil
War they formed national, state and local associations which
sponsored numerous periodicals and hundreds of revivals and
camp meetings and attracted a substantial following both inside and outside the Methodist church.   Horrified by the
growing formality and worldliness of urban Methodism and
bent on preserving the Wesleyan perfectionism and fervid
worship of the holiness camp meetings, by 1900 urban holiness believers were leaving denominational churches in increasing numbers and forming independent holiness churches
true to their rural tradition.

In these country churches, often located in the midst
of cities, newcomers found a substitute family, a religious
home away from home.   The estrangement and isolation
holiness people experienced presages the communication gap
which exists at the present time between the Eastern urban
establishment and the common man in the Midwest and South.
Distinctive personal styles arising from sectional differences
marked, for instance, Presidents Kennedy and Johnson and
to some extent explain the treatment accorded each by the
Eastern-dominated press.   A similar foundation seems to
underlie the dissimilar public treatment of Black Panthers
and of young upper-class white radicals.   Ostracism because
of stylistic differences attributable to sectionalism, religion
and national background has long existed in America and
presents one of the great barriers to a truly open society.

The history of the National Holiness Movement within
American Methodism is the story of how one displaced group
dodged this dilemma through self-segregation and sectarianism.   The story causes one to wonder if competition between
cultural styles even more than economic differences may not
be the determiner of social grouping.

Acknowledgments

I would like to take this opportunity to thank the host of people who contributed to making this book possible. Librarians at the State Historical Society of Wisconsin, the Library of Congress, the University of Wisconsin, the University of Michigan, Asbury College, Asbury Theological Seminary, Garrett Theological Seminary, Vennard College, Trevecca Nazarene College, Olivet Nazarene College, Nazarene Theological Seminary, and Bethany Nazarene College (my alma mater) were all helpful. The University of Michigan made considerable computer time for statistical work available, and James Klock, Robert Jones and William Miller, who were at that time students at the University of Michigan, provided technical know-how with the statistics. The Reverend John D. Abbott, then General Secretary-Treasurer, and the Headquarters staff of the Pilgrim Holiness Church in Indianapolis; and Miss Elizabeth Hughey, then librarian, and her staff at the Methodist Publishing House library in Nashville provided unusual help and hospitality. Thanks also are due to Russell and Carol Lundy, then of Lompoc, California, who provided a congenial place for revision of the manuscript in the summer of 1970. My colleagues at the Michigan Historical Collections of the University of Michigan assisted in innumerable ways. Robert Warner and Kenneth Scheffel read and criticized the entire manuscript and Caroline Wilton did the layout for the illustrations. Professor Timothy Smith, now of The Johns Hopkins University, read part of the manuscript and has been unfailingly helpful. Merle Curti, my major professor, and Tom Barton, Stephen Nissenbaum, and David Allmendinger, student colleagues at the University of Wisconsin, proved by their actions that there is indeed a community of scholars transcending airtight specialties. Above all I must thank my wife, Beverly, for continuous support and help during years of research, writing, and revision.

Charles Edwin Jones
Providence, R. I.
October, 1973

INTRODUCTION

This is a simple yet classic story of a well-known syndrome in religious history: the evolution of a sect into a church. Ernst Troeltsch was the first to describe this pattern. In this carefully-researched study, Charles E. Jones has applied it to the history of the Holiness movement in the United States.

Starting as a pietistic movement within Methodism (the attempt to recapture the perfectionist zeal of the early years of John Wesley's own pietistic movement within the Church of England), the first exponents of a new form of perfectionist holiness wanted to bring back an aspect of Methodism which they felt was being neglected in the 1850's and 1860's. To do this, they found, like Wesley, that they would have to establish extra-ecclesiastical organizations (the first holiness camp meeting associations). For thirty years these associations struggled to revive the older teachings and practices of Methodism only to meet increasing opposition from entrenched lay and clerical leaders who found the Holiness movement too extreme, too emotional, to fit into the new formalism of urban and suburban Methodist respectability.

As in the classic pattern described by Troeltsch, this pietistic movement within Methodism was forced to leave the church (or denomination) which would not accede to its demands. Some Holiness advocates left as come-outers; some were put out, and many, as Jones describes, found religious fulfillment in the extra-ecclesiastical missions and tabernacles (like Wesley's early chapels) without realizing that they were entering an incipient sectarian movement on its long road toward becoming a new denomination.

An added virtue of this study derives from the careful and insightful manner in which Jones has related the Holiness movement to the general pattern of American social and religious life in the years 1875 to 1925. During that half century the mainline Protestant churches and denominations underwent a revolution in thought and practice as a result

xvii

of the combined impacts of urbanism, industrialism, tech-
nocracy from the outside and higher criticism, Darwinism,
and Liberal theology from the inside. In this crisis the
Holiness movement met social and psychological needs for
many American churchgoers which the major denominations,
anxious to accommodate to the modern ways of which they
had become an established part, could not meet. In particular, the Holiness missions, tabernacles, and camp meetings
provided a religious home for thousands of rural Americans
who moved into the growing cities in these years. The
Fundamentalist-Modernist schism, which reached a delayed
climax in the Scopes trial of 1925, left many of these
rural Americans at odds with their established ministers and
churches. The Holiness movement offered them the kind of
hope, solace, joy, and mutual support they needed in their
own adjustment to urban-industrial life. Charles Jones tells
this story well because he grew up as part of it. Writing,
as few scholars can, from the inside, he does not sacrifice
scholarly objectivity on the one hand nor sympathy and under-
standing on the other. He knows the people of whom he
writes.

     With the 1920's the Holiness movement reached its
third stage. From a pietistic movement within Methodism,
to a sect drawing adherents from many other denominations
(notably Baptists, Quakers, Mennonites), the movement now
advanced toward full-fledged denominationalism: its members
left the shabby urban outskirts and moved to the suburbs;
its crude wooden tabernacles became brick and stucco
churches; its evangelists became respectable ministers and
pastors; its tent-meeting revivals became beautifully laid
out summer resorts. In part this resulted from the transi-
tion the Holiness people themselves made as they adjusted
to city ways and improved their socio-economic status; in
part it resulted from energetic and capable leadership, and
in part it was the inevitable result of the educational and
religious training which Holiness parents instituted to keep
their children in the path of righteousness. Come-outers
can be self-sustaining martyrs, but birth-right members
need to be taught their beliefs and trained in their practices.
The sect is self-sustaining through the battles it fights for
survival; the denomination must develop organizations and
institutions to sustain its membership. Like early Quakers
and Methodists, the Holiness churches have survived and
grown because they evolved institutionalized structures and
trained leaders to administer their denomination.

But institutionalized, denominational structure has not yet meant absorption into the mainstream of American society. In fact, one of the principal functions of sectarian institutionalism has always been to maintain the faith and practice (as well as the life-style) of the chosen by insulating the believers and their young from the corrupting influence of "the world." Jones amply demonstrates how the Holiness churches, Bible schools colleges, summer resorts, publishing houses, radio stations serve this purpose--providing a culture-within-a-culture for those who wish to remain separate and distinct.

Jones ends his story in 1930 when the outthrust of Holiness missions began to decline as money and energy turned inward to establish this institutionalized sub-culture. Since World War II, a continually rising standard of living has enabled these groups to turn once again outward to evangelize the world. Today the Holiness movement is making an enormous impact upon the religious life of Central and South America, Africa, and Southeast Asia, through its missionary, medical and educational efforts--the result of continuing faith, tithing, and dedication by a group which successfully resists total accommodation to an increasingly materialistic, Americanized world. Their story is an important one which prior to this has never been fully and accurately told.

One final word must be said about the appendices of this book. It is one of the marks of Jones's training as a student of religious history that he has utilized all of the tools of computerized statistics in his analysis. This is not old-fashioned church or denominational history. Its graphs and charts make use of the "hard data" of social science. This is, in the best sense, a study of the sociology of religion in America.

William G. McLoughlin
Brown University
August 15, 1973

Phoebe Worrell Palmer (1807-1874). Photograph from:
Simpson, Matthew, bp., 1811-1884, ed. Cyclopedia of
Methodism.... Philadelphia: Everts & Stewart, 1878
(c1876); p. 692.

The Beginnings:

1

METHODISM'S PECULIAR DOCTRINE

In 1729, two young men, reading the Bible, saw
they could not be saved without holiness, followed after it, and incited others so to do. In
1737 they saw that holiness comes by faith.
They saw likewise, that men are justified before they are sanctified; but still holiness was
their point. God then thrust them out, utterly
against their will, to raise a holy people. [1]*

The significant social consequences of the Methodist
movement, both in Britain and America, [2] sprang more from
the theological and behavioral reorientation of its converts
than from conscious efforts at social reform by its leaders.
Methodism's impact on secular society was in direct proportion to its effect on its own members. The Wesleyan revival diverted the interest of working class converts from
material inequities to evangelical perfectionism, thereby
cooling revolutionary tempers and generating an otherworldly
spirit.

Initially conceived as an agency for spiritual renewal
within the established church, Methodism stressed personal
religious experience in addition to the traditional sacramen-
tarianism of Anglicanism. Positing perfect love of God and
one's fellows as the essence of true Christianity, John Wesley thought of salvation as a journey from willful rebellion
to perfect love. [3] Attainment of perfect love in this life,
however, required the undivided commitment of the seeker.
Individually and collectively, therefore, the faithful must
ever be watchful lest arrogance, ambition or material advantage sidetrack the quest for Christian perfection. [4]

*See page 145 for references in each chapter.

Twenty-five years before John Wesley's death,
Methodism had spread to the American colonies where in
the haste of frontier expansion and institutional consolidation
it experienced numerical success undreamed of by the
founder. Barred by independence from remaining in the
Church of England, American Methodists formed a denomination and joined the race for sectarian survival. During its
first seventy-five years in the United States, Methodism
experienced phenomenal increase. From about fourteen
thousand members at the end of the War for Independence,
the Methodist Episcopal Church grew to six hundred thousand
in 1833, and to over a million (out of a total population of
twenty million) in 1845. [5]

For the Wesleyan perfectionist, however, the church's
future did not seem so bright. By 1845 L. L. Hamline, a
holiness advocate and bishop in the Methodist Episcopal
Church, was lamenting the widespread neglect of Christian
perfection among American Methodists. He claimed that the
doctrine of perfect love had become "mere speculation" to
forty-nine out of fifty Methodists. Since most Methodist
preachers did not profess Christian perfection themselves,
they were ineffective in leading others into the experience.
To combat apathy and doctrinal ignorance within the church
and the heretical perfectionism of utopian and free-love
sects outside it, Hamline urged that Methodism reaffirm
its peculiar emphasis. [6] Hamline's criticism was the out-
growth of vigorous proclamation of perfect love by a minority
in the church, a group that had led Hamline himself to profess entire sanctification as a second blessing. As early
as 1825 Timothy Merritt, a prominent member of the New
England Conference of the Methodist Episcopal Church, had
published The Christian's Manual, a Treatise on Christian
Perfection. In 1839 Merritt began his own journal, the
Guide to Christian Perfection. Published in Boston, the new
journal preached Wesleyan perfection in words nearly
identical to those of the Methodist founder himself. [7] Re-
named the Guide to Holiness, before Merritt's death in 1845
the paper became a major vehicle for holiness agitation
within American Methodism. [8]

In 1835 Sarah Lankford of New York City claimed
the second blessing and started a prayer meeting in her
home in the interest of encouraging seekers after perfect
love. When Sarah moved from the city, her sister, Phoebe
Palmer, the wife of Walter C. Palmer, a physician and
prominent Methodist layman, continued the meetings. Mrs.

Palmer's Tuesday Meeting for the Promotion of Holiness (so popular that it outlived her thirty years) influenced a dedicated core of the Methodist ecclesiastical elite, as well as prominent members of other communions. Her following included not only Methodists such as Stephen Olin, president of the Wesleyan University in Connecticut, Nathan Bangs, editor of the New York Christian Advocate; and bishops Edmund Janes, Leonidas Hamline, and Jesse Peck; but Congregationalists Thomas C. Upham, professor at Bowdoin, and Asa Mahan, president of Oberlin; Episcopalian Charles Cullis, a physician of Boston; Baptists E. M. Levy and A. B. Earle, ministers in Philadelphia and Boston respectively; and Friends Hannah Whitall Smith, author of the popular Christian's Secret of a Happy Life, and David B. Updegraff, leader in the Ohio Yearly Meeting. [9]

A publishing program and home meetings patterned after the New York Tuesday Meeting spread Mrs. Palmer's teachings throughout the country. In the years following 1840, when Mrs. Thomas C. Upham started a Palmer-type meeting in Brunswick, Maine, similar groups were organized in Boston, Trenton, Philadelphia, Wilmington and Baltimore. By 1886 over two hundred meetings were operating in the United States and a half-dozen other countries. In 1858 Dr. Palmer purchased the Guide to Holiness, moved the publication offices to New York, and installed his wife as editor. Under Mrs. Palmer's direction the paper reached the high point of its popularity, the circulation rising from thirteen to thirty thousand. [10] Providing a vehicle of discussion for scattered perfectionists, the Guide united holiness believers both inside and outside the church. [11]

In addition to Tuesday Meeting and publishing efforts, by 1858 Dr. and Mrs. Palmer had begun formal evangelism in revival meetings and camp meetings. At first, while his wife pursued her domestic and editorial duties and conducted the Tuesday Meeting, Walter Palmer cared for his homeopathic medical practice during the winter and evangelized only during the summer. Gradually, however, he freed himself from the restrictions of his medical practice and joined his wife in full-time evangelism. Although Phoebe Palmer felt it was improper for women to preach, she often gave lengthy exhortations in connection with her husband's sermons. Of the two, her talks always proved more popular. Like many other American revivalists, the Palmers extended their ministry to Europe, spending the years 1859 to 1863 there. [12]

Materially the Palmers enjoyed relative comfort. In
1855 their daughter, Phoebe, a gospel song writer of note,
had married Joseph Fairchild Knapp, a Methodist layman and
founder of the Metropolitan Life Insurance Company. Composer of musical settings for Fanny Crosby's popular "Blessed
Assurance" and her mother's "The Cleansing Wave, " Mrs.
Knapp took a deep interest in her parents' work. As she was
the recipient of an annual income of $50,000 from her husband's
estate upon his death, Mrs. Knapp's support may explain the
survival of the Guide to Holiness until 1902, twenty-seven
years after Mrs. Palmer's death. [13]

As much the benefactor of Wesleyan theology as was her
daughter of laissez-faire economics, Phoebe Palmer viewed the
experience of entire sanctification as a panacea for the spiritual
ills of Methodism. Recognizing that in accepting denominational
form American Methodism had largely substituted institutionalism for perfectionism, Mrs. Palmer sought to revive the
earlier emphasis. Passing over Wesley's emphasis on the
perfection of love as a process, the sponsor of the Tuesday
Meeting stressed entire sanctification as a present possibility.
Although John Wesley and Phoebe Palmer differed only on the
timing of perfect love, the two approaches produced markedly
disparate results: Wesley's, a generation of seekers after
Christian perfection; Mrs. Palmer's, a century of holiness
professors intent on reviving primitive Methodism. Wesley's
followers developed a discipline for seeking perfect love; Mrs.
Palmer's, a discipline for the sanctified life.

The contrast between the Wesleys' approach to perfection and that of the Palmers appeared strikingly in the hymns
each wrote. Representative of the Wesleys' thinking was
"Jesus Thine All Victorious Love;" of Phoebe Palmer's, "The
Cleansing Wave. "[14] Wesley's singer aspired to be endowed
with perfect love for God and man, so that his feet would "no
longer rove" in sinful desire, but be "rooted and fixed in God. "
For him the end of perfection was pure, godly intention: "I
only for His glory burn, and always see His face. " Mrs.
Palmer, on the other hand, emphasized sudden crisis accompanied by emotional exuberance. In "The Cleansing Wave"
she likened entire sanctification to baptism, an inward cleansing followed by a circumspect life. Reliving the experience
she claimed, "O now I see the crimson wave, the fountain deep
and wide, " then plunging in, claimed purity. Although Wesley
was certainly as puritanical as Mrs. Palmer, he anticipated
fewer behavioral changes than she as a result of perfect love.
Wesley's refining fire implied purgation of internal impurities;

Phoebe Palmer's baptism, external evidence of the internal
work.   The "polluted nature" died, and was replaced by a new
one divinely created, and the perfected Christian, ecstatic with
joy, exulted,

> I rise to walk in heav'n's own light,
> Above the world of sin;
> With heart made pure and garments white,
> And Christ enthroned within.

For him the life of perfect love was indeed a foretaste of
heaven.

While the holiness movement always regarded John
Wesley as its great authority, the movement owed many of its
distinctive ideas and practices to Phoebe Palmer.   The con-
fidant of powerful men in the church, she permanently modified American Methodist teaching on perfection through them.
Taken over by Methodist camp meeting promoters, Mrs.
Palmer's ideas were to pervade all future Methodist debate
concerning holiness.   Attractive to Methodist church leaders
at mid-century, her perfectionism was to create division by
the end of the century.

Phoebe Palmer's insistence on present availability
directly contradicted the theory of gradual attainment of
perfect love.   Regardless of the length of the process there
was a time when imperfect love was made perfect.   Since
the scriptures clearly promised deliverance from all sin to
believers, the process need take no longer than it took the
Christian seeker to meet divine conditions.   Once the scriptural requirements were met, the seeker had the right by
faith to claim perfect love.   In Mrs. Palmer's teaching the
Biblical injunction to living self-sacrifice[15] on God's altar
was closely akin to personal consecration at the Methodist
mourner's bench.   Having surrendered pleasures, ambitions
and thoughts to the divine will, the Christian seeker had every
right to claim the blessing.   In her spiritual autobiography
Mrs. Palmer said that in seeking entire sanctification, she
gradually came to realize that "instead of being an attainment
beyond her reach," holiness "was a state of grace in which
every one of the Lord's redeemed ones should live."[16]   Her
"altar terminology" which held that God's altar sanctified
every human self-sacrifice placed on it, was in reality much
like the covenant in Puritan theology.   Unlike Wesley who
believed that the Holy Spirit made the seeker conscious of
the attainment of perfect love, Mrs. Palmer taught that the

scriptural "promises" were witness enough.   Though some
seekers might have emotional experiences, all would not.
Heightened emotion was for edification, the Bible for evidence.

Holiness believers generally approved of contemporary
social standards and identified current taboos with the sins of
the spirit.   Like John Wesley, nineteenth-century perfectionists described inward sin in terms of undesirable personality
traits: pride, anger, envy, and slander.   Using Mrs. Palmer's consecration formula, evangelistic workers instructed
seekers after perfect love to forsake inward sins (pride,
covetousness, etc.) by adopting standards approved by the
already sanctified.   A seeker might detect pride, for instance,
in his reluctance to go to the mourner's bench or in his love
for fashionable clothes.   Long before the church required it,
Methodist ministers seeking to be sanctified gave up tobacco.[17]
Although at this time Methodist spokesmen for holiness did
not generally condemn membership in secret societies, seekers
often withdrew from lodges.   While the full flowering of holiness pietism was still in the future, its roots sprang from the
union of Christian perfection and popular culture in the Palmers' day.[18]

2

THE CHURCH CONTEXT

The revival of holiness teaching initiated by Timothy Merritt, the Palmers and others, met with a friendly response among many well-placed and prosperous people in the Methodist Episcopal Church. In his introduction to Bishop Foster's Christian Purity, Bishop Janes lauded holiness as "the greatest good, the highest destiny of the militant church, and the most precious interest of the race. A holy Church," he prophesied, "would soon make a holy world."[1] Led by bishops who preached and wrote about holiness,[2] the church itself was threatened by advocates of its peculiar doctrine. Jesse T. Peck, a future bishop, feared that schism would follow efforts at organized holiness promotion within the church. It would lead, he said, to "invidious distinctions," "jealousies, heart-burnings and divisions" not at all intended by holiness organizers. Himself a believer in entire sanctification, Peck advised the holiness brethren to "permeate the entire church," not to become a faction within it. "You must be distinct even from justified Christians," he admonished, "by being more deeply humble; by greater simplicity and sweetness of spirit; by loving" unsanctified brethren "more tenderly and laboring for them and the world more indefatigably and successfully" than would be possible without perfect love. "Strong and indissoluble Christian union" should "be the result of increased attention to the doctrine of holiness."[3]

Notwithstanding preachments about peace, controversy continued with tempers showing sufficiently to disturb the general quietude of the church.[4] Holiness Methodists continued to seek fellowship with like-minded believers, even outside the church. The containment policy, urged by Jesse Peck and others, proved to be nothing more than a rhetorical expedient, incapable of holding back a wave of holiness partisanship.

From the late 1830's forward, an increasing sentiment for the abolition of slavery paralleled the growth of holiness teaching. Methodist holiness leaders witnessed ultraist

7

groups leaving the church: the anti-slavery men to form the
Wesleyan Methodist Connection in 1843, and the radical perfectionists the Free Methodist Church in 1860. In 1845 holiness loyalists also saw the division of the main body of Methodists North and South. As moderates in these controversies
holiness believers adhered to the majority; as Northerners
they stayed in the Methodist Episcopal Church.

Holiness, as a doctrinal matter, played no part in
these divisions. Strong perfectionist contingents existed in
every faction, though the Free Methodists, by early inclusion of a statement on sanctification in their Discipline and
by insistence on rigorous standards of personal conduct, testified more dramatically than others to perfectionist predilection.
Acting as arbiters in these disputes, holiness bishops incurred
the lasting resentment of the dissenting brethren, not only
personally, but as representatives of the entire holiness group
in the church. Although after the war the Wesleyan Methodists joined the Free Methodists in explicitly espousing puritanical holiness and carried on an aggressive evangelistic
program, they continued to oppose unchecked church power,
even in the hands of sanctified leaders. Similarly, the liti-
gious role played by Northern holiness Bishops Simpson, Janes,
Peck and Gilbert Haven during Reconstruction earned the holiness movement the animosity of leaders of the Methodist
Episcopal Church, South.

During the same years that the Palmers were establishing the Tuesday Meeting and the Guide to Holiness, Orange
Scott, a pastor in the New England Conference and a delegate
to the General Conferences of 1836 and 1840, espoused the
cause of Negro freedom and tried to make the church recognize the "moral evil" of its compromise with human bondage.
Scott believed that the Methodist Episcopal Church's compromise[5] was maintained by an alliance of tyrannical ecclesiastical leaders with slaveholders. Convinced that no course short
of separation from the main Methodist body could unveil the
church's corruption, Scott announced that a convention would
meet February 1, 1843, in Andover, Massachusetts, for the
purpose of forming "a Wesleyan Methodist Church, free from
Episcopacy and Slavery."[6] After adopting numerous resolutions,
the convention adjourned to meet May 31 at Utica, New York,
where abolitionists from Boston, Providence, New York and
Pittsburgh joined a Michigan separatist group in forming the
Wesleyan Methodist Connection. The new church, having a
strong contingent in the "burned-over district" of western
New York, legislated many taboos. Forbidding slaveholding,

the use of alcoholic beverages and membership in secret
societies, the group substituted a president for bishops and
gave laymen representation in conferences and a voice in
selecting pastors. [7]

Sectional jealousy was far from dead in the parent body
and in 1844 contention over the status of Bishop Andrew, who
by marriage and inheritance had acquired slaves, split the
Methodist Episcopal Church. Bitterness generated in separation diverted attention from consideration of the morality of
slavery. Unwilling to recognize the legitimacy of the new
Methodist Episcopal Church, South, Northern Methodist leaders insisted that their group was still a national church, un-
restricted in its area of operation. In attempting to hold slaveholding border conferences, it sidestepped the slavery issue.
Participation by close friends of Phoebe Palmer in these ma-
neuvers showed them to be more interested in sectional domi-
nance than in racial justice. [8]

Concurrent with the Methodist Episcopal Church's conversion to Northern sectionalism in the 1850's, a group of
perfectionists in the Genesee Conference of western New York
pointed out the ambiguity between the church's actions and its
perfectionist professions. The forerunners of the Free Methodists (derisively called "Nazarites" by their opponents because
of their uncompromising attitudes)[9] struck out against the
church's accommodation with slavery and worldliness. Led
by Benjamin Titus Roberts, a graduate of Wesleyan University
who had recently converted to Palmer-type perfectionism, the
movement, which originated in protest against novel methods
of financing church building construction, condemned most of
the physical evidences of Methodism's growing affluence: pew
rents, choir singing, organs, elegant clothes, and costly meeting houses. Like Scott, Roberts condemned both slavery and
Masonry, practices condoned by the majority of Methodists,
including holiness believers. After appeals to the General
Conference had been curtly denied, Roberts and his "Nazarite"
associates institutionalized their criticism by forming the Free
Methodist Church at Pekin, New York in 1860.

While ministering to a Methodist congregation in Buf-
falo, Roberts had clashed with leading laymen in his congregation when he opposed selling pews as a means of financing
a new church building. Calling pewed churches "stock churches" because the contributors of seats acted like a joint stock
company in managing church affairs, Roberts so offended some
members that at the next conference they succeeded in getting

him removed to a "hard scrabble" circuit at Pekin. Roberts'
defense, an article entitled "New School Methodism" published
in a western New York anti-slavery journal in 1858, twice
earned him official charges of "un-Christian and immoral conduct" and finally expulsion from the Methodist ministry. [10]
Charging his enemies with Masonic secrecy in plotting against
him, Roberts held that cliques of prosperous members had
turned the churches into social clubs. The "lodge," he pre-
dicted, would soon "supersede the class meeting and love feast;
and the old-fashioned prayer-meeting" would "give way to the
social party."[11]

     The expulsion of Roberts and his followers from the
Methodist Episcopal Church laid bare the nearly limitless
power of nineteenth-century bishops. It also made plain the
gulf separating rural perfectionism from that of the Eastern
cities. Roberts' mistreatment was a strong indictment of the
perils of Methodist affluence and respectability, perils which
threatened the very foundations of vital piety.

     If Roberts' words left any doubt as to the ascetic per-
fectionism of the "Nazarites," the first Discipline adopted by
the new sect relieved it. Enjoining holiness, plain dress,
devotional rigor, free pews, and simple church buildings and
worship, the Free Methodist rules forbade membership in
secret orders, slavery, use of instrumental music and choirs
in the church, and ostentation in dress and behavior. The
Free Methodists' standard of piety was so rigorous in fact
that many Methodist holiness leaders, no less than others,
shied away from them as fanatics. Although mild-tempered
Bishop Janes, present in 1858 when Roberts was put out of the
ministry, assured him, "Do not be discouraged, Brother
Roberts--there is a bright future before you yet," he immediately bowed out of the controversy. Janes' episcopal colleague,
Matthew Simpson, who presided at the 1859 Genesee Conference session when six of Roberts' followers were disciplined,
seemed more intent on rooting out fanaticism than on judicious
procedure. Asked why he had voted for censure, one minister
explained, "Because Bishop Simpson told me to."[12] A lawyer
who attended the trials said he had "never before seen a presiding officer show 'such partiality'" as Simpson had. [13] Curi-
ously, had the outburst of extreme piety and anti-slavery sentiment occurred at a time other than when the Northern church
was struggling to retain the border conferences, it would
probably have been placated.

     While the slavery issue was soon settled by war, the

problem of Methodist worldliness remained. As editor of the
Western Christian Advocate, Matthew Simpson had denounced
Sabbath breaking, liquor licensing, and the theatre, and had
insisted that nothing but licentiousness could result from the
exhibition of Hiram Powers' nude sculpture, "The Greek
Slave" in New York. [14]   Jesse T. Peck, who in 1855 had
framed the first Genesee Conference resolution against Roberts'
extremism, now warned that the church, "satisfied without
going on to perfection, " had become inundated with a "mass of
backsliders. " Indeed, he charged that the once immaculate
"outward splendor of the church" had become "the attire of a
harlot ... revealing and inviting illicit intercourse with a
godless world. "[15]

    Rhetorically, the holiness bishops differed little from
the Genesee reformers; in reality the difference was immense.
With disparate interpretations of the Methodist tradition and
especially Christian perfection, the two vied unequally for a
leading role in shaping tradition and delineating discipline.

    Even if holiness leaders had not offended their radical
brethren by catering to the prosperous, their fashionably dressed wives would have. Once when Bishop and Mrs. Simpson
were to be entertained in a Presbyterian banker's home, their
hostess, never having seen them and believing that Methodists
were semi-literate, plain people, decided to dress so her
guests would feel comfortable. Twisting her hair into a tight
knot, the banker's wife donned a "big-flowered tycoon-rep
wrapper" and an apron. To her astonishment, however, the
bishop's wife appeared for dinner in a black silk dress embel-
lished with ruffles, lace and jewelry, her hair done in the
currently fashionable style. Embarrassed, the hostess re-
treated to the sidelines as Mrs. Simpson "charmed everybody"
with her conversation. [16]

    While Roberts wanted to restore frontier simplicity in
worship and behavior, Bishop Simpson advocated dignified
worship. In 1855 he encouraged the building of Christ Church,
Pittsburgh, the first gothic temple in American Methodism,
and toyed with the possibility of sanctioning liturgical worship
in selected Methodist congregations. [17]

    In order to raise money for new church buildings at
Dayton and Springfield, Ohio, John S. Inskip prior to his
sanctification decided to rent pews. Though approved by the
local congregations involved, the new system (known as "promiscuous" or family seating) generated a storm of opposition

among Inskip's ministerial colleagues who cited a church rule
enjoining free seats in all Methodist meeting-houses.   Charged
with "contumacious treatment" of the conference, Inskip appealed to the General Conference, and in 1852 that body nulli-
fied the Ohio Conference's action by revising the rule so as to
require free seats only when practicable. [18] Inskip was soon
called to be minister of the Madison Street Church, New York
City, and had his reward for standing with the rich and powerful in the church. [19]

The overt opposition of the Methodist majority to
the anti-slavery crusade and to straitlaced puritan perfectionism was a reaction not so much to the content of the
reformers' proposals, as to the uncompromising intensity
with which issues were put forward.   Years after B. T.
Roberts and his sympathizers had been put out of the Methodist Episcopal Church, holiness leaders within the church continued to fear the appeal of their strict ascetic piety and con-
sistently warned converts against dissent and fanaticism.

The leaders' attitude toward the rigorous perfectionism
of Free Methodism is illustrated in the case of Frances E.
Willard.   Miss Willard, as a student in Evanston, Illinois,
came into contact with holiness teaching through the ministry
of Randolph S. Foster and John Dempster and became a
seeker after her friend, Mrs. Leonidas Hamline, induced her
to read some books by holiness authors. [20] Miss Willard professed sanctification during a revival which Dr. and Mrs.
Palmer held in the Evanston Church.   Soon afterward, she
accepted a position at the Genesee Wesleyan Seminary, Lima,
New York.   On the eve of her departure for the job, a friend,
warning of the dangers of radical holiness teaching, cautioned:

> Sister Frank there is a strange state of things at Lima.
> The Free Methodists have done great harm in Western
> New York by their excess in the doctrine and experi-
> ence of holiness.   You know I believe thoroughly in
> and profess it, but just now our Church has suffered
> so much from the 'Nazarites, ' as they are called, that I
> fear that if you speak and act as zealously at Lima in
> this cause as you do here it may make trouble. [21]

In light of the situation, the friend advised Frances to hold
to her experience, but at the same time to be "very careful"
what she said about perfect love.   Soon after her arrival in
Lima she overheard a professor tell an enquiring student that
holiness was a subject they did not mention there.   Later,

Miss Willard testified that in the restricted environment of
the Genesee Wesleyan Seminary she "kept still" about holiness until she found she "had nothing in particular to keep
still about!" Years afterward she lamented,

> Since then I have sat at the feet of every teacher of
> holiness I could reach; have read their books and com-
> pared their views. I [feel] love and reverence and am
> greatly drawn toward all, and never feel out of har-
> mony with their spirit.... But that sweet pervasive-
> ness, that heaven in the soul, of which I came to
> know in Mrs. Palmer's meeting, I do not feel. [22]

Despite overt prejudice against their "free" brethren,
holiness believers subscribed to standards of conduct as
personally demanding as did the Free Methodists. At the
1864 General Conference a future holiness minister, J. B.
Foote, introduced the first official resolution condemning the
use of tobacco. [23] In an age when Methodists were enforcing
contemporary social standards with moral sanctions, holiness
believers increasingly shied away from ostentatious dress and
"prideful" behavior. While in the process of seeking sanctification, Frances E. Willard, for instance, was made to feel
that the "simple bits of jewelry" she wore, "gold buttons,
rings" and a "pin, all of them plain and 'quiet' in their style, "
were "separating" her from the Savior. [24] George D. Watson,
a Methodist minister seeking perfection, felt that as a pre-
condition of his sanctification God required him not only to
give up tobacco but to be willing to accept the poorest preaching appointments or be sent as a missionary to the freedmen.
Concerning his consecration in December 1876, Watson wrote:

> That Friday night ... as I lay on the edge of the bed
> ... The Lord began to talk to me. 'Will you do all
> for my glory?' 'Yes, Lord. ' 'Suppose your wife will
> not believe and accept it, will you receive it?' ...
> 'Yes, Lord; give me the blessing. ' 'Will you let me
> take your health in my hand--give you bronchitis or
> consumption?' 'Yes, Lord....' 'Will you consent to
> leave those large appointments you have been having?
> Will you consent to take a poor appointment for me?'
> 'Yes, Lord, I will take the poorest appointment in
> Indiana if it is Thy will. ' (And there were some poor
> ones.) 'Suppose I want you to go and preach among
> the Freedmen, will you go?' I said, 'Yes, Lord, if
> it is thy will. ' 'Will you give up your tobacco, that
> your body may be my clean temple?' I had tried sev-

eral times to give it up, but would go back to it
again.... 'Yes, Lord, I will give it up. I will do
anything. Give me the blessing.' When I got all
through I dropped to sleep.... When I waked up next
morning I found the appetite for tobacco was gone. I
never have taken back that consecration. [25]

The difference between the holiness element in the
church and the reformers was not, therefore, in the issues,
but in the intensity and exclusiveness with which each group
espoused them. Total commitment to ascetic piety and slavery reform isolated issue-oriented dissidents from a multitude of potentially sympathetic holiness believers in the church.
Sole emphasis on any issue ultimately led to schism. In order
to stay in harmony with the church, Methodist holiness believers sided with the majority, accepting compromised social
stands.

With a few striking exceptions, holiness believers re-
acted to slavery[26] and the Civil War with marked passivity.
Although at least four future holiness evangelists, Alfred
Cookman, John S. Inskip, Gilbert Haven, and Lucius C. Matlack, [27] served for short periods as chaplains in the Union
army during the war; and although a future holiness leader
in Iowa demonstrated his loyalty to the Union by draping his
pulpit with the American flag, [28] such actions were exceptional. Concentrated in the Philadelphia and Baltimore conferences where legal slavery continued throughout the war, most
holiness preachers stayed in their pastorates and shared the
booming wartime prosperity with their congregations. [29] The
Palmers, Andrew Longacre, Gilbert Haven, and William
Taylor spent all or part of the war years in religious work
abroad. [30]

As the war progressed expansion of the Northern
church into the South became possible. In 1864 Bishops
Ames and Simpson persuaded Secretary of War Stanton to direct generals to place all church buildings belonging to the
Methodist Episcopal Church, South "in which a loyal minister
... appointed by a loyal Bishop" did not officiate, in the hands
of bishops of the Northern church. [31] These developments,
coupled with the organization of the Methodist Episcopal
Church's own Freedmen's Aid Society, paved the way for expansion southward.

Led by Alfred Cookman and Gilbert Haven[32] and armed
with a program of providing the freedman with the "spelling-

book, the Bible, equal rights before the law, and the elective
franchise, "[33] a few holiness Methodists pushed the movement in the South. Apart from promotion of Freedmen's Aid
Society institutions, however, holiness contributions to South-
ern betterment were slight. Immediately after the war,
Lucius C. Matlack, a holiness minister recently returned
from the Wesleyan Methodist Connection, filled a Northern
Methodist pulpit in New Orleans.[34] In the 1870's Bishop
Simpson appointed William B. Osborn, founder of the National
Camp Meeting Association for the Promotion of Holiness and
of Ocean Grove Camp Meeting, presiding elder of the Saint
John's District in Florida.[35] And from 1875 to 1881 Joseph
H. Smith, future National Association evangelist, nearly
starved while ministering to poverty-stricken Northern churches
in Georgia.[36]

Whatever the effect upon the future of perfectionism in
Methodism, holiness participation in the church's reconstruction program paid off. The 1872 General Conference of the
Methodist Episcopal Church was a great triumph for respectable urban holiness people. In the episcopal elections that
year, five of the eight new bishops chosen were unabashed
friends of the holiness group. Having denounced fanaticism
and avoided schism, Methodist holiness believers now had
strong spokesmen in the councils of the church. Their year
of majority had arrived.

The Camp Meeting:

3

THE EVANGELISTS

Invented by Presbyterians on the Kentucky frontier, by the Civil War the camp meeting had become largely a Methodist institution. The earliest meetings drew an unsorted section of the community and many people attended who seemed more intent on sensual enjoyments than on spiritual edification. Embarrassed by impious behavior and hysterical emotionalism, Presbyterians and Baptists abandoned the camp meeting. The Methodists brought it under control.[1] Each year they brought their entire local denominational family together for a summer grove meeting. In 1849, James Porter explained that camp meetings were "a golden link" binding distant Methodist "societies together in a holy brotherhood." The "strictly religious" meeting held "amid waving trees" and "purling streams" was "conducive to health," furnishing a change of air, scenery, society, and style of living which was "most ruinous to hypochondria, and invigorating to the whole man."[2]

Methodist camp meeting organizers encouraged attendance of families and maintenance of regular domestic discipline. Usually camp regulations reiterated the prohibitions of the General Rules. They required attendance at services and outlawed alcoholic beverages, promiscuous courting and Sunday money transactions. To maintain nocturnal decorum, ministers patrolled the grounds. Religious services and devotional activities filled the waking hours.

Long before the Civil War, the revivalistic novelties of the camp meeting had become the tradition of American Methodism. Although John Wesley sent the Americans a formal Sunday service,[3] Americans venerated New World innovations and regarded practices a generation or two old as ancient traditions. American Methodists quickly convinced themselves that currently popular evangelical notions represented primitive Wesleyan belief.

In no area did Wesley's position in American Methodism appear more anomalous than in the propagation of his
theory of Christian perfection by means of specially designed
camp meetings. After the mid-century revival of evangelical
perfectionism, most Methodist camp meetings included special
"Holiness" meetings. Featuring "clear," "direct" testimonies
to perfect love, the special meetings soon attracted large audi -
ences. According to John S. Inskip, pastor in New York City,
multitudes "thronged" daily to hear of "the wonders of grace."[4]
Encouraged by the success of these meetings, a group of ministers in the New York East, Philadelphia and Baltimore conferences of the Methodist Episcopal Church, set out to create
a camp meeting devoted entirely to holiness. Convinced that
"a sanctified church would soon secure a converted world,"
the sponsors proposed "spiritual revolution" without "modification of church polity." They felt that such a camp meeting,
led by men free from partisanship or theological "shibboleth,"
might be instrumental in leading Methodism to her theological
heritage.[5]

Socially a wide gap separated the holiness camp meeting
proponents from earlier camp meeting backers. Educated in
Methodist academies, the new promoters had spent their early
careers in rural charges. Most of them ministered in Eastern
commercial and industrial towns then receiving large numbers
of rural immigrants.[6] While professional success had separated them from the evangelical fervor and free worship of rural
Methodism, urban residence had brought them into contact with
the Palmers and the holiness bishops instrumental in their es-
pousal of Christian perfection. Sharing the benefits of an affluent society, the holiness pastors feared the loss of Wesleyan
simplicity. Nostalgic middle-aged participants in a commercial and industrial revolution, they longed to reinstate evangelicalism of the countryside in their city congregations.[7]

In April 1867, W. B. Osborn, a presiding elder in
southern New Jersey, became so filled with enthusiasm for
the holiness camp meeting idea that he went to New York City
to enlist the support of J. S. Inskip, then pastor of the Greene
Street Methodist Episcopal Church. Finding Inskip in his study,
Osborn announced: "I feel that God would have us hold a holiness camp-meeting." During prayer the two believed they received divine command to hold a meeting that summer and
covenanted to do so even if the encampment consisted of only
"two tents."[8]

Despite the role attributed to faith in the decision to

National Camp Meeting Committee for the Promotion of Holiness about 1869.   Photograph from: McLean, Alexander, 1826-1910, ed.   Penuel; or, Face to Face with God, co-edited by J. W. Eaton.   New York: W. C. Palmer, Jr., 1869; frontispiece.

promote a camp meeting, in this instance substance preceded faith.   In the summer of 1866 the Reverend John A. Wood of Wilkes-Barre, Pennsylvania, while enroute to a camp meeting at Red Bank, New Jersey, told Mrs. Harriet E. Drake about opposition to "the doctrine and distinctive experience of entire sanctification" he had felt in some Methodist camp meetings.   Wood said that to combat the trend he felt that camp meetings especially devoted to holiness should be held. Mrs. Drake countered by saying that if Wood would start such a camp meeting, she personally would underwrite one-half of the expense.[9]   It was with knowledge of Mrs. Drake's offer that Wood's friend, W. B. Osborn, sought other backing for the venture.

On June 13, 1867, an exploratory meeting was held in

Philadelphia.   Chaired by G. C. M. Roberts, a "venerable"
local preacher and physician from Baltimore, the group
proved so amicable "as to convince all present" that "God had
taken the affair into his hands. " At the suggestion of Osborn,
the group selected Vineland, New Jersey, near Philadelphia,
as the site of the 1867 encampment and designated it as a
National Camp Meeting to set it off from ordinary Methodist
summer grove meetings.   The encampment was to be held
early in the season (July 17 to 26), so that campers might
attend other summer meetings carrying the "blessings" of the
special holiness meeting with them.   Such harmony prevailed
in choosing a site, naming the organization, and preparing for
the meeting, that John S. Inskip declared, "It was the most
fraternal and religious business meeting any of us" had "ever
attended. "[10]

        Vineland, easily accessible by rail from the major
Eastern cities, was also the seat of Vineland Seminary,
center of Methodist activity in southern New Jersey. [11] The
village offered a well-shaded forty-acre grove, "The Park, "
for the meeting.   Adding moral to physical inducements, the
village and surrounding township had by local option banned
the sale of intoxicants and an aura of Methodist utopia pervaded the place.   Between services pious action was to oc-
cupy campers' time.   The "arching trees" provided "a beauti-
ful and extensive 'Bower of Prayer. '"

        In his address at the dedication of the grounds, John
S. Inskip announced that he hoped "religious interests of this
extraordinary Camp-Meeting" would extend throughout Chris-
tendom.   He admonished campers to brush aside "all differences" in the "spirit of mutual forebearance and brotherly
love. " Since political discussion could only produce division,
he suggested that "all secular matters be kept entirely out of
sight. " Having left worldly affairs "down yonder in the valley"
and having "come up" to the "mountain to worship the Lord, "
campers could here find a retreat from secular life, a veritable pastoral fortress for primitive Methodist worship, free
from worldliness, sectarianism, sectionalism, politics, and
controversy. [12]

        Most of the twenty-six speakers at Vineland were
Northern Methodists from seven Middle Atlantic conferences.
The presence of Bishop Matthew Simpson demonstrated the
tacit approval of the church's leaders and that of a Presbyterian minister hinted at ecumenicity. [13] Inskip declared that
if "Christian purity were generally prevalent, " "a catholic and

fraternal spirit" would pervade "all sects and parties" and
sectionalism would be tempered by "unity and friendship."[14]
Speaking for the majority, A. E. Ballard, presiding elder in
the New Jersey Conference declared, "I understand this to
be a Methodist Camp-Meeting for the promotion of holiness. "

Ministers supporting the Vineland meeting included
pastors of New York, Newark, Brooklyn, Philadelphia, Trenton, Wilmington and Baltimore. The central and accessible
location, an attractive site, and the prominence of the evangelists, guaranteed a large attendance. Sponsored by well-
established, urban middle-class people, the meeting attracted
listeners similarly situated. Although not consciously exclusive, post-war camp meeting organizers located meetings
in places most attractive to the families of entrepreneurs
and professional men able to afford formal vacations. The
ordinary working man not in the immediate vicinity simply
could not afford to attend the new camp meetings. Even if
he had been able to manage the transportation costs to attend
on the weekends, he would likely have been frustrated in his
plans, for holiness evangelists generally felt that Sunday travel
violated the Sabbath. As a result they forbade Sunday rail
service to camp sites. The crowds that thronged these early
Eastern meetings represented the comparatively few urban
Methodists affluent enough to afford rural escape from the
city heat.

Though Methodist evangelism always aimed at radical
changes in personal behavior, holiness camp meeting speakers
found that their audiences were largely made up of churchgoers. Bishop Simpson explained that when camp meetings
had first been introduced near cities, they attracted "vast
multitudes" of unchurched people. Many sinners then had
been "arrested by the preaching. " After the Civil War,
crowds which formerly had attended camp meetings out of
curiosity, instead frequented the "theatre, the ball-room, the
public garden, the horse-race, " the very "haunts of dissipation. " Since the "very wicked seldom" attended camp meetings,
there were now "fewer instances of those remarkable conversions" and personal transformations which had characterized
earlier gatherings.[15] Increasingly, camp meetings specialized
in evangelizing the children of believers and in calling the
devout to perfection. During the course of the Vineland
meeting Simpson saw his son, Charles, converted.[16] Holiness revivalism had become the evangelism of the already
convinced.

Encouraged by the results of the Vineland camp meeting, and intending to conduct a similar meeting the next summer, twenty-one principal proponents organized the National
Camp-Meeting Association for the Promotion of Holiness.
The Association arranged for the 1868 encampment at Manheim, Pennsylvania, in the heart of an area of old German
settlement. An excellent location, the "majestic forest, excellent water and well-prepared grounds, "[17] attracted Christians of many denominations. By his presence, Bishop Simpson again lent an aura of official approval to the proceedings.
A reporter observed that "fear of failure had been dispelled"
by the success of the Vineland camp and the meeting at
Manheim progressed with mounting "fervency and power."[18]
People came from nearly every state in the Union. On the
final Sunday over 25,000 people, including three hundred ministers, attended. A fraternal spirit so markedly prevailed that
one supporter claimed "he was utterly unable to distinguish
... one denomination from another."[19]

Despite ecumenical pretensions, the Association
leaders viewed camp meeting evangelism as an instrument
of Methodist reform. After Manheim, loyalty to the church
caused the Association to hold camps only in response to
local groups in the Methodist Episcopal Church. With about
one hundred official invitations from 1870 to 1894 it conducted
fifty-two camp meetings. Tying itself ever more tightly to
the leaders and fortunes of the Northern church, the National
Association doggedly declared and carefully maintained denominational allegience. It defined itself simply as a committee of evangelists, acquired no property and studiously sought
not to compete with official Methodist activities.

In most particulars National Camp Meetings resembled
church sponsored meetings. They appealed to the same Methodist audiences, and shared nostalgia for the religious culture
of a day recently past and passing. Except for their emphasis
on Christian perfection, neither the preaching nor music was
strikingly different. Neither William Cowper's hymn "There
is a fountain filled with blood," the so-called theme song of
the National Camp Meetings, nor "I am coming to the cross,"
written by William McDonald, second president of the National
Association and first sung in 1870 at the Hamilton, Massachusetts National Camp Meeting, contained a distinctive message. The latter's sole allusion to the camp meeting was
that one who came to the cross knelt in the dust.[21]

During the first years, National Association ministers

accepted regular pastoral appointments, and evangelized at
large only in the summer. In March 1871 however, President John S. Inskip, with the approval of Bishop Ames, left
the pastoral ministry to become a full-time evangelist. That
spring, Inskip accompanied the bishop on his official visits
to hold holiness meetings in conjunction with sessions of the
St. Louis, Missouri, Kansas, and Nebraska conferences.
Throughout the tour he enjoyed receptive audiences and at
St. Louis nearly every minister present sought the second
blessing at the altar. "Fully assured of success," President
Inskip exulted, "I have greater confidence in the church than
ever."[22]

When in early April Inskip joined twelve other National
Association workers bound for California, he demonstrated
his intention of making the movement national in scope as
well as in name. A standardized pattern of operation was
becoming clear. With the approval of local church officials,
meetings would be held near population centers. Continuing
to hold summer meetings near Eastern cities, the leaders
planned to invade other sections of the country as well. In
1869 the National Camp Meeting Committee held its camp on
the Troy Conference grounds at Round Lake, New York. In
1870 it conducted meetings at Hamilton, Massachusetts, near
Boston; at Oakington, Maryland, near Baltimore; and at Des
Plaines, Illinois, near Chicago. Successful meetings in 1870
led the Association to undertake another far western campaign.

In the spring of 1871 the evangelists took a 4000-seat
tent with them to Sacramento. Here despite "ranters" who
disturbed the peace of the meeting, the preachers reported
converts from many social groups: gamblers, dope addicts,
some very rich as well as very poor people, Baptists, Presbyterians and Methodists. Claiming over two hundred professions of entire sanctification in the capital city, the Association evangelists moved on. Supported by Methodist leaders,
meetings at Santa Clara and San Francisco proved even more
fruitful. Prominent ministers, including the agent of the
Methodist Book Concern in San Francisco and the editor of the
California Christian Advocate, claimed the second blessing.
On their return, the evangelists stopped in Salt Lake City
(where they denounced polygamy) and in Indianapolis, Urbana,
Ohio, and Round Lake, New York, en route. At the end of
their first full year of evangelism, Inskip and McDonald reported that they had traveled 20,000 miles, had conducted six
hundred services and had witnessed twelve hundred conversions,
and thirty-seven hundred professions of perfect love.[23]

Although the first holiness camp meeting promoters assumed that their primary task was to save Methodism, they soon found themselves as busy defending their own ideas and methods as reviving the church. Fearful of fanaticism within their own ranks and pricked by criticism from without, the Association, acting corporately as the National Publishing Association for the Promotion of Holiness, decided during the Vineland camp meeting to launch the Methodist Home Journal. Operating from Philadelphia, the National Publishing Association aimed at flooding "the land with inexpensive holiness literature." Still troubled by criticism from outside, the 1869 annual meeting of the National Camp Meeting Association proposed a magazine to correct misrepresentations of holiness work and appointed a committee to study the possibility. The committee, consisting of McDonald and Boole of the New York East conference and Charles Munger of the Maine conference, persuaded John Bent, a Boston printer, to assume personal financial liability during the first year of publication provided that McDonald would edit the paper without pay. Issued in July 1870 as the official organ of the National Camp Meeting Association, the Advocate of Christian Holiness[24] gained over eight thousand subscribers the first year. When the National Publishing Association bought the paper in 1874, every minister in at least eight Methodist conferences subscribed.[25]

Near-bankruptcy necessitated merger of the two papers. The Advocate moved to Philadelphia and President Inskip assumed the editorship.[26] Well acquainted with business men in the church, Inskip enlisted the aid of Washington C. DePauw, a New Albany, Indiana, glass manufacturer, and soon put the publishing business in better financial condition. Solvency, however, diverted the leader's attention from evangelism. The financial crisis proved an omen of pressures for greater institutionalism in the future.[27]

No less than publishing interests, revivalism forced National Association leaders into administrative roles. Between 1867 and 1883 Inskip personally directed forty-eight of the fifty-eight National camps held. In 1875 the National evangelists, like the Palmers before them, extended their ministry to Canada. In 1880 they embarked on an international evangelistic tour, holding meetings in Great Britain, India and Australia. Popular everywhere, in India they saw the whole Methodist conference, including the bishop, at the mourner's bench seeking perfect love.[28]

The National Association leaders, loyal sons of mid-

century American Methodism, sought to define the true nature
of Wesleyanism. Unable or unwilling to utilize church ma-
chinery for their purposes, they worked outside the church's
confines to reform its alleged backsliding. Early success
and popularity which necessitated publishing ventures and
year-round evangelism lured Association leaders out of the
regular Methodist ministry into administrative jobs on the
edge of the church's activity. Well recommended in the
church, early leaders wore themselves out in the holiness
cause, established its doctrine and worship, but failed to
father spiritual sons to lead the movement in the church.
Despite their intentions, they failed to save Methodism from
change, unwittingly becoming agents of faction rather than
fraternity within its ranks.

4

THE BEULAH LAND[1]

The mid-century commercial and industrial revolution
had marked effects on the physical organization and social
role of American camp meetings. Alongside rural camp
meetings which continued with vigor until the turn of the century, new suburban encampments sprang up. Patronized by
people who within the last few decades had migrated to the
cities, the new meetings testified to the substantial prosperity
of their supporters. Promoters, nostalgic for the primitive
camp meetings of their youth, hoped to escape from the con-
gestion, heat and sin of the city in the morally guarded atmosphere of the suburban camp meeting. Like their forebears
who had used the camp meeting as a temporary refuge from
the isolation of the frontier, urban Methodists, prosperous
enough to afford extended vacations, sought renewal in permanent lakeside and ocean shore encampments which sprang up
as prosperity increased.

By the Civil War, a conventional pattern for ordering
camp meeting grounds had evolved which provided guide lines
for all future camp site development. In the center of the grove,
the preacher's stand, a raised platform containing a pulpit
stand and seats for the ministers, faced a large grassy area
where the congregation sat on rough-hewn benches. In a cir-
cle or rectangle surrounding the stand, the campers pitched
the tents where they slept and prepared their meals. As
camp locations became permanent, lots and streets were laid
out, a large tent or board tabernacle covered the preacher's
stand area and simple frame cottages replaced some of the
family tents, giving the meeting site the appearance of a rural village.[2] The story of the camp meeting at Wesleyan Grove,
Martha's Vineyard Island, Massachusetts, the oldest permanent camp meeting in the United States, illustrates this process.

Although a camp meeting had been conducted at Martha's Vineyard nearly every summer from 1835 on, no design
for a permanent encampment was put forward until 1850, when,

BEULAH LAND (1875)

I've reached the land of corn and wine,
And all its riches freely mine,
Here shines undimm'd one blissful day,
For all my night has pass'd away.

[Refrain:]
O Beulah Land, sweet Beulah Land,
As on thy highest mount I stand,
I look away across the sea,
Where mansions are prepared for me,
And view the shining glory shore,
My heav'n, my home, for evermore!

My Savior comes and walks with me,
And sweet communion here have we;
He gently leads me by His hand,
For this is heaven's borderland.

A sweet perfume upon the breeze,
Is borne from ever vernal trees;
And flow'rs that never fading grow
Where streams of life forever flow.

The zephyrs seem to float to me
Sweet sounds of heaven's melody,
As angels with the white-robed throng
Join in the sweet redemption song.

Edgar Page Stites
(1836-1921)

with eighty-seven tents pitched, the voluntary camp meeting
association negotiated a ten-year lease of the grounds at
$30.00 per year. Put under the supervision of neighboring
Methodist presiding elders in 1854, the camp continued to
grow. In 1865 the campers purchased the grounds, and incorporated as the "Martha's Vineyard Camp-Meeting Association" three years later.

The continuance of the meeting year after year encouraged campers to seek more dependable shelter than
could be provided by tents. After the Rev. Frederick Upham
erected the first small cottage in 1856, campers gradually
replaced tents with permanent cottages. By the mid-1870's
Wesleyan Grove presented "the appearance of a regularly
laid out" permanent "summer city of elegant" and "expensive"
cottages. [3]

Construction of permanent housing signaled another
persistent trend: the tendency of camp meeting grounds to
become summer resorts. Years before the construction of
the first cottage at Martha's Vineyard, some campers started
arriving for camp meeting a few days early in order to relax
in the quiet of the grove and to enjoy clam bakes. As housing on the grounds increased, campers lengthened their visits.
Gradually, extended stays became the rule and the religious
meeting, at best, of secondary importance. Despite the camp
meeting association's pronouncement that the holding of a
"strictly religious" annual camp meeting was the paramount
object of the development, the stream of "strangers" who
had "no particular sympathy with the religious objects of the
gathering" annually increased. In fact, by 1875 Martha's
Vineyard was well on its way to becoming nothing more than
a seaside resort. The attempt to blend evangelistic exercises
"with the cultivation of physical vigor, wholesome recrea-
tion, and rational, innocent amusement" steadily gravitated
toward the latter. Two neighboring resorts opened in 1867
attracted numerous residents apathetic to the evangelistic purposes of the community. [4]

Consequently, when in 1870 the National Camp Meeting
Association evangelists decided to hold meetings on church-
controlled grounds, they were choosing (in the East at least)
physical settings like Martha's Vineyard. Determined to hold
"strictly religious" meetings, Association evangelists conducted
camp meetings only if they had control over all activity on the
grounds. Fearful that the camp meeting would degenerate into
a "picnic, "[5] the day's schedule was [continued on page 32]

Ocean Grove Camp Meeting of the Methodist Episcopal Church. Left: an early scene (Ellwood H. Stokes, long-time president of the Ocean Grove Association, and Alfred Cookman, noted abolitionist and holiness evangelist, in left foreground). Right: a late scene. Photographs from: Daniels, Morris S. The Story of Ocean Grove.... New York: Methodist Book Concern, 1919; 136-137.

Ocean Grove Camp Meeting. Left: First Tabernacle, 1870's. Right: Second Tabernacle, 1870's. Photographs from: Daniels, The Story of Ocean Grove... (1919), 56-57.

Ocean Grove Camp Meeting. Top: Third Tabernacle, 1880's.
From: Daniels, The Story of Ocean Grove... (1919), 58. Bot-
tom: John S. Inskip's cottage. From: Osborn, Lucy Reed
(Drake), 1844- . Pioneer Days of Ocean Grove. New York:
Printed for the author by the Methodist Book Concern, 19--;
opposite p. 26.

Ocean Grove Camp Meeting of the Methodist Episcopal Church.
Top: Fourth Tabernacle (exterior), 1894. Bottom: The
same (interior). From Daniels, The Story of Ocean Grove...
(1919), 60-61.

Ocean Grove Camp Meeting.   Cottages on Ocean Pathway,
with tabernacle.   From: Osborn, Pioneer Days... (n.d.),
opposite p. 28.

filled with religious activity: a prayer meeting before breakfast, a testimony or experience meeting (generally called the
"love feast") in mid-morning, preaching services before lunch,
in mid-afternoon, and in the evening.   In short, campers
were "expected to devote nearly all their time to religious"
activities. [6]

In addition to positive provision for abundant religious
activity, the leaders issued an extensive set of rules to regu-
late activity on the grounds.   Typically, these rules not only
outlawed the sale of intoxicants and tobacco, but forbade the
running of Sunday trains to the grounds and the conducting of
Sunday business.   They also discouraged athletic and recreational activities and, in some places, restricted admission
by requiring tickets and by denying admittance to all vehicles
from Saturday evening to Monday morning.

While the National Association regulated the use of
camp facilities in meetings where its workers preached, the
Association itself did not maintain camp grounds.   Some of
its members as individuals served as trustees of particular
camps, however.   Notable was William B. Osborn, an
original National Association member who was also a founder
of Ocean Grove, one of the most ostentatious encampments
in the country.   Since the Ocean Grove Camp Meeting, with
several National evangelists on its committee of control, served
as a model for numerous other post-war encampments, [7] its
practices may be used to illustrate holiness promoters' ideas

concerning the camp community.

Inspired by the success of the first National Camp
Meeting at Vineland, Osborn became enchanted with the idea
of securing a seaside camp meeting ground where "desired
rest and the great salvation" could be "secured at the same
time."[8] With the cooperation of several ministerial colleagues of the New Jersey Conference, Osborn in 1869 obtained an unimproved site on the coast six miles from Long
Branch. The site included high ground with a good beach
and an excellent grove free from mosquitoes.[9] In 1879 with
twelve other ministers, including seven associated with the
National Association,[10] and thirteen laymen, Osborn petitioned
the New Jersey legislature for incorporation as the Ocean
Grove Camp-Meeting Association of the Methodist Episcopal
Church.[11]

The charter described the Ocean Grove project as a
"permanent Camp-Meeting ground and Christian seaside resort" controlled by a self-perpetuating board of trustees composed of members of the Methodist Episcopal Church. The
charter gave immunity from taxation as a religious institution,
and allowed camp appointed and paid peace-keeping officers
full police powers. Adopting by-laws for "the holding of Camp-
Meetings for the Promotion of Christian holiness,"[12] the
trustees also obtained special legislation forbidding the sale
of alcoholic beverages within a mile of the entrance.[13]

Although the charter professed a love for nature and a
desire to have "a portion of land skirting the sea consecrated
to sacred uses," Ocean Grove became a stronghold of Methodist Victorianism rather than a rural utopia. In 1883 the
New York Sun attributed Ocean Grove's success to the "remarkable beauty of the locality ... the firmness" of the
management in enforcing charter provisions concerning alcoholic beverages, and to "the suppression of amusements ...
classed as immoral" in the Methodist Discipline.[14] From the
beginning undesirables were turned back at the gates and
Ocean Grove authorities early used licensing powers to ex-
clude unwanted vendors. A 1878 report recorded 38 eye-glass
and pack pedlers, 21 prize package vendors, 3 Punch and Judy
shows, 4 bird shows, 2 gymnastic shows, 199 back peddlers,
28 organ grinders, 2 brass bands, 36 eye-glass pedlers, 7
flashy shows, and 56 tramps fined, put off or turned away.[15]
Even after the development had obtained all the marks of a
substantial resort community, the camp meeting association
leaders enforced sabbatarian decorum. They forbade card

playing, dancing, and most other amusements during camp meeting and on Sunday, and closed the gates to vehicular traffic from 11:00 P.M. Saturday until daylight Monday morning. [16]

Although to the outsider the regimen of holiness camp grounds must have seemed less than liberal, the Methodist perfectionist believer found there the disciplined fellowship which he considered essential to the maintenance of genuine freedom. Two youths who were apprehended at Ocean Grove for playing cards and accused the Association of being "the narrowest-minded and most bigoted" men ever heard of, were told by the police that the camp authorities were actually very liberal, for having established the camp for religious purposes which did not prevail in the general society; the Association neither compelled the boys to come, nor forced them to stay, if they did not like it. [17] Convinced that social ills sprang directly from personal sins rather than the structure of society, the prosperous believer felt the camp community offered a wholesome temporary alternative to the general dissipation of urban society. Given the Wesleyan belief that sin issued from disobedience to know commands of God, the sincere Methodist hardly compromised the Decalogue. Assuming that running Sunday trains violated the fourth commandment, he had no alternative but unqualified opposition to running them.

Success crowned success. Every year crowds increased; every year more campers came; and every year numbers of ever more ostentacious cottages were built. Fast moving away from rural simplicity, campers in increasing numbers described the holiness camp meeting as a foretaste of heavenly bliss. In 1874 one camper likened Ocean Grove "to Mount Pisgah," from whence a clearer glimpse of the promised land could be obtained. [18] He had reached the Land of Beulah.

5

THE PILGRIMS

Following the lead of Phoebe Palmer who used the
mourner's bench as a symbol of the relationship between
personal consecration and entire sanctification, later holiness writers used the camp meeting as a metaphor of the
exuberance which characterized truly sanctified Christians.
Impressed by the joyful atmosphere of holiness camp meetings, preachers and gospel song writers posited a spiritual
camp meeting. Inhabited by fully sanctified believers alone,
this internal camp meeting was a veritable heaven on earth.
Testifying to its reality, in 1877 Sheridan Baker, a Methodist evangelist, declared that despite "very great" physical
suffering, he "enjoyed" an "almost ... continuous" spiritual
"feast--a kind of 'National Camp Meeting'" in his soul all
the time. [1]

Expanded to include other analogies drawn from the
Bible and John Bunyan's Pilgrim's Progress, [2] the internal
camp meeting metaphor informed connections holiness writers
established between the pilgrimage of Bunyan's Christian and
the Exodus; between the Wesleyan theology of salvation and
Israel's journey from Egypt to Canaan; and between the experience of entire sanctification or perfect love and the
believer's residence in the Promised Land, also referred to
as Canaan or Beulah. Having come into the experience of
entire sanctification during a camp meeting, many holiness
believers identified their religious feelings with the physical
setting in which they had first been aroused. As a consequence holiness song writers used the Beulah metaphor in the
testimonies which filled their songs. Representative are

> I've reached the Beulah land,
> The summer-land of love,

and

> I have found the land of Beulah
> The blessed land of perfect rest.

35

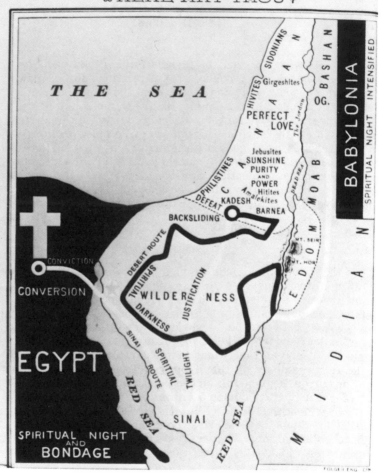

"Out of Egypt into Canaan." Photograph from: Knapp, Martin Wells, 1853-1901. Out of Egypt into Canaan; or Lessons in Spiritual Geography. Boston: McDonald, Gill & Co.; Albion, Mich.: Revivalist Publishing Co., 1889 (c1887); frontispiece.

Not content with affirmation of spiritual rest, the second
writer explained the role of Christ in the internal camp
meeting.

> He has wrought my perfect freedom
> From the pow'r of inbred sin,
> He's my soul's eternal Eden,
> I have paradise within.

Echoes of Eden, present in John Bunyan's Beulah land,
could also be heard in holiness gospel songs. Connecting the
Beulah metaphor with entire sanctification and camp meetings,
such reverberations could be heard in Edgar Page Stites'
"Beulah Land." Written in 1875 while Stites, a New Jersey
shipbuilder, was enroute to the Ocean Grove Camp Meeting, [3]
this song described a heavenly place having most of the characteristics of a camp meeting ground on the seashore. Upon
reaching this rich "land of corn and wine," darkness disap-
peared and an "undimm'd ... blissful day" dawned. Christ
joined the traveler and "gently" escorted him through Beulah
land. Evidence that this was a "borderland" of heaven abounded. Every "breeze" carried the scent of the "vernal trees"
and "never fading" flowers of heaven. "Zephyrs" from the sea
nearby brought "sounds of heaven's melody" causing the en-
raptured pilgrim to pause,

> As angels with the white-robed throng
> Join in the sweet redemption song.

Surrounded thus with delights of sight and smell, the sanctified pilgrim contemplated heaven and sang:

> O Beulah Land, sweet Beulah Land,
> As on thy highest mount I stand,
> I look away across the sea,
> Where mansions are prepared for me,
> And view the shining glory shore,
> My heav'n, my home, for evermore.

Camp meetings were as often located in the mountains
as at the seaside. Holiness gospel songs placed the Land of
Beulah in both settings. Harriet Requa's "Is Not This the
Land of Beulah," issued about the same time as Stites' song,
described the delights of a mountain-top Beulah.   There a

pilgrim mountain climber rested and enjoyed pleasures he had
never before experienced. Basking in "golden sunlight, "
drinking the "pure" water of fountains flowing under "amaran-
thine bow'rs, " and breathing air "laden" with the scent of
"flowers, " the satisfied pilgrim exclaimed,

> Is not this the Land of Beulah?
> Blessed, blessed land of light;
> Where the flowers bloom forever
> And the sun is always bright.

While Stites' pilgrim was so enchanted with the Land
of Beulah that he forgot his past existence, Requa's mountain
climber reminisced.

> I can see far down the mountain
> Where I wandered weary years
> Often hindered in my journey
> By the ghosts of doubts and fears.

At the mention of past failures, however, he recalled that
"great salvation" which had lightened his load and made
"worldly honors" easy to forsake. Cheered by the knowledge
that Christ had recently preceded him up the trail and strength-
ened by His presence which lingered "near, " the triumphant
pilgrim now had little sympathy for defeatists who complained
because of "heavy crosses" or "burdens hard to bear. "

The didactic purpose of most songs in the Beulah land
tradition was but thinly veiled. Published in 1879, Annie
Turner Wittenmeyer's "The Valley of Blessing" straight-
forwardly preached regeneration as a prerequisite of entire
sanctification, complete cleansing from sin, and "perfect love"
as an instrument for casting "out fear. "[4] Other texts required singers to testify about religious experiences and, on
occasion, even to shout. The singer of Henry J. Zelley's
"The Sweet Beulah Land"[5] was required to do both. After
testifying

> I am washed in the blood
> And my soul is made white,
> And I know I am sanctified,

he shouted

> Glory, glory to God
> My heart now is cleansed from sin,
> I've abandoned my self to the Holy Ghost,

And His fulness abides within.

Although such songs were undoubtedly designed with the edification of the saints in mind, they obliquely suggested a trip
to the mourner's bench by those who could not claim the experiences described or did not feel like shouting. By dividing
the congregation into saints and sinners, didactic songs
helped to weld the faithful into an ever-more close-knit fellowship.

As the century advanced, condemnation of worldliness
increasingly characterized holiness preaching and singing.
Many gospel songs pictured holiness Christians as forsaking
popular habits and customs. Entering the holiness repertoire
about 1879, "The Pilgrim Company" enunciated the belief
that acceptance with God depended on separation from the
world. With music arranged by William McDonald, second
president of the National Association for the Promotion of
Holiness, it gloried in otherworldliness. The chorus reiterated the theme:

> I had rather be the least of them
> Who are the Lord's alone,
> Than wear a royal diadem
> And sit upon a throne.

Reflecting the growing exclusiveness of the holiness element
within the church, the text consisted of a series of questions
and answers concerning Christian pilgrims. Asked to identify
some "poor despised ... travelers, " the guide answered that
they were "children of a King, " "heirs of immortal crowns
divine. " Why then were they so poorly clothed and "lacking
daily bread?" the worldling asked. Because, though ill-
clothed and ill-fed by worldly standards, they possessed "rich"
spiritual "robes" and feasted on "heavenly manna" invisible to
natural eyes. Following their "Leader" the pilgrims took the
"thorny" path of righteousness and avoided the "pleasing"
worldly "path" which led to "hell. " "No other road to Salem's
happy ground?"[6] "No other Way, " the guide replied, "Christ
is the only way to God. "

The wayfarers had found company. Exclusive, ascetic,
and suffering from real or imagined persecutions, holiness
believers warmed to the prospect of heaven. "Going Home"
written about 1845 by William Hunter spoke with jubilant an-
ticipation of celestial glory.

> My heavenly home is bright and fair;
> Nor pain nor death can enter there.

Seeing heaven as an escape from the "earthly prison, "
Hunter exclaimed,

> Let others seek a home below
> Which flames devour, or waves o'erflow;
> Be mine a happier lot to own
> A heavenly mansion near the throne.

Then contrasting the present with the future, he capped each
stanza with the refrain "I'm going home to die no more. "

As the end of the century neared, however, editors
replaced the old refrain with an optimistic one and inserted
"I feel like traveling on" between lines in the stanzas.   Exuberance now characterized the whole text and exultant congregations chanted.

> The Lord has been so good to me,
> I feel like traveling on,
> Until that blessed home I see
> I feel like traveling on,
>
> My heavenly home is bright and fair,
> I feel like traveling on. [7]

In addition to the pilgrim community analogy, a soli-
tary sanctified believer resembling Bunyan's Christian early
appeared in holiness hymnody.   In the 1870's "Deliverance
Will Come, " first published by the Rev. John B. Matthias in
1836, became popular in holiness circles.   This song pictured
the sanctified Christian as poor, sick and weighed down with
earthly cares, yet like Bunyan's hero cheered continuously by
the prospect of heaven.   "In tatter'd garments" the way-worn
traveler struggled "up the mountain" toward "home. "   Oblivious alike of the "summer sun, " "worn" "dusty" clothing, a
sweaty brow, and physical exhaustion, repeatedly he reminded
himself of promised "deliverance" by reciting: "Then palms
of victory, crowns of glory ... I shall bear. "   Ignoring "song-
sters in the arbor" which bade him pause, he hurried forward
and at dusk reached the crest of the mountain.   He had just
sighted "his everlasting home" far away when a band of angels
suddenly appeared and carried him over the river of death.
On the celestial shore a multitude of saints sang, "Jesus has
redeemed us to suffer nevermore. "

Like William Hunter's "Going Home," John Matthias'
song met revision in the closing decades of the century.
And as in the case of Hunter's song, editors aimed at en-
hancing the optimism of the text.   Experimentation begun by
1882 reached its climax in 1886 when Captain R. Kelso Carter, teacher at the Pennsylvania Military Academy and frequent participant in the Mountain Lake Park Camp Meeting
in Maryland, copyrighted a modified version of the words.
In the new version "a bloodwashed pilgrim" replaced the
"way-worn traveler," and the pilgrimage took place on a
highway rather than a mountain trail.   Unlike the exhausted
traveler of the earlier version, now the pilgrim, his counte-
nance "peaceful" and "shining," appeared oblivious to worldly
opposition and derision.   Impressed by the bloodwashed pilgrim's boldness and humility, an observer reported,

> I saw him in the furnace;
> He doubted not, nor feared,
> And in the flames beside him
> The Son of God appeared;
> Tho' seven times 'twas heated
> With all the tempter's might,
> He said, 'Thy yoke is easy,
> The burden, it is light.'

In the midst of "storms, and clouds and trials, in prison"
and "at the stake," his faith remained unshaken. And in the
flames he "leaped for joy" and rejoiced that his suffering
was "all for Jesus' sake."

In Carter's "Bloodwashed Pilgrim," a refrain which
described the pilgrim as wearing "palms of victory" and
"crowns of glory" helped maintain the hopeful tone.   At death
the "bloodwashed pilgrim" passed over "the threshold" into
the heavenly throne room, there to reign forever with Christ.
At last

> The Crown, the Throne, the Sceptre,
> The Name, the Stone so White, [9]
> Were his, who found, in Jesus,
> The yoke and burden light.

For the sanctified pilgrim the journey had lost its hazards.

In the 1890's and the first decade of the new century
holiness song writers carried the trend toward optimism to
the ultimate.   First published in 1906 by J. M. Harris, [10] a

well-known holiness song evangelist, Florence Horton's
"Walking in the King's Highway"[11] forecast an almost unbe-
lievably happy spiritual journey ahead.   It said that "salvation" would enable Christian pilgrims to see both earthly and
heavenly things in a new light, "the desert" for instance "as
a rose."   Secure in the knowledge of divine protection, "ran-
somed" and "purified" saints passed through well-watered
country unmolested by "rav'nous" beasts, singing

> There's a highway there and a way,
> Where sorrow shall flee away,
> And the light shines bright as the day,
> Walking in the King's highway.

Now the pilgrims were exultant.

Breaking with a long tradition of walking pilgrims,
Charlie D. Tillman, a Southern song evangelist, mechanized
the journey.   In his "Life's Railway to Heaven" copyrighted
in 1891, Tillman pictured the pilgrim as a railroad engineer.
Bound for heaven over a serpentine route, an inner voice
repeatedly directed the Christian engineer,

> Keep your hand upon the throttle,
> And your eye upon the rail.

"Grades," "fills," "curves," "obstructions," "bridges,"
"tunnels" and "tressels" combined with "wind and rain"
storms to complicate the job.   When conditions seemed unbearable, however, the engineer renewed his confidence by
praising God.   Then he exclaimed,

> Blessed Saviour, Thou wilt guide us
> Till we reach that blissful shore;
> Where the angels wait to join us
> In Thy praise for evermore.

"Christ" the "conductor" gave directions and as long as the
pilgrim-engineer remained prayerful and teachable he could
look forward to successful completion of the run.   Hopefully,
on arrival at "Union Depot" the heavenly "Superintendent"
would greet him "with the hearty joyous plaudit, 'Weary
pilgrim, welcome home'."

Alongside the trend toward ever more specific applica-
tion of the Beulah pilgrim metaphor was its use in connection
with the Exodus analogy.   Drawn from the Old Testament in

much the way that the Land of Beulah had been extracted
from Pilgrim's Progress, this analogy likened the individual's flight from sin to sanctification to Israel's journey from
Egypt to the Promised Land.[12]   According to this schema
the sojourn in Egypt represented the life of sinful indulgence.
The passover[13] and escape through the Red Sea, stood for
conversion.   Israel's forty-year residence in the wilderness
symbolized the justified Christian's life before he attained
perfection, a period during which the believer was continually tempted to sin.   The propensity to sin which remained
after conversion was compared to Israel's continual grumbling
in the wilderness.   The disobedience at Kadesh-Barnea paralleled the situation of Christians who having light concerning
entire sanctification, failed to go on to perfection.   Death
of all except Caleb and Joshua[14] in the wilderness symbolized the secession of pride and selfish ambition in complete
consecration.   Finally, the crossing of Jordan stood for instantaneous attainment of entire sanctification.   Freed from
divided affections thereby, the sanctified Christian began to explore the Promised Land.   Symbolic of this state of undivided
love for God and man was Canaan's natural bounty: corn,
wine, milk, honey, pomegranates, and figs.   Human imper-
fections: ignorance, poor judgment, indiscreet behavior,
products of man's fallen nature not eliminated by sanctification, were likened to the residents of Canaan--at the time
of Israel's arrival--who must be driven out if the people of
God were permanently to possess the land.

"I've Pitched My Tent in Beulah, " by Mrs. M. J.
Harris, wife and co-worker of J. M. Harris, stated in autobiographical terms the doctrinal substance of the Exodus
analogy.   Written at the Hollow Rock, Ohio camp meeting
in 1908,[15] Mrs. Harris' song recounted the entire journey.

> I long ago left Egypt
> For the promised land,
> I trusted in my Savior
> And ... His guiding hand,
> He led me out to victory
> Thro' the great red sea,
> I sang a song of triumph,
> And shouted I am free.
>
> I followed close beside Him
> And the land soon found,
> I did not halt or tremble,
> For Canaan I was bound,

> My guide I fully trusted
> And He led me in,
> I shouted hallelujah,
> My heart is free from sin.
>
> I started for the highlands
> Where the fruits abound,
> I pitched my tent near Hebron,
> There grapes of Eschol found,
> With milk and honey flowing,
> And new wine so free,
> I have no love for Egypt,
> It has no charms for me.

Then, as was characteristic of later Beulah songs, at the
end of each stanza she shouted,

> You need not look for me
> Down in Egypt's sand,
> For I have pitched my tent
> Far up in Beulah land.

Utilization of the Exodus analogy paved the way for
a sequence of gospel songs recounting every step of the
journey from sin to entire sanctification. In "Tis Good
to Live in Canaan," Mrs. C. H. Morris claimed that re-
sponding to God's command to go up and possess the land,
she fled "Egypt's cruel bondage."[16] About 1902 John G.
Foote made the passover a metaphor of individual repentance. In "When I See the Blood," Christ became the
paschal lamb:

> Christ our redeemer died on the cross,
> Died for the sinner, paid all His due;
> Sprinkle your soul with the blood of the Lamb,
> And I will pass, will pass over you.

In 1886 Joshua Gill, an editor for the National Association, and in 1896 Henry J. Zelley, New Jersey Methodist
pastor, celebrated the Red Sea crossing as a symbol of God's
grace. While in "I'm in the Promised Land," Gill spoke of
personal salvation:

> I passed between the billows,
> Walled up on ev'ry hand,
> I trusted to my captain,
> And sought the promised land.

In "He Rolled the Sea Away, " Zelley spoke both of divine
deliverance from sin and of supernatural relief from sorrow
and death.   After narrating the Red Sea miracle, Gill continued the autobiographical rehearsal:

> I came to Sinai's mountain,
> I trod the desert sand,
> I drank at Horeb's fountain,
> Seeking the promised land.

Despairing of entering at Kadesh-Barnea because he had no
guide, he continued aimlessly wandering in the wilderness
many years.

> The spies bro't back their message,
> Some wept, some said "we can";
> The land was all 'twas promised,
> But who would lead the van?
> At last my heart dispairing,
> Of entering with this band,
> I cried aloud to Jesus,
> To show the promised land.

While confessing that they themselves had long sought
the blessing before receiving it, most song writers reminded
audiences of the uselessness of lengthy seeking.   Haldor
Lillenas, a Norwegian immigrant converted in the Peniel
Mission at Astoria, Oregon, who later became a prolific
song writer, [17] implored, "Why wander in the wilderness, O
fainting soul?" then exhorted, "Come over into Canaan land."

Finally singers of Joshua Gill's "I'm in the Promised
Land, " "found the river-crossing" and saw the Land of
Canaan ahead.   Waiting on the bank of Jordan, pilgrims in
I. G. Martin's "Out of Egypt into Canaan" heard those who
had crossed before them singing,

> I'm over the Jordan tide,
> The waters did there divide;
> I'm in the land of Canaan,
> Abundantly satisfied.

Indescribably happy over their new experience, holiness songs
compared it to heaven. Issued in 1903, J. E. French's "This
Is Like Heaven to Me" described the celestial joy experienced
by the sanctified.   French explained that when he found "people" who failed to understand why the sanctified were "so

happy and free," he told them that they had "crossed over
over Jordan to Canaan's fair land," and it seemed "like
heaven" to them.   Exuberant religious expression then was
natural.

> So when we are happy
> We sing and we shout,
> Some don't understand it I see;
> We're filled with the Spirit,
> There isn't a doubt,
> And this is like heaven to me.

During an era when masses of Americans had been
wrenched from a settled farm environment by removal to
new areas or to the city, songs which reiterated the familiar
imagery of camp meeting provided a bridge to the old life.
By this means holiness proponents were able to gain audience with many first generation rural immigrants, although
such people may at first have been opposed to the Methodist
perfectionism they preached.

6

THE COME-OUTERS

During the first decades of its existence, the National Camp Meeting Association for the Promotion of Holiness hewed rigidly to its original purpose: the restoration of Wesley's teaching on perfect love by means of camp meeting revivals. As a "committee of evangelists," holiness promoters adopted methods similar to those of Dwight L. Moody, yet provided for continued evangelistic efforts through the National Association, an organization similar to contemporary reform agencies such as the Young Men's Christian Association and the Woman's Christian Temperance Union. Disclaiming any desire to spawn a separatist movement within the church, the Association evangelists ranged widely, making the Association national in influence as well as name.[1] Success in camp meeting promotion and publishing eventually led Association officers to seek release from Methodist conference appointments.[2] While professing deep loyalty to the Methodist Episcopal Church, National Association leaders moved continually toward the periphery of church activity. To aid converts, National Camp Meeting leaders increasingly used agencies independent of the church's control. Though sincerely loyal to the church, National evangelists demonstrated that their Methodist allegiance was grounded in nostalgia. Having by divergent direction lost real contact with present conditions in the church, they failed to provide converts with bridges between the camp meeting and the church. Instead, the aid which they provided outside the church's official program foreshadowed the independent churches of the future.

Association evangelists early recognized the necessity of continued contact if their converts were to remain true to their perfectionist profession. To meet this need, the National Assocation endorsed regional, state, and local associations modeled after the national organization. These associations, designed to provide occasional services, conventions, revivals and camp meetings, were to promote brotherly watch care among holiness adherents. In communities containing several

47

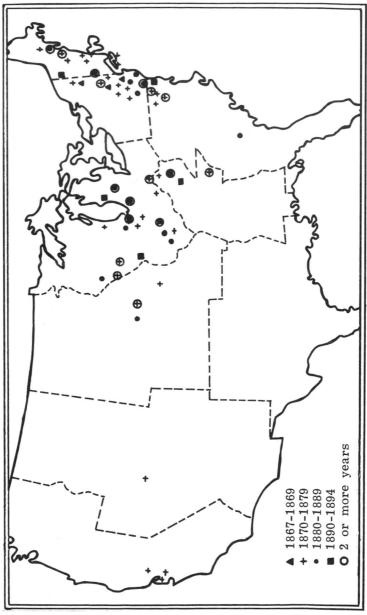

Figure 1. Sites of National Holiness Camp Meetings, 1867–1894, by Geographical Regions.

◀ 1867–1869
+ 1870–1879
● 1880–1889
■ 1890–1894
○ 2 or more years

individuals who professed perfect love, Association leaders
encouraged the formation of holiness bands (prayer groups
similar to Mrs. Palmer's Tuesday Meeting) where believers
might be nurtured and seekers after Christian perfection be
encouraged in their quest.

Clustered in four great metropolitan areas in the
East--Boston, New York, Philadelphia and Baltimore--but
intent on reinvigoration of old-time Methodism on a national
scale, the Association expanded into other sections in the
1870's and 1880's. Meeting with cordiality beyond the fondest
hopes of the Easterners, this thrust resulted in the organization of many local groups as instruments for establishing
converts and consolidating the movement within the church.
Approved by leading western preachers who attended the
Association-endorsed Holiness Conferences held at Cincinnati
and New York in the fall of 1877,[3] the association methodology soon proved less productive of unity than some Easterners
believed it to be. Midwestern holiness leaders denounced urban
and ecclesiastical power. In an address to the Cincinnati Holiness Conference, John P. Brooks, editor of the Banner of
Holiness, listed urban conditions and antagonistic churchmen
as main stumbling blocks to rapid extension of holiness
teaching in the West. He claimed that "country communities"
and "rural people" generally were "readier and freer to hear,
believe and embrace the truth of holiness, than the populations
within the cities." Church leaders were as inamicable to
holiness teaching as country folk were receptive. Consequently,
the speaker advised, "Where entrance has not been secured,
and cannot for the asking, then should entrance be procured
anyhow, independent of all considerations and all conditions"
excepting "the command of God."[4]

Starting in 1872 with the Western Holiness Association
in Illinois, regional associations, modeled after the national
one, sprang up in the Midwest, South, and Southwest. Organization of the Western Association was quickly followed by the
Texas Holiness Association (1878),[5] the Iowa Holiness Association (1879),[6] the Southwestern Holiness Association in
Missouri and Kansas (1879),[7] the Georgia Holiness Association
(1883),[8] and the Pacific Coast Holiness Association in California (by the mid-1880's). Periodicals helped to unite the
regional associations and to provide necessary direction. The
Western Association issued the Banner of Holiness; the Iowa
Association, The Highway; the Southwestern Association, The
Good Way; the Michigan Association, the Michigan Holiness
Record; the Georgia Association, The Way of Life, and the

Pacific Coast Association, the <u>Pacific Herald of Holiness.</u>

Although in structure regional associations differed
little from the National one, they fellowshipped non-Methodist believers more readily[9] and were less restrictive concerning faith healing and the millenium. Composed almost
entirely of Easterners, the National Camp Meeting Association itself was a kind of regional association.[10] Loyal to the
doctrine, methodology and example of their Eastern mentors,
Midwestern regional leaders were independent in spirit from
the beginning. While seniority set the National evangelists
at the top of a pyramid of bonds and associations, submis-
sion to the National program was voluntary, and the convention called annually by the National officers possessed no
disciplinary prerogatives. Faced with novel methods, heretical teachings, scandal, or indiscreet action among their followers, National Association leaders could only admonish,
rebuke, or disown.

By the end of the century, National Association leaders
had become aware that their interests lay with the Midwesterners. At the same time they discovered that holiness-sym-
pathizing bishops, elected in the 1870's with their support,
had been forced by the exigencies of office to be more objective
toward special groups than they otherwise might have been.
To favor perfectionist teaching in the church and to favor
holiness associations independent of the church were two distinct, sometimes contradictory, things. Ten years before
the National Association was formed, Jesse T. Peck,
a leading advocate of teaching perfect love in the church,
warned that he regarded the "organization of the friends of
holiness, as a distinct work" as "undesirable and highly
dangerous" to the welfare of the church.[11] Troubled by those
who agreed with their doctrine but questioned their methods,
National evangelistis had no choice except to look to the
emerging regional leaders who sometimes pushed the Association idea more heartily than did original National leaders
themselves.

Skepticism toward associationism generally characterized Methodist leadership. The one exception was Bishop
William Taylor, the inventor of "self-supporting" missions.
Perhaps the most controversial bishop in Methodist history,
Taylor got his start during the gold rush by preaching to
miners and sailors on the streets of San Francisco. After
pastoring the first Methodist congregation in San Francisco,
he returned East where he itinerated as an evangelist for five

years.[12] In 1862 he left for Australia, spending several
months in England, Ireland, and Palestine en route. With
gratifying results, he moved through Australia, Tasmania,
Ceylon, then to Cape Colony, Kaffraria, and Natal in Africa.
Finally in 1870 he went to India, where his idea of "self-
support" found wide acceptance. Handicapped because he did
not know the language, Taylor decided first to aim at conversion of Europeans and English-speaking natives who in turn
could effectively evangelize the native populace. An additional
advantage would be the ability of such workers to provide their
own support. Preaching at bazaars and in market-places,
Taylor was so successful that within a few years he attracted
many free-lancers into Indian service and laid the foundation
for the South India Conference of the Methodist Episcopal
Church.[13] Despite opposition by church officials, in 1884
Taylor won election as missionary bishop for Africa.[14] The
inclusion of prominent holiness people among his workers won
Taylor the support of the holiness press[15] and National Association leaders.

Holiness workers associated with Taylor included
Amanda Smith, a Negro washerwoman sanctified during John
S. Inskip's pastorate at the Green Street Church in New York
City[16] and William B. Osborn, a founder of the National Camp
Meeting Association and of the Ocean Grove Camp Meeting.[17]
The relationship between Osborn's wife and Amanda Smith il-
luminates the process by which Taylor's workers were sometimes recruited. Before her marriage, Lucy Drake, rejected
for missionary service by the Methodist board because of
poor health, went to India on her own, where she served
several terms. Once, she was in London en route back to
the field when she heard that Amanda Smith was also in England. During a visit with Miss Drake, Amanda learned that
Lucy "had a conviction that the Lord wanted" her [Amanda]
"to go to India. I [Amanda] told her I didn't see it in that
light at all" and left. Amanda confessed, "I never prayed a
bit about it, although she told me to do so." "A few days
later" Amanda received a letter from Lucy saying that in
answer to prayer money was coming in for her expenses. "As
I stood by the mantel shelf reading" that "letter," Mrs. Smith
later recalled, "I said to myself, 'I know the reason Miss
Drake thinks the Lord wants me to go...; she ... doesn't
like to travel alone, and it is easy to see the Lord in it...;
I have enough to do ... and I'm not going'." But then "a
voice" seemed to rebuke her for failing to ask "the Lord what
His will" was. She repented and accompanied Lucy Drake.[18]

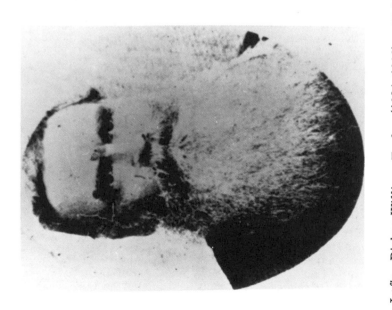

Left: Bishop William Taylor (1821–1902). Right: Amanda Berry Smith (1837–1915). Photographs from: General Holiness Assembly. Chicago, 1901. Echoes of the General Holiness Assembly Held in Chicago, May 3–13, 1901, ed. by S. B. Shaw. Chicago: S. B. Shaw, 1901.

Left: William Bramwell Osborn (1832-1902). Right: Lucy Reed Drake Osborn (1844-). From: General Holiness Assembly. Chicago, 1901, Echoes... (1901).

In 1875 William B. Osborn went to India where he married Miss Drake. Instrumental in founding the Lanowli camp meeting, in 1880 Osborn persuaded National Association evangelists to come to India. Returning to America with them, he joined Association leaders in a campaign for adoption of Taylor's self-help methods in domestic as well as foreign fields. [19]

On the boat en route to the United States, Osborn weighed the possibilities of self-supporting work in the homeland. He commented to Mrs. Osborn: "What a fine thing it would be" for there to be a special "gathering of returned missionaries of all denominations where every address should be delivered by a returned missionary." The resulting encampment, Wesley Park located near Niagara Falls, Ontario, Canada, close by Lucy Drake Osborn's birthplace, not only quickly became an annual affair, but spawned the International Missionary Union, which specialized in foreign evangelism in much the same way that the National Camp Meeting Association did domestically.

Wesley Park[20] and the Union Missionary Training Institude of Brooklyn, New York, [21] founded by the Osborns in 1882, consumed their attention for the remainder of their lives. The Brooklyn Institute attempted to develop self-reliant missionaries who trusted God to provide food and material necessities while pursuing missionary work, independent of denominational boards. Along with Taylor University in Indiana which helped staff independent mission projects, the Missionary Training Institute broke ground for a score of self-supporting missionary training schools founded by the constituency of the National and state associations during the next thirty years.

Although National Association members endorsed Bishop Taylor's quasi-independent methods and although their own activities lay for the most part outside the church, nineteenth-century evangelists never forgot the National Association's original purpose. While they recognized that Christian sanctity was not a Methodist monopoly and preached the value of interdenominational fraternity, Association leaders felt that their primary mission was to preserve old-time Methodism. [22] By means of the camp meeting they attracted many non-Methodists to perfectionist belief, yet insisted that the camp meeting was no substitute for the church. Upon recommendation of the evangelists, converts normally joined denominational churches. The new members soon found, however, that while their own camp meeting experiences made a crucial difference in what they thought the church should be doing, older members resisted change.   Frustrated in attempts to reform the existing churches, by the mid-1880's holiness converts had started considering the possibility of a distinctively holiness church.

On at least three occasions, groups agitating for an independent church succeeded in calling conventions to consider closer formal ties among the brethren.   Each of the meetings attracted a cross section of the holiness constituency.   At each, National Association officers chaired the business sessions and were able to steer deliberations away from separation.

The first of these, the Western Union Holiness Convention, held at Jacksonville, Illinois, in 1880, [23] sought means for holding converts.   J. W. Caughlan, editor of The Good Way, suggested that holiness believers in every community form bands similar to Mrs. Palmer's cottage meetings, for mutual edification during intervals between camp meetings and revivals.   "It is a noteworthy fact, " he declared, that the results of "faithful Holiness testimony" remain "only in those places" where "regular Holiness" bands have been organized. On the other hand, "in places where, out of regard for ecclesiastical" leaders, the band organizations have been neglected, "Holiness work has come to nought. "   When the demands of the church and Christ came into conflict, Caughlan insisted that holiness workers must "consecrate" the demands of the church on the altar and follow the Lord's leadings instead. [24] Endorsing the idea of regional, state, and local associations and bands, the Western Convention was a first step toward creating a potentially separatist group within the church.

Trouble arising from fanaticism and independent churches led to the calling of the first General Holiness Assembly to meet in Chicago in May 1885.   George Hughes, the National officer who chaired the meeting persuaded the Assembly to spend most of its time seeking a "gigantic" spiritual "baptism. "[25]   The chairman barred from consideration a letter from B. A. Washburn of the Southern California and Arizona Holiness Association calling for the Assembly's endorsement of the organization of independent churches. [26] Instead, the "Declaration of Principles" contained a doctrinal statement and advice about personal behavior, tithing, camp meetings, and publishing enterprises, and recommended that holiness believers become members of denominational churches "to lay a molding hand upon the great body of Christian people"

and to "bring the church to the realization of the glorious
ideal of the New Testament--perfect holiness." The "Declaration" provided a doctrinal statement based on a consensus of
holiness opinion.   It distinguished orthodox belief from the
gradual perfection taught in many churches of the time as
well as from innovations of some believers in instantaneous
attainment who thought that the second blessing would be followed by other crisis experiences.   Completing its business
by appointing a "Committee on Correspondence" empowered
to call a future meeting, the General Holiness Assembly of
1885 proceeded to its declared task of evangelizing the "whole
city" of Chicago, complacent in its "sin and formalism."27

As evinced by the chairman's tactics at the 1885 Assembly, National Association leaders adamantly refused to be
party to any schismatic movement.   Most of them loyally clung
to this conviction until death.   The 1885 meeting demonstrated
the inordinate respect accorded the National officers generally.
Even though many holiness believers in the West shared the
prejudices of their section against Eastern ways and though
many left or would eventually leave the mother church against
the admonition of the National officers, they never forsook
personal loyalty to the founders.   Sixteen years after the
first meeting, the committee called for another General Assembly to meet in Chicago, this time with the obvious purpose
of exploring the possibility of founding a distinctively holiness
church.   National Association President C. J. Fowler was
elected chairman.   The Assembly passed resolutions designed to console perfectionists forced out of denominational
churches, yet offered no alternative courses of action.   Again
the leaders turned the meeting into a revival meeting.   Although the leaders hewed closely to original commitments,
their loyalty cost them leadership.

Meanwhile regional leaders struggled with the tension
between personal admiration of the National leaders and their
own unhappy circumstances.   The advice which the National
Camp Meeting Association leaders gave reflected their own
well-placed position in the Methodist Episcopal Church.   They
had excellent personal relationships with bishops, editors of
the church's periodicals, seminary professors, and leading
pastors.   The General Conferences of 1872 and 1884 had in-
ducted holiness sympathizers into the bishop's office.   Randolph
Sinks Foster of Drew Seminary and Daniel Steele of Boston
University led in the defense of the doctrine of Christian perfection in the church.   Asbury Lowrey, early National member
and editor of the Christian Standard during its early years, 28

climaxed a distinguished career by editing Divine Life, a widely-read perfectionist journal.

While the Midwestern movement was yet in early adolescence, the Eastern movement was experiencing the slackening pace of full maturity. When J. N. Fitzgerald[29] and Phoebe Palmer Knapp, [30] the children of early holiness promoters, rallied to the defense of holiness within the church, National leaders may have thought they were seeing the return of Methodism to her old paths.

Regional holiness leaders faced a vastly different situation. Those within the Methodist Episcopal Church found their church ties strained. Having joined the church upon the advice of holiness evangelists, converts judged the organized church by special criteria. They complained endlessly about the lack of fervor, formality in worship and manner, and the growing ostentation of Methodist meeting-houses and dress. Inexperienced, they were often assigned to poorly paying rural circuits, to places where formality and ostentation were least manifest. There, in recently settled areas, they evangelized their congregations continuously. Troubled by the wealth and urban bias of church but encouraged by periodic pronouncements[31] about the necessity of Christian perfection, most preachers drawn into the holiness movement before 1890 lived and died in the church. Younger Methodists and converts who joined other denominations faced serious problems. The rhetoric of Methodist loyalty developed by the National Association evangelists took little cognizance of recent developments. Those joining the Southern church suffered stigma as disciples of Yankee evangelists and found that church authorities maintained surveillance over methods of Christian work as well as over doctrine. At least holiness believers in non-Methodist churches found appeal to Wesley and Methodist tradition inappropriate.

New emphases coming out of the camp meeting occasioned the first outright breaks with the older denominations. Following the National Association's example, regional associations also elected members and published religious papers. In addition they organized local bands as auxiliaries. They opened Bible training academies, acquired real estate, adopted written doctrinal statements, and permitted the discussion of faith healing, the nature of the church, and the millennium. [32] Such practices opened the movement to criticism from without and to division within. And as early as the 1880's their sect-producing potential was evidenced by independent groups in Missouri, Kansas and California.

In 1882 the Southwestern Holiness Association decided
to allow the local bands to obtain meeting houses and call
pastors. Feeling that this action did not go far enough, a
minority of the Southwestern Association members, convinced
that they had discovered the New Testament plan of church
government, in 1883 started "setting in order" autonomous
churches in rural areas of Missouri and eastern Kansas.
With the editor and key officers of the association on their
side, the church faction gradually took over the enterprises
the Southwestern Association had sponsored: The Good Way,
a holiness school at College Mound, Missouri, and several
camp meetings. Contending that the principles of church
government which it advocated had been practiced by early
Christians and by American Methodists before the establishment of the Methodist Episcopal Church, the new group believed that the bishop's function was in no way different from
that of other ministers. In June 1883, six local preachers
of the Methodist Episcopal Church, South, who presented
themselves to the newly formed Church of God at Centralia,
Missouri, were ordained by a self-constituted presbytery
headed by Isaiah Reid, a leader in the Iowa Holiness Association. Decentralized so that it had few options in dealing with
heterodox teaching or unethical behavior, the group was racked
by controversy over sacraments, church order, and belief
in "the fire" as a third work of grace. As a result, the
Church of God long served loyalists as an example of the
deleterious effects of "come-outism."[33]

By 1883 California independents led by J. W. Swing,
Hardin Wallace, and James F. Washburn gained ascendancy
in the infant Southern California and Arizona Holiness Association and organized holiness bands auxiliary to it into independent churches. The Holiness Bands admitted to membership only persons professing entire sanctification. Incorporated in 1896 as the Holiness Church, this California group required prospective members to forsake lodge affiliations, tobacco, gold ornamentation, and ostentatious dress. With the
development of the Pentecostal movement, which stressed un-
known tongues as evidence of baptism with the Holy Ghost,
the Holiness Church lost hundreds of members. Never
numbering as many as a thousand members, this uncompromising, loosely organized and rural group diminished steadily.
In 1946 it merged with the Pilgrim Holiness Church.[34]

The "come-outers," plagued by internal dissentions,

were shunned by Methodist officials and holiness leaders.
Reaction to independency and the advancing age of National
leaders inspired conservatism and kept most holiness believers in the church for the remainder of the century. On the
other hand, holiness converts outside Methodism found the
loyalty rhetoric irrelevant. They also discovered that camp
meeting experiences, while not changing their own loyalties,
tended to modify their ideas about theology, liturgy and church
order. Upsetting traditional beliefs concerning the sacraments, healing, the millennium, and worship, holiness evangelists directed converts to go home after having made the
situation there unbearable for them.

Increasing estrangement marked holiness converts.
S. B. Shaw, who in 1881 founded the Michigan Holiness
Association, wandered from the Methodist Episcopal to the
Wesleyan Methodist, then to the Free Methodist Church,
seeking an appropriate ecclesiastical setting. Shaw found,
however, that even among the Free Methodists, who from
their beginnings had been believers in the second blessing,
there was opposition to evangelistic efforts when pursued outside the bounds of the church's discipline. The 1887 and 1888
Michigan conferences of both the Free Methodist and the Wesleyan Methodist churches passed resolutions which in essence
forbade their members to join any non-church group specializing in holiness promotion. As a result, Shaw felt obliged to
withdraw from the church. Although he claimed that the
Primitive Holiness Mission, a church association he founded
in 1889, was "not quite" a church, the new body assumed
churchly functions. Ordaining ministers and administering
the sacraments, the Primitive Holiness Mission's distinctiveness lay in insistence on an unsalaried ministry, and permis-
siveness in regard to faith-healing and foot-washing as sym-
bols of Christian brotherhood. Persisting until the turn of the
century, the Primitive Holiness Mission broke a path for
evangelistic associations which sprang up in the wake of ecclesiastical conflicts in the 1880's and 1890's.[35]

In 1884 several Baptist preachers returned to Nova
Scotia from the Old Orchard Beach Camp Meeting claiming
entire sanctification. Opposed by colleagues who were offended
by their testimony, four years later they, with several others,
were disfellowshipped by the New Brunswick Baptist Association. Joined by other holiness Baptists, they re formed a
church. Called the Reformed Baptist Alliance, this group,
which eventually spread over the Maritime Provinces and
northern Maine, furnished numerous workers for independent

holiness work in New England. Organized according to Baptist
principles, it adopted Wesleyan theology and sponsored camp
meetings. In 1966 when it merged with the Wesleyan Methodist Church, the Reformed Baptist Alliance had about 3500
members.[36]

By the 1880's the National Holiness movement had made
its Methodistic mark on Mennonites and Quakers. Because
these groups depended heavily on tradition and social consensus,
holiness believers tended to cluster around a few strong
leaders. The Mennonite Brethren in Christ, for instance,
came into contact with Wesleyan perfectionism through the
activities of the National and regional holiness associations
and the Free Methodists, United Brethren, and Evangelicals
in the northern Midwest. In addition to entire sanctification as an instantaneous experience, they accepted belief in
divine healing and premillennialism, instituted an administrative hierarchy for control of ministers and churches, and
conducted camp meetings. Eventually the Mennonite Brethren
drifted far away from the Dordrecht Confession,[37] becoming
ever more like the Methodists.

Numerous German Baptists in Indiana and Ohio espoused the Methodist doctrine of perfection. Led by Daniel
Sidney Warner, who in the mid-1870's came under the influence of National Association evangelists, several members of
the Church of God in North America (General Eldership)
seceded. In 1878 they formed the Northern Indiana Eldership to promote new ideas about holiness and secret societies.
In the belief that it was a sect, the founders soon withdrew
from the new church also. Warner's followers, who called
themselves the Church of God, maintained no membership
rolls but recognized as members professing Christians who
habitually attended their services. Seeking to avoid sectarianism the group barred members of denominational churches
from fellowship. As a consequence the Church of God reformation movement lost vital contact with other groups which
shared its beliefs about Christian perfection.[38]

Holiness evangelists also proselytized among Midwestern Friends. Moved by the testimony of an acquaintance,
in 1869 David B. Updegraff, a birthright Quaker of Mount
Pleasant, Ohio, professed entire sanctification and started
meetings in his home. Soon in demand as a camp meeting
evangelist, he for many years preached in holiness meetings
at Mountain Lake Park in western Maryland and at Pitman
Grove, New Jersey. A worker in many Methodist revivals,

he advocated congregational singing, preaching and baptism, practices at variance with Quaker tradition. In 1887 Updegraff became editor of the Friends' Expositor. With his friend Dougan Clark, professor at Earlham College in Indiana, he succeeded in getting the international Quaker assembly which met at Earlham that year to adopt an evangelical doctrinal statement that included a Wesleyan article on sanctification. Supported by Calvin Pritchard, editor of the Christian Worker, Wesleyan perfectionists gained a strong footing in the yearly meetings of Indiana and Ohio. By 1894, however, the evangelicals were on the run. Earlham fired Clark; David Updegraff died; and liberals got control of the Christian Worker. Having lost the positions where general leadership might be exercised, the holiness faction fought as guerrillas. They opposed the efforts of Rufus Jones and other liberals to unite independent yearly meetings in a Friends church committed to social rather than evangelical concerns. Constituting a majority of yearly meetings in Ohio, Indiana, Kansas and Oregon, holiness Quakers either refused to enter or soon withdrew from the Five Years Meeting, a Friends denomination created in 1902. Supporting the Cleveland Bible Institute in Ohio, the George Fox College in Oregon, and academies in Idaho, Kansas and Indiana, Quaker evangelicals stressed Wesleyanism in theology, polity, and worship.[39]

Thus, the National Camp Meeting Association for the Promotion of Holiness which began by proposing to revive Wesleyan perfectionism in the teaching and expectation of Methodists, ended by becoming virtually independent of the church. Led by men who conceived the organization's mission in terms of the church establishment, the National Association made few attempts to nurture converts in the church. Instead, the leaders encouraged the development of regional and local holiness associations modeled after the national one, which unwittingly became instruments for pooling local grievances. By providing an alternative to the denominational church, holiness associations posed a threat to Methodist officials. Success in making converts among members of non-Wesleyan churches introduced controversy in those churches over entire sanctification, church government, the sacraments, worship, and eschatology. Thus, conventional ministers in search of reform within Methodism unwittingly became agents of controversy and disunion both inside and outside their own communion.

FAITH WORK

Wanted! Ten thousand to labor in every land.
Wanted! Those who will work without salary.
Wanted! Those who will take the fare by the
way /and shout, 'Glory to God!' Amen! They
are coming.... There is a call from Jamaica,
West Indies. Who will fill it? There are calls
from Australia, Tasmania, and New Zealand.
Who will go? Calls from Sweden and Germany
wait for workers.... Let all the faint-hearted
pack their satchels and leave quickly to make
room for the Gideons, the Shamgars, the Daniels, the Davids and the Deborahs, the Marys,
the Priscillas, and the Dorcases, who are
coming.... With fingers in your ears, eyes
on the mark, feet on the Thorny path, hands
filled with pitchers and lamps, hearts aflame,
on to victory! Fellow-workers, I am with you
on the battlefield and will be in the triumphal
march.[1]

The impact of the holiness movement on the denominationalism of the Gilded Age transcended formal sectarian divisions of the time. For the National Camp Meeting movement,
originating in native reaction to the growing urbanism, com-
mercialism, and industrialism, provided more than pastoral
respite for the nostalgic Methodists of the cities. The practices of holiness camp meetings, coupled with those of Bishop
Taylor's self-supporting mission work, offered appropriate
methods for evangelistic endeavors among native migrants
flocking into the cities and settling the last frontiers.[2]
Adopted during the period of independent holiness secessions,
the Taylor-derived faith methodology ushered in a new era in
the holiness movement.

During the nineteenth century, the leaders of the

national and state associations spent much time declaring
their loyalty to Methodism. They felt that the basic purposes
of the holiness movement were being undermined by those
who sought to restore apostolic Christianity through independent church schemes. Methodist officials lashed out at holiness believers, calling them "come-outers" and equating
voluntary separation from the Methodist church with fanaticism. In 1894 the bishops of the Methodist Episcopal Church,
South issued the sharpest official rebuke the holiness movement ever received. Addressing the General Conference, the
episcopal spokesman chastised associationism as a step
toward schism. He declared,

> There has sprung up among us a party with holiness
> as a watchword; they have holiness associations, holi-
> ness meetings, holiness preachers, holiness evange-
> lists, and holiness property. Religious experience is
> represented as if it consists of only two steps, the first
> step out of condemnation into peace and the next step
> into Christian perfection.... We do not question the
> sincerity and zeal of their brethren; we desire the
> church to profit by their earnest preaching and godly
> example; but we deplore their teaching and methods
> in so far as they claim a monopoly of the experience,
> practice, and advocacy of holiness, and separate them-
> selves from the body of ministers and disciples. [3]

Insinuations that the National Association was the instrument of schism so agitated Methodist holiness leaders
that they saw potential disloyalty everywhere. Theirs was a
lover's quarrel, however, and they seldom broke fellowship
with separated brethren. Not all who left the church did so
voluntarily: some were expelled on heresy charges, others
eased out.

Although during the 1890's National leaders began speaking sympathetically of "put-outers" they at no time approved
independency. To be put-out of the church was one thing; to
leave voluntarily, quite another. "It is a sorrowful spectacle, "
Carradine observed,

> to see people ridiculed, oppressed and sometimes
> ejected from the church on account of possessing a
> heart-warming, soul-overflowing religious experience.
> The Bible tells us about putting away the member who
> committed sin, but where will we find a Scripture that
> can cover and defend the course of thrusting people out

of the ministry and church because they have received
the Baptism of the Holy Ghost and are sanctified?4

When independents adapted Bishop Taylor's methods
in domestic missions, they escaped the frown of loyalist leaders by doing work spurned by denominational agencies. This
self-help system provided the foundation of much later holiness institutionalism. Faith ventures that grew up out of
regional and local holiness associations in the 1880's and
1890's represented the same concern which had motivated the
founders of the National Camp Meeting Association a generation earlier. Devoted to evangelistic social service, the
evangelistic associations, like the National Association, did
not regard their organizations as churches. Usually, they
allowed constituents to maintain membership in denominational
churches. Functionally, they resembled the Salvation Army
which developed from similar motives and promoted similar
activities during the period. Evangelistic associations operated rescue missions, homes for unwed mothers and Bible
training academies; published religious periodicals, books and
tracts; and sponsored foreign missionary work.

An independent school, started at Coldwater, Michigan,
in 1884, provides a striking example of the use of the faith
principle in institutional administration. The project of Lura
Mains, a sanctified Free Will Baptist minister, this boarding
school for orphans depended mainly on prayer to provide daily
necessities. Miss Mains started the school with "five dollars
and a few cents" she had received for preaching. "With the
five dollars I paid two weeks rent, " she recalled, "and with
the few cents bought some crackers and sugar. " I knew
nothing of where a single loaf of bread was coming from" but
decided "to take all students free that wanted to come that
way" and to trust God for living expenses. Lura and Belle,
an orphan girl who lived with her, moved their trunks into
an unfurnished house they had rented and started unpacking.
"The first afternoon, " Miss Mains recounted, "I said to Belle
... 'Do you believe if we ask God for anything we shall receive it?' She said, 'Yes, Ma'am, " so "I said, 'Then let us
ask God for some seats, for you see we have no place for any
one to sit down'. " After praying that God would send chairs,
Lura and Belle had begun work again, when "in about five
minutes" a gentleman appeared at the door and asked if they
wanted a half dozen chairs. Miss Mains reported that such
incidents happened repeatedly. "We prayed for tables, stoves,
bedsteads, " even a cow, "and just as mysteriously everything
came. "5

Like other holiness associations, faith groups conducted camp meetings, cottage prayer meetings, revival campaigns and street meetings. Much of their work overlapped
that of the older National and regional associations and faith
groups often engaged National or state association evangelistic
for revival meetings. The distinctiveness of the evangelistic
associations rested rather in emphasis on lay responsibility
and in strong disapproval of a "hireling" ministry. Protest
against ministerial professionalism did not, in most cases,
amount to anticlericalism, however. Evangelistic associations
made use of ordained clergymen as well as laymen and eventually ordained their own ministers. They objected to a
salaried clergy because of the adverse effect that they felt a
stipulated financial return would have on evangelistic zeal.
Preachers should receive as much in voluntary contributions
as the people could afford, but mission, not money, should be
the motivating factor in Christian service. Consequently,
workers in the evangelistic associations were expected to demand no more than subsistence. If the people prayed earnest-
ly enough, God would reward faith with needed provisions.
Evangelistic workers were expected literally to "pray in" the
groceries. Attracting recent converts who chafed at the leth-
argy of denominational churches, evangelistic associations
assumed responsibility for nurturing new converts in the man-
ners and mores of perfectionism. They put converts to work
evangelizing former companions and running social service
agencies.

While ministering to rough elements in newly settled
areas of the West, rural associations, like their urban counterparts, used rescue mission methods. They interspersed such
endeavors with school house revivals and camp meetings. The
rural faith associations utilized the services of zealous young
people drawn from several denominations which traditionally
had made little place for lay participation in evangelistic efforts. Drawing on holiness camp meeting constituencies,
rural holiness faith workers itinerated in the Midwestern and
Southwestern states. Stressing the relation between the demands of Wesleyan perfection and personal ethics, entertain-
ment, dress and behavior, faith workers sought to instigate a
revival of the earnest piety and asceticism so central to the
late Victorian religious ideal. 6

Driving motives of rural faith associations varied
immensely. They encompassed reaction against ecclesiastical
hierarchies; desire to nurture converts of holiness revivals;
evangelization of orphans and unfortunates; and desire to escape

from traditional sectarian discipline.

In the mid-1880's the Pentecost Bands and the Primitive Holiness Mission challenged the emphasis of the Free Methodist Church, an avowed holiness body, on its regulation of laymen and unsalaried workers. Separating in 1889 over Michigan Free Methodist conference strictures against state holiness association activities, the Primitive Holiness Mission followed the traditional Methodist practice of stationing workers by appointment of the conference. At the time of its organization, the secretary of the Primitive Holiness Mission reported that it utilized the talents of those specially called to general evangelism or colportage work. Such workers would "be expected to hold public services every day when ... health and circumstances permit." The next spring the Conference officially discountenanced a salaried ministry: "We disapprove of the hiring of preachers for a stipulated amount, as we believe it tends to hinder deep spirituality and promote a dependence upon circumstances instead of perfect reliance upon the promises of God for temporal support."[7]

Members of the Pentecost Bands on the other hand, remained in the Free Methodist Church until after the death of their original leader, Vivian A. Dake, in 1892. Then, refusing to submit to rules adopted by the 1890 Free Methodist general conference which would have put the bands under the governance of local pastors, Dake's followers reluctantly withdrew. Incorporating in 1898 under the name Pentecost Bands of the World, workers accepted annual unsalaried appointments at the hand of the officials of the conference. Changing its name in 1925 to Missionary Bands of the World, the Bands continued as an independent body until 1958 when it merged with the Wesleyan Methodist Church. In 1906 the United States Bureau of the Census reported that the Pentecost Bands had about seventy-five domestic missionaries and seventeen foreign missionaries in the field. Although at one time or another this group operated missions in several countries, strong permanent work was developed only in India and Jamaica.[8]

Other rural evangelistic associations discarded the appointment system altogether. The Hephzibah[9] Faith Missionary Association, a group of independent churches and individuals with Mennonite backgrounds organized at Greenwood, Iowa, in 1892, allowed much freedom in selection of fields by workers. By 1894 Hephzibah faith workers had reached foreign territory, and in 1906 the Association reported work in India, China,

Japan and Africa.   At the same time the superintendent reported that supplies "sufficient for food, clothing, fuel, and
traveling expenses" for about sixty domestic missionaries was
being supplied.   In 1948 this group merged with the Wesleyan
Methodist Church.   Centering in Iowa and Nebraska, it sponsored training schools at Tabor, Iowa, and Hot Springs, South
Dakota (the latter for American Indian students), as well as
foreign missionary work in Haiti.[10] Similar in background and
program was the Missionary Church Association.   Organized
by former Mennonites at Berne, Indiana, in 1898, this group
permitted much freedom to workers.   In 1969 when it merged
with the United Missionary Church to form the Missionary
Church, it had about 7500 members in the United States and
foreign work in Africa and the West Indies.[11]

The Southeast Kansas Fire Baptized Holiness Association, which believed in the baptism by fire as a third work of
grace, grew out of the anti-ordinance faction of the Southwestern Holiness Association.   Originating in the 1880's in a
dispute over the necessity of sacraments, the anti-ordinance
protest soon grew to encompass a wide variety of other issues.
From Missouri to Texas they were said to teach a series of
religious experiences beyond entire sanctification: "The Second
Blessing was to be characterized by fire; the third by dynamite;
the fourth by lyddite; the fifth by T. N. T. , and so on. It was
power, power, power, that should be sought, power that would
be manifested in outlandish demonstrations. "   Conventional
holiness people attributed other fanatical acts to the "fire baptized" element.   They charged that some who believed in "mari-
tal purity" (the belief that sexual intercourse even in marriage
was sinful), and others who believed that they, through religious
experience, had escaped death; were merely carrying to its il-
logical conclusion the fanaticism present in the third blessing
idea.   Whatever its corrolaries, "fire baptism" seems to be the
only belief that survived in the Southeast Kansas Association.
In 1945 the group changed its name to the Fire Baptized Holiness Church (Wesleyan).[12]

The circumstances which attracted workers to faith
work and the conditions under which they labored were recounted by F. B. Whisler, who served for five years in Indiana, Iowa, and Nebraska under the Pentecost Bands of the
World.   Converted in a church in Iowa which taught neither
entire sanctification nor the possibility of divine healing, as
a youth Whisler felt called to be a missionary to India and
realized that he must prepare for foreign missionary work in
an environment conducive to his belief in holiness.   When he

Left: Hephzibah Faith Mission at Yokohama, about 1900. Right: Camp Meeting Tabernacle at Tabor, Iowa, headquarters of Hephzibah Faith Missionary Association, erected in 1940. Photographs from: Worcester, Paul W. The Master Key; The Story of the Hephzibah Faith Missionary Association. Kansas City, Mo.: Printed for the Author by the Nazarene Publishing House, 1966; 41.

was about twenty, Whisler went to a convention in Indianapolis sponsored by the Pentecost Bands. During the meeting he
repeatedly felt prompted to give offerings until money for his
fare home ran out. Deeply impressed by the zeal and piety
of the Pentecost Bands workers, young Whisler joined them.
Assigned with several other bachelors to a mission conducted
in a country schoolhouse about sixty miles east of Indianapolis, the new missionary was given money for transportation,
then expected to depend upon God to provide groceries and
other necessities. "None of us boys knew how to cook, "
Whisler explained. "We lived largely on potato soup" and
"whatever we could make from cornmeal and flour...." " "I
gained twenty pounds in a month's time!"

Whisler recalled, "The usual routine after the dishes
were washed, beds made up, floors swept, etc., was to read
our Bibles, study, and pray until time for lunch. " "We fasted
for breakfast on Tuesday and Friday mornings" and at those
times "had a searching, old-fashioned class meeting among
ourselves." In the afternoon they visited in the neighborhood,
reading the Bible and praying in as many homes as they could,
then conducted public evangelistic meetings in the evening.
The workers met continual harassment. One night "someone
punched a window out just back of" Whisler's seat "and spat
tobacco juice down" his neck. Opposition created interest,
however, and the youthful workers "never lacked for crowds."
Even "while the persecution was going on, converts would run
the aisles ... shouting the praises of God. " Pentecost Bands
workers stayed in one place eleven months and generally were
assigned to a new location at the convention at the end of the
year. [13]

Although in Texas some holiness workers spent summers conducting camp meetings and school house revivals,
and worked in city missions in the winter, rural evangelists
usually steered clear of cities. [14] Several groups specializing
in urban evangelism emerged in the 1880's and 1890's, however. Employing social services as an adjunct to evangelism,
holiness workers in city missions from Boston to Los Angeles
combined the practices of the rescue mission with the rhetoric
of the camp meeting. In addition to the Peniel Missions on
the West Coast and the International Holiness Union and Prayer
League in the Midwest, urban evangelistic associations included the Metropolitan Church Association in the Chicago area;
the Heavenly Recruit Church and the Holiness Christian Association in Pennsylvania and Indiana; the Pentecostal Union in
Colorado and New Jersey; the Vanguard Mission of St. Louis;

the People's Mission of Colorado Springs; the Pentecostal
Alliance centered in Nashville; the Holiness Union of Louis-
ville; the Young Men's Holiness League of Indianapolis; the
Pentecostal Rescue Mission of Binghamton, New York; and
loosely federated churches and missions identified with the
New Testament Church of Christ in Tennessee, Arkansas and
Texas; the Central Evangelical Holiness Association in New
England; the Association of Pentecostal Churches of America
in Brooklyn, and the Independent Holiness Church in Texas.

The Heavenly Recruits were typical of the city mission associations. The group formed in 1882 when "several
preachers, impressed with the lack of spirituality ... in the
churches, began preaching on the streets of Philadelphia."
In order to hold converts they secured a hall for services,
and in 1885 incorporated as the Heavenly Recruit Association
of Philadelphia.[15] Another sponsor of city missions was the
Metropolitan Church Association. Commonly known as the
Burning Bush movement, this group grew out of a revival in
1894 in the Metropolitan Methodist Episcopal Church of Chicago. It specialized in slum missionary work and operated
on the faith principle. Preferring rented halls to church
buildings, the Metropolitan group early adopted communal
features in its work. In 1906 a report noted,

> Members are ... to possess nothing which can be
> sold and the proceeds applied to evangelistic work.
> Ministers receive no salaries, nor do they solicit any
> gifts. All money received ... goes into the treasury
> and is distributed for the various causes of the associa-
> tion.

Headquarters at Waukesha, Wisconsin, included an orphanage,
a day school and family quarters. In 1906 the Metropolitan
Association claimed 466 members in six organizations and
missions in Africa, India and Wales. In 1958, 443 members
in fifteen congregations were supporting work in India, Africa,
Mexico and the Virgin Islands.[16]

Often led by recent arrivals from the country who had
succumbed to temptation in the unfamiliar life of the city, the
urban evangelistic associations bent their energies toward
sheltering new converts from the temptations of alcohol, sloth-
fulness and worldly amusements and sought to reconstruct
the discipline of the pious farm family. The concept of the
extended family pervaded the program of the rescue missions
and served as a means of preserving rural culture in an urban
environment.

Although missions tended to spawn auxiliaries, most of them originated in a single rescue mission run by an individual or a man and wife. Typically, the founder of the mission recruited workers from his converts and depended on offerings from the mission clientele and from subscribers to the house publication to meet expenses. Depending on personal resources or patronage to provide for emergencies and buildings and equipment, the founder tried to expand both the support and the program, establishing with his wife a parental relationship to workers as well as converts. Usually he placed great store in Spirit guidance and special providence and, having committed himself to the "life of faith," expected the complete subordination of workers under him.

This pattern of paternalistic evangelistic endeavor prevailed in holiness missions established in Los Angeles, St. Louis, Nashville, Cincinnati, and Cleveland during this period. Rescue homes, orphanages and Bible training schools sprang up in connection with the mission. Adopting many of the ideas which religious liberals were also using, urban holiness promoters developed institutions to save young people from the sins of the city and at the same time to put them to work at the evangelistic task. Projects varied immensely, ranging from faith missions operated by individuals to complex operations which required significant outside support. Peniel Missions, a federation of rescue missions on the West Coast, was representative of the successful individually sponsored project, while the God's Bible School complex in Cincinnati typified operations commanding wider support.

Like many of his future converts, T. P. Ferguson, who founded the first of the Peniel Missions in Los Angeles in 1886, espoused holiness and entered mission work after a life-long grounding in earnest Christianity. Born in 1853 at Mansfield, Ohio, to pious Presbyterian parents, Theodore was converted in 1875 while a student at Oberlin College. (Coincidentally, Charles Grandison Finney, long-time professor of theology at Oberlin and inventor of many techniques widely used in revivalism, died at Oberlin, August 16, 1875.[17]) Moving to California in 1879, Ferguson settled at Santa Barbara where, during a revival conducted by the Holiness Bands, he was instantaneously sanctified. That winter he evangelized in Oregon. Attending the camp meeting at Round Lake, New York, the next summer, Ferguson was deeply impressed by Bishop Taylor's account of the use of self-help in foreign missionary work. He returned to California convinced that such methods might as well be used in domestic missions as on

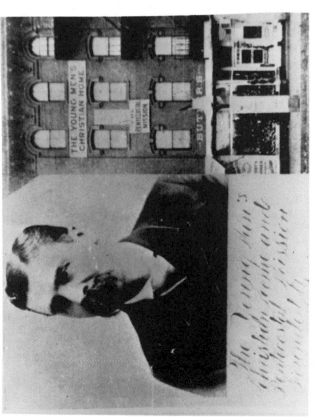

Left: Isaac W. Hanson, harnessmaker, and the Pentecostal Mission, Haverhill, Mass., which he founded in 1896. Right: Church of the Nazarene, Haverhill, Mass., organized in 1900 out of the constituency of the Pentecostal-Mission; building purchased from the First Methodist Church in 1907. From: Haverhill, Mass. Church of the Nazarene. [Brochure] "Fiftieth Anniversary of the Church of the Nazarene . . . organized May 1, 1900." Haverhill, Mass.: 1950.

foreign fields.

In June 1883 Theodore married Manie Payne, an
Irish-born girl from Santa Barbara, and resumed his itiner-
ate endeavors. During part of 1885 and 1886 he had charge
of a school for mission workers connected with the Newton
Mission in San Francisco.[18] Manie developed a severe chest
cold during the winter. No less than prayer, practical considerations influenced the Ferguson's direction; they returned
to Southern California to seek Manie's recovery and to start
their own mission.[19]

Arriving in Los Angeles in March 1886, Ferguson
and his wife found the town in the midst of a population ex-
plosion which transformed "a respectable-sized town" into
"a respectable-sized city." Later Mrs. Ferguson recalled,
"Ordinary accommodations bore no proportion to the influx
of people that crowded everywhere ... sleeping on floors, in
R. R. cars, and many more comical places."[20] Fascinated
by the restless crowds roaming the streets, the Fergusons
longed for a chance to do every-night evangelism. The
Salvation Army had not yet arrived in Los Angeles, and
evangelical activities were limited to the regular services
of the churches. "The rest of the week," Mrs. Ferguson
complained, "there was not a door open for God."

The Fergusons spent the spring and summer of 1886
looking after some rental properties they owned and attending
camp meetings. "My husband was full of love and zeal for
God," Manie later explained, "but my chest seemed to be
going to pieces, and I could see" that a "laborious Mission did
not look very practical to him." By October, however, Manie's
cough was gone and the Fergusons waited "on God for an open
door." "Things were booming away," Mrs. Ferguson reported,
"and I had not heard of anything to rent in the center of the
city for eight months." Then "on the first of November, my
husband came bounding up the stairs.... 'The Masonic Hall
is for rent,' he said, 'vacated this morning ... it is seventy-
five dollars a month'." After scraping together about half the
money, Mr. and Mrs. Ferguson started praying. After three
days nothing had happened, so they decided to fast the fourth
day. That day "we continued to wait on God till 3 P. M.,
when we heard a wagon stop at the gate and a familiar voice
calling 'Hallo'." Coming into the house, the visitor asked
about their plans for the winter, inquiring about the availability
of a mission hall, the amount of the rent, whether they had a
sufficient number of chairs to seat it, etc. Then sitting down,

he wrote out a check for a hundred dollars. Manie exultantly
recalled, "I assure you my husband went wonderfully quickly
up town" and rented the "old Masonic Hall, on Spring street,
and on November 11, 1886, the work long known as the Los
Angeles Mission ... opened."21

    The new mission was an immediate success. "Many
were converted and many sanctified." Only "a few days after
he had been brightly saved," the mission's first convert was
killed in a landslide set off by construction on Temple Street.
"So, you see," Mrs. Ferguson commented, "we began to lay
up treasure in heaven from the very beginning."22

    During its first eight years of existence, high rent
repeatedly forced the mission to find new quarters. From
the Masonic Hall, it removed to the basement of the Nadeau
Hotel; then to a roofed-over burned-out church building which
the landlord soon razed; then to a store room.

    Finally in 1894 it occupied Peniel Hall, a permanent,
specially designed mission building. The construction of
this building was a monumental testimony that the Fergusons
and their fellow workers hardly expected an early cessation
of downtown mission work. With the exception of $1384.75, 22
G. B. Studd, an Englishman who joined the mission staff
soon after Peniel Hall opened, underwrote the entire cost of
construction.

    Mrs. Ferguson's quaint accounting of the $1384.75 in
gifts testified obliquely to the familial atmosphere which pervaded even the fund raising efforts of the Los Angeles Mission.
Gifts

> included a gold medal, 'an alabaster box,' sold for
> $78.40, and a ring from one of the missionaries that
> brought $5. The largest sum was from a most pre-
> cious friend, now in glory, who had volunteered $5 a
> month when we started in '86, and only paid $15--and
> when it became possible to bring this $500 to Peniel it
> was done with great joy and the exclamation, 'Now I
> am out of debt to the Los Angeles Mission.' One hun-
> dred and twenty dollars was given by the same dear
> brother, who gave the first $100 in '86. The next
> largest amount was from a good German brother, who
> gave $40 to Peniel, even though he belongs to a church
> in another tongue. Three gave $25 each, two Metho-
> dist brethren and a lady who still drops in to noon

meeting and has done so for a dozen years.   There
were four twenties, one from an old friend, a Professor up north; one from a loved Presbyterian brother,
now in heaven; one from an Italian brother, and one
from some dear holiness workers whom we meet on
the field betimes ever since 1880.   The rest was in
smaller sums.   Two $15; a few tens; eight dollars
each from several friends who heard that a window
cost that much.   A number of fives, and many little
sums, presumably the precious offerings of the poor,
$1, 50¢, 25¢, 10¢.   Many of these are warm friends
to the work and workers today.   Some have gone
home to God.   Some are scattered to distant places;
some were strangers whose names we do not recognize, and some worship elsewhere, but we pray that
we may meet them all again 'in the land beyond the
river, where the mists are cleared away'. [24]

Completed, the three-story building contained an audi-
torium capable of seating a thousand people, two small store
rooms fronting on the street, "half a dozen suites" and "a
row of very small bedrooms." The Fergusons rented the
suites and most of the rooms. They found, however, that
maintenance and "expensive city" taxes consumed most of the
rental money, leaving no surplus for use in "spreading the
work."

Mrs. Ferguson recalled the origin of the mission's
tract fund. "One night a lady asked me if we wanted some
tracts, and gave me six big dollars to start a tract fund telling me" this bit of "touching history. She was a wealthy
woman, living in an eastern city, and had recently lost a lovely
little daughter, about eleven years old. This child had been
blessedly saved for some time, but somehow failed to make
her parents understand about the rest that Jesus gives. She
saved her pocket money for tracts and missions, and after
she had gone to the upper fold her mother found" the "six
dollars laid away for God.... Wild with grief, her husband
had brought her to California for a change.... Distracted
with sorrow, they were walking on Spring street and followed
our crowd to the hall where she found her daughter's Savior,
and the sainted child's sacred savings began our tract work.
It seemed," Manie confessed, "like money from heaven."[25]

From its beginning the mission held evangelistic services every night. Preceding the regular service, workers conducted street-corner meetings, where by hymn singing, testi-

monials, and tract distribution they drew a crowd. At the end
of the street meeting workers encouraged the street congregation to follow them to the mission hall where a second,
more conventional evangelistic service was held. The service
ordinarily included songs of contemporary revivalists and
camp meeting singers. They featured special musical numbers by small ensembles of singers or instrumentalists even
more often than camp meetings because of the unfamiliarity
of the audience with gospel songs.[26] The music set the
mood for the sermon and the invitation to seek salvation at
the mourner's bench.

After the service, workers commonly served a simple
meal to those who desired it. The Fergusons did not mention
it or any other social service, however. Building arrangements, the nature of mission services, and statements made
by the Fergusons, all point to concern with soul-saving and
institutional solvency rather than social reform. Mr. Ferguson spent much of his time praying for the success of the
mission. Later his wife remembered, "He would drop on
his knees beside a chair.... Pretty soon I would see the
perspiration starting on his forehead, then he would slip down
on the carpet and laugh and cry. He talked real reverent love
talk to the Lord, and laughter, tears, and praises would all
mingle together.... Then up and out to the battle again--
invincible ... and such a glory face." Sometimes as an "ob-
stinate" person was leaving a service, Ferguson would tell
him that the mission door was always open and that the preacher would pray for him until he returned. Manie declared, "the
fellow always came back, " sometimes "on the run and bawling. "
As he grew older he refused to slacken his pace and met all
words of caution with "Maybe I will get a soul. " When he did
secure a convert, Mrs. Ferguson said "he would caper all
around our little sitting room like a boy, crowing over me, 'I
got my soul, I got my soul'. "[27]

During the years 1891 to 1899 Fergusons' organization
spread to other California towns; to the mining district of
Colorado; to Memphis, and New York City, and to Alaska,
Hawaii, India, and Egypt.[28] Manned by an unpaid staff of
converts, this far-flung enterprise depended largely on the
founders' initiative. Operating on the principle that the Lord
Himself would provide for the workers He had called, branches
of the Peniel Mission often originated from the donation of
funds for unstarted projects and the appearance of volunteer
workers for such projects. Before opening the Rescue Home
in San Francisco, Manie had been given a $20 gold piece for

the work. Impressed that the money was for rescue work,
she combed the city without success looking for a suitable
house to rent. Then, she recalled,

> a good woman called on me and offered herself for
> midnight work, and rescue work too. I told her to
> look for a little house and report to me. After faith-
> ful searching, she told me of a nice, clean flat in a
> good location, $17.50 a month. I knew that she was
> poor, and asked if she had any bedding, etc., of her
> own. She said she had a mattress and bedding of her
> daughter's, and a blue flame oil stove. "Well, " I
> said "there is an old bedstead and wire mattress at
> one of the mission homes, and a rag carpet in another,
> neither in use.... If you can take this twenty dollars,
> pay a month's rent and start a rescue home on the two
> dollars and a half left, and GOD, you can go ahead. "
> She answered very decidedly, "Sister Ferguson, I
> can. " I gave her the capital, and left for Los Angeles.
> And the midnight meetings were started at one of our
> Mission halls in San Francisco, September 17th, '98,
> and have been held every night since; and the little
> rescue home has sheltered a few of God's weary, lost
> lambs, and many have been led to Him. [29]

Most of the branches were both small and short-lived. Housed
in rented halls and staffed for the most part by single women
missionaries who soon married or headed for the foreign field,
branches of Peniel seldom outlasted the tenure of the founding
missionary.

Until well into the 1890's, most missions remained in
the hands of individual workers, who like the Fergusons took
personal responsibility for financial affairs. These superintendents administered mission affairs as private business,
resented any inference that their efforts might lead to schism,
and carefully guarded against competition with denominational churches. They refrained from conducting services
during the normal hours for Sunday morning worship and from
offering the sacraments and ordaining workers. Ordinarily,
they neither maintained membership lists nor required workers
to sever ties with denominational churches. Regarding the
mission as a "soul saving station" they expected most converts
to unite with denominational churches. In short, they regarded
the mission institution as a private concern, supported by private gifts and sacrificial effort. But as evangelistic associations
acquired property and developed institutions, more effective

means of establishing administrative control and gaining
financial support became imperative, forcing missions either
to curtail expansion or to move toward formal church organization.

THE EXODUS

Country people moving into the cities in the last decades of the nineteenth century faced a vastly different situation from their predecessors a generation before. In place of the compact walking city familiar to the Civil War generation, newcomers found a sprawling development surrounding a central business district and tied together by a network of streetcar and interurban lines. Instead of owner-operated shops and factories, they found department stores and factories overseen by salaried managers and supervisors. The familiar homogeneous community where rich and poor, employer and employee jostled together freely, had been supplanted by a strange, stratified, impersonal society. Forty years before, the new urbanite's neighbors and fellow workers had likewise usually come to the city from nearby farming areas; now the newcomer found that many of them had come from the ends of the earth, spoke strange languages, and adhered to strange religions.[1]

In place of the evangelicalism which was native to urban workmen and employers at mid-century, the newcomer now discovered that he was in a community of diverse national and religious backgrounds. In place of agreement concerning behavior which he had known in his home community, the newcomer found disagreements and contradictions. And in place of the country church which had supported his assumptions about the common life, he found a status-conscious one, little concerned with perpetuating the evangelical tradition of the countryside. By 1890 even church officials noted the increasing formality in worship. Disapprovingly, Bishop Foster asked,

> Is not worldliness seen in the music? Elaborately dressed and ornamented choirs, who in many cases, make no profession of religion and are often sneering sceptics, go through a cold, artistic, or operatic performance which is as much in harmony with spiritual

worship as an opera or theatre.   Under such worldly
performances spirituality is frozen to death. [2]

In face of change some newcomers took advantage of
the anonymity of the city to explore pleasures denied or
frowned upon at home.   Others joined denominational churches
and accommodated to the new environment.   A few, however,
held to beliefs from home and felt ill-at-ease and unwelcome
among the expensively dressed, status-conscious members of
the city churches.   Out of this group came the first urban
independents. [3]

Urban congregations were fast forsaking older neighborhoods for new developments at the far ends of the streetcar lines, leaving most of the newcomers in their wake.   In
1893 Josiah Strong declared, "Those parts of the city which
need the most churches have the fewest."   For instance,

> there was a district in New York containing a larger
> population than Detroit, in which there were [almost]
> no Protestant churches....   In some wards there are
> one or two hundred times as many saloons as churches.
> In the Thirteenth Ward of Boston with upwards of
> 22,000 souls there is not a single Protestant church;
> while in the Eleventh--the Back Bay--with a smaller
> population, there are thirty.   Ten of the wealthiest
> wards of Cleveland, having a population of about
> 53,000, contain one half of all the Protestant church
> members of the city; while the other half is scattered
> through thirty wards, having a population of about
> 215,000.   The worst portions of our cities are fear-
> fully destitute of churches, and generally growing
> more so.   [For example,] during the twenty years pre-
> ceding [1888] 200,000 ... moved in below Fourteenth
> Street, New York [at the same time] seventeen Prote-
> stant churches ... moved out....   This is an illustra-
> tion of the 'uptown' movement ... taking place in all
> our large cities. [4]

Meanwhile they were beginning to subscribe to the tenets
of the Social Gospel which strongly encouraged established
churches to support missions in poorer areas.   Viewing the
churches as a positive deterrent to the salvation of urban
multitudes, newcomers sought to rescue their neighbors from
the onslaughts of city life.   Newcomers denominationally loyal
enough to identify with suburban churches, composed the bulk
of the volunteers at these missions.

In older neighborhoods pious country folk discovered young girls working as prostitutes, [5] and young men engrossed in fleshly, alcoholic and narcotic pleasures. Convinced that such departures led to total personal and social disintegration, holiness workers set about reconstructing the familiar safeguards of old-time Methodism by means of every-night mission activity. [6]

The effect of city life is illustrated in the experience of U. E. Harding who later became a holiness evangelist. In 1899 as a seventeen-year-old lad, Harding went to Indianapolis from southern Indiana in search of work. Upon arrival, acting on his mother's advice, he sought the aid of a minister in finding a boarding place and found accommodations in the home of church members. Supposing he "was in a religious crowd" he felt safe. On "the second night," however, his landlord explained that he was entertaining the "cinch club" and wondered if Harding would like to join. Having already "made up" his mind that he was not going to be a hayseed, he said he "could play seven-up, and a little poker." After "a few games, the city people brought in beer. To young Harding's utter amazement "those church members, some of them young girls, drank like they were pouring it in a hole cut in their shoulders." Disillusioned, Harding said he began to have "doubts" about the validity of all religion. "I began to think it was a bad man's story, or a Santa Claus affair," and "quit going to church altogether." Pursuing pleasure instead, Harding testified the total result of his first stay in Indianapolis was that he "learned" to wear "tailor-made clothes," "to part" his hair in the middle, to tip "his hat to the girls and blow smoke through" his "nose by turning it towards the sun." Harding later observed, "If a fellow keeps that up long," he "will soon blow out what brains he has." The urban experience heightened the desire of youthful Harding for rural religion, however, and upon returning home, he claimed conversion during a revival meeting, never again to stray. [7]

Re-location produced similar effects whether people moved from rural Indiana to Indianapolis or from Indiana to Oklahoma, Texas or California. [8] In addition, Midwestern farm areas experienced heavy emigration, draining many established congregations of members and vitality, resulting in consolidation of out-lying charges. Since the holiness message appealed largely to people away from home, holiness evangelists first concentrated their efforts in new urban and agricultural areas. Converts of these meetings, realizing the evangelical void in their home communities, returned home.

Armed with a rhetoric familiar to their hearers and a boldness attained during recent sojourn in strange surroundings,
new converts set about re-establishing the old-time religion
in their home communities.

       A similar process took place in new agricultural areas.
In frontier districts of the southern Great Plains where free-
lance revivalism met with early and sustained successes, the
primary attraction seems to have been the nostalgic quality of
holiness preaching and worship. In new settlements as the
bonds of civilization seemed on the verge of snapping, the
formal apparatus of official Methodism must have appeared
unnecessary to many. In light of urgent desire to preserve
evangelical practices remembered from childhood in settled
agricultural areas, the unconventional methods and ecclesiastical independence of the revivalists might be tolerated.

       Despite numberless holiness camp meetings conducted
in country places during the summer months and mission work
carried on in cities year around, [9] the holiness movement
might still have died with its original leaders or have succumbed to the fanaticism of over-zealous converts, had changing conditions in the church not driven established holiness
ministers into independency. At most only a few hundred established Methodist ministers ever went independent, but they
defined the goals and set the future course of the holiness movement both inside and outside the church. Although ministerial
politics, formality in worship, reaction against urban fashions
and sophistication, and doctrinal differences contributed to the
separation process, most holiness believers attributed church
troubles solely to theological matters. Complaining endlessly
about the church's backslidings, the holiness faction insisted
that the remedy for the church's spiritual ills was a widespread
revival of Christian perfection, a solution, it turned out, which
included reckoning with worship and behavior as well as theology.

       Theologically, late nineteenth-century Methodist per-
fectionists started where Phoebe Palmer left off. Reaffirming
the Wesleyan belief that salvation was accomplished through
a spiritual process encompassing two stages, regeneration
and entire sanctification, holiness spokesmen after the Civil
War delineated both the processes and results of full salvation.
Like their predecessors, later perfectionists taught that true
repentance would be evinced by reformed behavior. Believing
that sin was conscious disobedience to a known law of God,
holiness believers were convinced that the true Christian, having

repented of every known act of sin, did not and could not
wilfully sin again and remain a Christian.   They believed that
the Christian, having forsaken his sins, was still troubled by
a sinful nature[10] which tended to thwart his most righteous
intentions, making him vulnerable to temptation and backsliding.
Holiness evangelists taught that man's natural propensities to
sin were so great that, short of a second spiritual operation,
the regenerated man almost inevitably would go back into sin.
But backsliding was really unnecessary, they claimed, since
Christ died to save man from bondage to sin as well as from
acts of sin, [11] making it possible and necessary for modern
disciples, like those present on the first Day of Pentecost, to
receive the Holy Ghost and power.

The experience thus described and known variously
as entire sanctification, the second blessing, Christian perfection, perfect love, heart purity, the baptism with the Holy
Ghost, the fulness of the blessing, full salvation, and Christian
holiness, [12] was regarded as being prerequisite to earnest
Christian living.   To holiness writers it was the crowning
glory of Methodism.   Regarding themselves as true followers
of Wesley, holiness people inevitably looked upon churchly opposition to their ideas as rejection of Methodism's essential
beliefs and likened the vicissitudes of the nineteenth-century
holiness movement within American Methodism to the fate of
the eighteenth-century Methodist movement within Anglicanism. [13]

Later perfectionists based their teaching on the work
of their mid-century forebears, modifying their own presen-
tation to fit contemporary evangelistic exigencies.   Relying on
Mrs. Palmer's altar terminology which analogically reduced
the quest for salvation to a contractual agreement between the
seeker and God, holiness apologists spelled out the terms of
salvation in ever-increasing specificity.   While holiness
teachers distinguished between acts of sin and an inward
bent toward sinning, they believed that after conversion the
unsanctified believer would by behavior demonstrate to himself his need for heart cleansing.   Undesirable personality
characteristics, habitual or compulsive behavioral patterns,
and dispositional or social tendencies were considered evidence of carnality. [14] An already converted person might
recognize his need of entire sanctification after an uncontrol-
lable outburst of temper, a continued or seemingly unmanage-
able appetite for tobacco or alcohol, or a continuing desire to
conform to current fashions and to be popular with the "world."
Most autobiographical testimonies cited inner struggle over one

of these tendencies prior to attainment of entire sanctification.

Charles A. McConnell, a Texas printer sanctified in 1898, said that had anyone told him after his conversion that he still had "a principle of evil" hidden in his heart, he "would have vigorously denied it." He explained,

> I was in the local courtroom, when it developed, in the hearing of a case, that a man in whom I had placed implicit confidence, was planning to defraud me.... My sudden anger burst forth. I sprang to my feet and cursed the false friend before the court. In the next moment the enormity of what I had done crushed down on me. My heart broke. I did not know such a foul passion remained in me. [15]

Holiness literature abounded with instances of such recognition of carnality by individuals. Concerning deliverance from tobacco, M. L. Haney, an Illinois evangelist, related the experience of "Guss" who before conversion

> had been a rough man and was a vile tobacco user. The habit had become so all controlling that he had to rise from his bed each night [to] smoke or chew.... He had been several times to the altar crying for a holy heart, when one day he sprang to his feet and walked up and down the aisle. His feelings seemed too deep for utterance, but by and by he gave vent to his soul by puffing, as a steamboat pours forth steam....

The next morning through habit he reached into his pocket for tobacco, then withdrew his hand without touching it. Again, after dinner "he thought he would taste it" but "found he abhored the filthy stuff, and has probably testified ... one hundred times that he has never desired it" since he was sanctified. [16]

While holiness writers never claimed that any particular manifestation of inbred sin was normative, they felt that every unsanctified person would at some time see outward signs of a corrupt inner nature. They felt that failure to seek perfection after such manifestation ultimately led to total backsliding. Maintaining that no behavioral superiority marked off perfect Christians from the unsanctified ones, holiness leaders held to a single standard of behavior for all, regardless of religious profession. No antinomians, they maintained

that no religious state could be attained in this world from
which man by sin could not fall.   They urged converts immediately to seek entire sanctification in the belief that once
in an experience of perfect love the Christian, though still
subject to temptation, would be free from inward compulsion
to sin.   In the belief that corrupted desire lay at the base of
all sinful actions and that the already converted believer no
less than the man in outbroken sin retained a diseased nature,
holiness evangelists continually urged upon their congregations
the dual necessity of rigorous personal discipline and persistent seeking after Christian perfection.

Popular culture left its deepest mark on holiness teaching in the area of personal conduct.   In much the same way
that the exuberance of the camp meeting had permanently impressed itself upon holiness worship, the denial of fashion
left a lasting mark on later holiness teaching.   Rejecting intel-
lectual formulas such as the social gospel, the higher criticism,
the theory of evolution, and socialism, holiness spokesmen
vigorously contended for "the Old Paths."[17]   They identified
the holiness movement with ideas and customs then past or
passing, rejecting as "modern," worldly, and un-Christian
much of their present environment.

Nowhere was the withdrawal more apparent than in
terms which now entered the holiness vocabulary.   While
generally accepting the doctrinal formulation inherited from
mid-century, holiness teachers in the 1880's and 1890's in
everyday practice used a new, more vivid nomenclature.   The
process of consecration, whereby the seeker after Christian
perfection surrendered to God's design for him, became known
as "dying out."   Similarly, the seeker's unsanctified disposition
was dubbed "the carnal nature" or "the old man of sin."   Elim-
ination of carnality by entire sanctification became known as
the "eradication of inbred sin, root and branch" or "the death
of the old man."[18]

While adoption of new terms signalled no significant
theological change, new terminology pointed to a new method
of determining the loyalty of individuals within the holiness
camp, a method which ultimately delineated social requirements for admission to the holiness group.   Identifying inward
purity with decorous conduct, holiness evangelists often confused the two.   In the belief that extravagant dress indicated
inward haughtiness, some condemned ruffles, feathers, jewelry
(including wedding rings), and corsets.

Wide differences existed within the holiness group, so wide indeed that holiness people had been known to dub others fanatical because of particularly stringent preaching on externals. Nevertheless, even M. L. Haney, an evangelist generally known for moderation, spoke against corsets which, he claimed, exchanged "the beauty of the 'human form divine' ... for the similitude of the wasp." "Dress which cramps the vitals, by so changing the form of the body as to fetter the action of the lungs, of the stomach, and of the heart, is unquestionably of the devil." Rather, "if your heart is right with God, you will" purchase no article "without first asking" divine counsel. The Christian should "seek to combine neatness with plainness, and get wisdom to attire" himself "without superfluous ornaments."[19] After quoting Wesley to the effect that arrogance in dress "engenders pride," breeds and increases vanity, "begets anger, and every turbulant passion," "creates and inflames lust," and "is directly opposite to being adorned with good works,"[20] one writer went on to claim that extravagant dress "impoverishes families, begets dishonesty, leads to crime, and ends in temporal and eternal ruin."[21]

Denunciations were also levelled against the use of tobacco, alcoholic beverages, and attendance at expensive or frivolous entertainments. Membership in fraternal societies and secret orders was condemned because of oaths which theoretically committed members to lie for one another, and because of alleged competition between lodges and the church. Such reasoning led some holiness groups to frown upon, even to forbid membership of their people in labor unions. The somewhat ambiguous statement of the Pilgrim Holiness Church was: "We are opposed to organizations, whether of labor or capital, which involve Christians in unscriptural alliances," while that of its more radical offshoot, the Emmanuel Association, enjoined abstaining "from all worldly associations and unscriptural alliances" which "include, among others, secret societies, and lodges which are oath-bound, and organizations both of capital and labor. No dues-paying member of a labor union shall be allowed to belong to the Emmanuel Association or take any appointed part in public service."[22]

Thus, by defining the external manifestations of inward perfection, holiness spokesmen delineated the social style as well as the religious discipline of holiness believers, a style and discipline well described in 1899 by W. E. Arnold, a Methodist minister in Kentucky. In an article in the Pentecostal Herald, he explained,

Holiness is more than a blessing ... much more than
a clean heart. A holy man or woman ought to be as
perfect a man or woman as it is possible for that man
to be. It will clean up and round up a person in his
whole being, and will show itself in all the manifestations of his life. It will make relentless war upon
everything that is of doubtful propriety, or that allied
itself with things sensual or worldly.... It will cause
a person to lay aside every filthy and useless habit;
it will cleanse his lips of all foul speech; it will lead
him to discontinue the use of all bywords and exaggera-
ted forms of expression; in short, it does away with all
that is hurtful to the soul, body or influence, and
places before us the highest ideal of perfect manhood
and womanhood. It is opposed to everything that would
not be proper in the Lord Jesus Christ, and is the friend
of everything that will make us like him. Oh, to be
perfect men and women in Christ![23]

While to the outsider the stringent discipline must have
seemed like moral slavery, to the convinced the life of holiness
afforded the essence of freedom. Characterizing the worship
of the "old line" churches as "cold, " "formal, " and "dead, "
holiness spokesmen charged that most conventional churches
regularly stifled the spirit of God in worship. They pictured
a musically sophisticated but spiritually dead paid choir, chor-
ister, and organist, capable of rendering an operatic performance, but utterly insensitive to the Holy Spirit.[24] Similarly,
they felt the new preacher, seminary-trained, tainted with the
higher criticism, the social gospel, and attendant liberalism,
poorly prepared for the central ministry of the church, the salvation of souls.[25]

Holiness people felt that "when churches" got "filled
with the Holy Ghost, " evangelistic zeal would become "uncon-
tainable" and preaching and mission work would supplement
church services. Under such conditions evangelistic effort
(to use Carradine's mixed metaphor) "overflows" banks created
by the church institution and the swollen "stream sends the
locomotive flying. The fire-filled man cannot keep still, and
so sweeps over the land. "[26] In short, the Methodist perfectionist felt that the church stood between him and the commands
of God. Increasingly dependent upon Spirit guidance for direction in decisions concerning worship, personal behavior, voca-
tion, and political and social affairs, the holiness believer felt
that freedom could only be attained by "dying out" to human
opinions and institutional compromises. Since the Holy Spirit's

directions in all these areas coincided with contemporary
rural ideals and mores, the dislocated holiness believer soon
sought spiritual "freedom" among like-minded and similarly
situated people. In missions and tabernacle churches, urban
newcomers found a family-like fellowship which provided both
the discipline and enthusiasm requisite for admittance to the
turnpike from piety to prosperity.

I'M GLAD I'M ONE OF THEM

There are people almost ev'rywhere,
Whose hearts are all aflame,
With the fire that fell at Pentecost,
Which cleans'd and made them clean;
It is burning now within my heart;
All glory to His name,
And I'm glad that I can say I'm one of them.

[Refrain:] One of them, one of them,
I am glad that I can say I'm one of them;
Sanctified, sanctified,
I am glad that I can say I'm sanctified.

Tho' these people may not learned be
Nor boast of worldly fame,
They have all received their Pentecost
Thro' faith in Jesus' name;
And are telling now both far and wide
That His pow'r is yet the same,
And I'm glad that I can say I'm one of them.

Come, my brother, seek this blessing,
That will cleanse your heart from sin,
That will start the joy-bells ringing
And will keep the soul aflame;
It is burning now within my heart;
And glory to His name,
And I'm glad that I can say I'm one of them.

Isaiah Guyman Martin
(1862-1957)

THE PUT-OUTERS

> When we are turned out of the synagogue and
> all the forces of hell are turned loose on us,
> we may rest assuredly [sic] our preaching is
> pleasing to God and that we are stirring the
> devil and his gang. When we preach true
> Holiness, the devil will howl and groan. I had
> rather enjoy the Holiness of God than to burn
> in hell forever. [1]

Commitment to authenticity through separateness, which
by the 1890's pervaded holiness teaching and behavior, led to
demands for a new, distinctively holiness church. Simply
stated the argument was that converts won in holiness meetings
soon backslid when entrusted to pastors opposed to holiness
teaching. In much the same way that holiness advocates had
convinced themselves that abstinence from worldly pleasures
was requisite to spiritual freedom, they now reasoned that the
way to preserve the doctrine of Christian perfection was to
re-create the primitive Wesleyan church outside the confines
of official Methodism. Few of the advocates of a pure church
relied solely upon theological arguments as justification for
independence, however. Rather they alleged that opposition to
entire sanctification had ushered in worldliness, unbridled
political machinations, preferment of the rich, neglect of the
poor, and theological modernism. Such conditions, coupled
with expulsions of holiness promoters from the church, made
further accommodation within established Methodism impossi-
ble, they said. Beginning in the mid-1890's holiness people
tended to trace every disagreement to doctrine. Little men-
tioned were differences concerning church government, the
millennium and standards of conduct which prevented holiness
independents from uniting in a single separate body.

Separations resulting from the holiness Methodist impact on members of other denominations and from faith missions

went on apace. After 1882 the formation of independent congregations regularly augmented the separatist movement. In New
England, independent groups developed at Rock, Massachusetts,
in 1882; at Providence in 1887; at Attleboro, Massachusetts,
in 1888; at Lynn, Massachusetts, and Keene, New Hampshire,
in 1889; and at Malden, Massachusetts, in 1890. Uniting in
1890 to form a loose federation called the Central Evangelical
Holiness Association, [2] these New England churches came into
contact with three infant holiness congregations in Brooklyn
known as the Association of Pentecostal Churches of America. [3]
In 1896 most of the Central Association churches joined the
Brooklyn association, taking the name of the latter.

In 1885 five holiness workers in Philadelphia, who for
three years had been holding street meetings, rented a hall
and organized the Heavenly Recruit Association of Philadelphia. Spreading to other Pennsylvania towns and eventually
to Indiana and Illinois, the Heavenly Recruits re-organized in
1894 as the Holiness Christian Association; three years later,
as the Holiness Christian Church. Part of the group continued
as Heavenly Recruits and in 1906 reported 927 members in 27
churches. The Holiness Christians continue in mountainous
areas of Pennsylvania. Many members of both groups eventually found their way into the Church of the Nazarene and the
Pilgrim Holiness Church. [4] Similarly, the Pentecostal Rescue
Mission founded in 1897 at Binghamton, New York, soon spread
to other industrial towns including Schenectady, New York, and
Allentown, Pennsylvania. [5]

In Michigan an independent holiness church was started
at Kalamazoo in 1895; another began at Battle Creek in 1899.
Between 1894 and 1900 holiness evangelists established missions in Cincinnati, Nashville, St. Louis, and Colorado Springs
and formed churches in Tennessee, [6] Texas and California.
Like their Eastern counterparts, separatist congregations in
other sections joined like-minded groups in support of missionary activities, publishing enterprises, and educational or
benevolent institutions.

The new independence sprang largely from splits in
individual Methodist congregations and the growth of unspon-
sored missionary work. By 1894 it became evident that some
church officials even equated membership in holiness associations with disloyalty. That year the bishops of the Methodist
Episcopal Church, South, cautioned,

There has sprung up among us a party with holiness as

a watchword; they have holiness associations, holiness
meetings, holiness preachers, holiness evangelists,
and holiness property. Religious experience is represented as if it consists of only two steps, the first step
out of condemnation into peace and the next step into
Christian perfection.... We do not question the sin-
cerity and zeal of their brethren; we desire the church
to profit by their earnest preaching and godly example;
but we deplore their teaching and methods in so far as
they claim a monopoly of the experience, practice, and
advocacy of holiness, and separate themselves from
the body of ministers and disciples. [7]

Again holiness leaders repeated old disclaimers of schism.
Yet under attack themselves, they limited preachments against
separatism to condemnation of "come-outers." Association
spokesmen denied the legitimacy of independent holiness
churches, yet fraternized with separatist ministers and accepted invitations to preach at independent tabernacles. In
short, holiness loyalists flailed an abstraction while condoning
its concrete manifestation.

The New England Union Holiness Convention demon-
strated this tendency in dealing with the People's Evangelical
Church, an independent holiness congregation of Providence,
Rhode Island. Organized in 1887 by former members of Saint
Paul's Methodist Episcopal Church, [8] the People's Church kept in
touch with holiness Methodists through the New England Union
Holiness Convention. Present in 1889 at the meeting of the
Union in Boston, representatives of the People's Church
secured H. N. Brown and E. M. Levy as evangelists for a
revival meeting but met rebuke of the assembly. An official
resolution declared, "We favor no come-outism from the
churches because of opposition or indifference" to the doctrine of Christian perfection, "but ... approve rather of
remaining in our providential places and there witnessing" to
both "small and great..., doing as best we can to aid all the
work of the church." However, when the New England Conference of the Methodist Episcopal Church in 1892 adopted a
resolution which declared that all meetings conducted by church
members without the express consent of the pastor were "in
conflict with the order and discipline of the church," even
loyalist leaders conceded that in some localities independent
churches might provide the only alternative available to holiness people. At this conference Daniel Steele, professor of
theology at Boston University and a holiness writer, delivered
a minority report urging pastors either to take charge of holi-

ness meetings in their churches or to appoint leaders for
them. 9

The rhetoric of Methodist loyalty which long characterized the National Association was beginning to lose its bite
by the mid-1890's, a weakening apparent in holiness response
to the church's treatment of Henry Clay Morrison. In 1890
Morrison, descendant of John Durham, a Methodist pioneer in
Kentucky and himself a life-long Methodist, finished a two-
year term as pastor of the fashionable First Methodist Episcopal Church, South, of Frankfort. He then requested location
from the Kentucky Conference to devote full-time to evangelism and to The Old Methodist, a holiness paper he had started. 10 A member of the National Association, Morrison
rapidly developed stature both as editor and evangelist. Ac-
claimed as an orator, he annually spent the winter months
conducting revival meetings, his summers in camp meetings.
He was well on his way to establishing a national reputation,
when just before a lay-sponsored camp meeting at Dublin,
Texas, in 1896, the local Methodist officials informed him
that they would consider his preaching there a violation of
church law. Assured of public support by a petition signed by
230 local residents, Morrison went ahead with the meeting.
At this point the Methodist presiding elder assembled a committee of ministers which drew up charges against him. "The
amusing feature" about the whole censuring procedure, Morrison afterward declared, "was that the wife of one of the local
preachers" on the presiding elder's committee "came to the
tent while the committee was at work, and while her husband
was preparing charges ... was most gloriously sanctified.
She shouted and testified with great joy. 11

The dispute centered on a provision in the Discipline
of the Methodist Episcopal Church, South, which gave a pastor
charge over his pulpit, interpreted to imply that no Methodist
minister should conduct services in the territory surrounding
a church without the consent of the pastor. 12 Forwarded to
the Hill Street Methodist Episcopal Church, South, in Lexington, Kentucky, the charge resulted in the evangelist's expulsion
from the church. Although the next session of the Kentucky
Conference cleared Morrison, eight years later a similar situation led him to organize the Holiness Union, a loosely constructed federation of holiness bands in Southern and Southwestern states similar to the National Association for the
Promotion of Holiness. Devoted to supporting independent
foreign missionary activity and to nurturing converts of holiness revivals, the Holiness Union would likely have developed

This page: Henry Clay Morrison (1857-1942). Facing page:
Asbury College, established at Wilmore, Ky., in 1890, largely
supported by Methodist loyalists. Morrison was president,
1910-1925 and 1933-1944. Photographs from: Nee, Gilbert
Chibee, ed. Voices from Many Lands. Louisville: Pentecostal
Publishing Co., c1936; 11, 14.

into an independent church, had Methodist officials again brought the issue of Morrison's independent revivalism to a head.   The crisis, however, passed without incident and the Holiness Union faded into oblivion. [13]   Although in later years Morrison was repeatedly honored by the church, [14] his experiences convinced holiness supporters that the church was aligned against them.   Such knowledge tempered holiness reaction to the separations of Phineas F. Bresee, a Methodist pastor who in 1895 founded the Church of the Nazarene in Los Angeles; and of Martin Wells Knapp, a Methodist minister who in 1897 assembled a handful of like-minded individuals in Cincinnati to form the International Holiness Union and Prayer League, ancestor of the Pilgrim Holiness Church.

Bresee, who, like Morrison, served as an evangelist with the National Association for the Promotion of Holiness, was also a life-long Methodist.   Born in 1838 at Franklin, Delaware County, New York, at age seventeen Bresee moved with his parents to Iowa.   Two years later he accepted appointment as pastor of a circuit of tiny rural churches.   He rose steadily during the next twenty-five years, serving as pastor of some of the largest Methodist congregations in the state, and as presiding elder and editor of the conference paper.   Successful in promoting building programs and in liquidating indebtedness, Bresee maintained exceptional rapport with businessmen in the church.   With Joseph Knotts, an old ministerial colleague, he invested in Mexican iron mines, but was left bankrupt when subterranean flooding destroyed expensive equipment.   Feeling these troubles had irreparably damaged his

ministry in Iowa, Bresee decided to move to California
where professional recovery seemed more probable.[15]

Arriving in Los Angeles on Saturday afternoon,
August 26, 1883, Bresee was surprised when the pastor of
the First Methodist Church invited him to fill his pulpit the
next day. The following Sunday the pastor of the church on
the campus of the University of Southern California invited
Bresee to preach for him. As a result of these invitations,
during the few days between his arrival and the opening session of the Southern California Conference, Bresee had become relatively well known. The Conference itself did not
disappoint him, for when the pastoral appointments were
read, he was listed as the pastor of the First Church in
Los Angeles.[16]

Similar good fortune marked all Bresee's activities
during his first years in California. He held prominent
conference appointments and offices: pastor of First Church
in Los Angeles, 1883-1886; and pastor at Pasadena, 1886-
1890; delegate to the 1892 General Conference; presiding
elder, Los Angeles District, 1891-1892; president of the
Southern California Conference board of church extension
and president of the trustees of the conference corporation;
chairman of the board of the College of Liberal Arts of the
University of Southern California; director of the Long Beach
Methodist Resort Association; and member of the editorial
committee of the Southern California Christian Advocate.[17]

While minister in Los Angeles, Dr. Bresee first
came into contact with the organized holiness movement.
This proved to be the turning point in his life. Within the
membership of the church, he discovered a "fully sanctified"
minority. Later Bresee confessed, "I instinctively ... allied
myself with them, and, while they must have known that I
was not in the clear enjoyment of the blessing, they seemed
to appreciate whatever efforts" I made "in assisting them in
the work of holiness. They were very kind and gentle," and
persuaded the pastor to call George D. Watson and William

Facing page, left: Phineas F. Bresee in 1878. Right:
Methodist Episcopal Church, Red Oak, Iowa, constructed in
1874 while Bresee was pastor. Photographs from: Girvin,
Ernest Alexander, 1857- . Phineas F. Bresee: A Prince
in Israel; A Biography. Kansas City, Mo.: Pentecostal
Nazarene Publishing House, 1916; opposite pp. 64, 72.

McDonald, evangelists identified with the National Holiness
Association, for a revival meeting. Bresee remembered
that during this meeting, he was "crying to God for some-
thing that would meet" his "needs," while "not clearly realizing what they were, or how they could be met." Consumed
with inward uncertainties, Bresee recalled, one day

> I sat alone in the parsonage, in the cool of the even-
> ing, in the front parlor near the door. The door
> being opened, I looked up into the azure in earnest
> prayer, while the shades of evening gathered about.
> As I waited and waited, and continued in prayer,
> looking up, it seemed to me as if from the azure
> there came a meteor, an indescribable ball of con-
> densed light, descending rapidly toward me. As I
> gazed upon it, it was soon within a few score feet,
> when I seemed distinctly to hear a voice saying, as
> my face was upturned towards it: "Swallow it; swal-
> low it," and in an instant it fell upon my lips and
> face. I attempted to obey the injunction. It seemed
> to me, however, that I swallowed only a little of it,
> although it felt like fire on my lips, and the burning
> sensation did not leave them for several days. [18]

While never claiming that such mystical experiences were
normative, Pastor Bresee believed this experience marked
the turning point of his ministry. "There came with it into
my heart and being, a transformed condition of life and
blessing and unction and glory, which I had never known before." "A new element of spiritual life and power" now
came into "my ministry." "People began to come into the
blessing of full salvation; there were more persons converted;
and the last year of my ministry in that church was more
consecutively successful, being crowned by an almost con-
stant revival." In fact, "when the third year came to a
close, the church had ... nearly doubled in membership."[19]

In California Bresee conducted "Home Camp Meeting"
revivals and encouraged modern gospel singing and spontaneous congregational responses, practices which had characterized his ministry in Iowa.[20] He emphasized soul-saving as
the principal activity of the ministry. A consistent foe of
long pastoral appointments, he felt that the ideal Methodist
minister was one who continually and vigorously evangelized.
Despite mounting opposition, Bresee followed a revivalistic
program ever more faithfully, especially after his sanctification experience. Following A. W. Bunker, a fellow National

Association member, as pastor at Pasadena, he discovered
that the building under construction when he arrived was in-
adequate to house the crowds attracted by pre-service street
meetings and by his preaching. As a result, he recommended that a tabernacle seating 2000 be constructed adjacent to the sanctuary to accommodate the crowds. [21]

His pastoral activities clearly identified Phineas Bresee
as an advocate of the traditional evangelistic methods of rural
Methodism and as presiding elder of the Los Angeles District
during the 1891-1892 conference year, demonstrated belief
that such methods represented essential Methodist practice.
Appointed to this supervisory post by Bishop Willard F.
Mallalieu, himself an unabashed supporter of the holiness
cause, Bresee immediately began conducting revivals in the
main churches under his charge. Ignoring the hostility of
some leading ministers, he enlisted the assistance of National Association evangelists John A. Wood, William Mc-
Donald, and D. Cobb and travelled with them from church
to church. Invitations to hold meetings were not always
spontaneous. For instance, the pastor of the First Church
in Los Angeles requested Bresee's assistance only after
Bishop Mallalieu insisted that he do so. Climaxed by a
campmeeting at Long Beach led by National Association
workers, Bresee's term as presiding elder, which in more
propitious times might have been a stepping stone to advance-
ment in the church, became a first step on his way out of
the church. Since Bishop Vincent, the presiding officer at
the next conference, was as much repulsed by the incum-
bent's perfectionism as Bishop Mallalieu had been impressed,
Vincent relieved Bresee of the presiding eldership and
appointed him pastor of the debt-ridden Simpson church in
Los Angeles. Assigned the following year to another finan-
cially difficult post, a congregation in the Boyle Heights
section of Los Angeles, in 1894 Bresee decided to seek relief from conference appointment (supernumerary status) to
go into mission work. The bishop denied the request, however, and after thirty-seven years, Bresee withdrew from
the Methodist ministry. [22]

In the meantime, Martin Wells Knapp, a youthful
member of the Michigan Conference, was also in trouble
for taking part in the holiness evangelistic program. Born
to pioneer Methodist parents in Calhoun County, Michigan
in 1853, Knapp was nurtured from earliest childhood in the
mores of frontier Wesleyanism. Entering Albion College at
age seventeen, Martin rebelled and tried for a time to be an

infidel. His apostasy was short-lived, however, for the
next year during a brief attempt at school teaching, he was
overcome with introspection about death-bed agonies and
funerals. Repentance, culminating in a pledge to God that
he would henceforth open school with prayers, led Martin
to profess conversion, to join the Methodist Episcopal
Church, and to announce his calling as a minister. Alter-
nating study with farm work and school teaching, Knapp remained in the vicinity of Albion until 1877. Then he married and spent the next eight years in the pastorate. Always more intent on getting seekers to the mourner's bench
than in gaining the praise of prosperous and influential
church members, Knapp mercilessly bore down on worldliness. While attacks on the formality, sociability, and
fashionability of contemporary Methodism generated opposition in every pastorate he served, skill as an evangelist made him the darling of conservatives. An evangelist
of sufficient repute to receive calls for meetings as far as
a hundred miles from home, in 1886 he withdrew from the
conference to devote full-time to revival work.[23] Uncere-
moniously sanctified while reading his Bible April 21, 1889,
Knapp rapidly developed as a champion of the holiness
cause. In the mid-1880's he started a printing office in
Albion, which issued a stream of religious tracts and books.
Also in 1888 he started The Revivalist (re-named God's
Revivalist and Bible Advocate in 1901), a journal devoted to
the renewal of holiness teaching in the church. Knapp's
book titles mark stages of his thought and indicate his
attachment to imagery derived from rural life and the holiness camp meeting; they include Out of Egypt and into
Canaan (1888); Revival Kindlings (1890); The Double Cure
(1895); Pentecostal Preachers (1897); Lightning Bolts from
Pentecostal Skies (1898); and Holiness Triumphant; or,
Pearls from Patmos, Being the Secret of Revelation Revealed
(1900). These publications received appreciative attention
outside Michigan and rapidly brought Knapp into prominence
in the Midwestern holiness movement.

In the fall of 1891 James L. Glascock, a Methodist
evangelist, visited Albion and persuaded Knapp that it was
God's will to move the publishing work to Cincinnati. Glascock
explained that although this city had previously been noted
as a "burnt over" district, it had recently been backsliding.
Accepting the challenge, in September 1892 Knapp moved,
locating both his family and editorial offices in rented quarters at 520 Chase Avenue, Cincinnati. He demonstrated continuing cordiality to the church, contracting with Cranston &

Stowe, the official Methodist publishing agent, to do the printing, and aided by family and friends, wrapped and mailed the Revivalist from his home. 24

Knapp agitated for an aggressive holiness evangelistic program in Cincinnati. The Knapps opened their home for a weekly prayer meeting which within a month grew into a holiness association organized in St. John's Methodist Church with Knapp as president. Meeting on Sunday afternoons in various churches, carefully avoiding conflicts with regularly scheduled church services, the Cincinnati holiness association soon decided that its principal activity should be union revival campaigns in the spring and fall each year. At the first of these, a meeting held May 7-14, 1893, at the Trinity Methodist Church, the Central Holiness League was organized. 25 Similar to the Cincinnati holiness association but designed to sponsor union holiness revivals in a larger area, the League provided Knapp with a convenient tool for marshalling wider support. In addition, the International Revival Prayer League, formed in 1894 by scattered readers of the monthly Revivalist, pooled moral support for the workers. 26

In demand as an evangelist for camp meetings, conventions, and revival meetings in the Midwest, East and upper South, by 1895 Martin Wells Knapp had decided to make Cincinnati his permanent headquarters. That year, because of growth in the subscription list of the Revivalist, he rented rooms on the second floor of the Y.M.C.A. in downtown Cincinnati for his publishing activities and the Thursday night meetings of the holiness association. (The association continued Sunday afternoon services in various churches.) At that time he also purchased a home in the prosperous Mount Auburn section. 27

Up to this time, Evangelist Knapp had remained scrupulously "loyal" to the Methodist Episcopal Church. In 1893 and 1894, when he served with the Revival Band of the Michigan Conference, of the "four thousand four hundred souls" who professed conversion "through its agency" "two-thirds" joined the Methodist church. 28 Like the National Association men with whom he worked during these years, Knapp avoided conducting meetings without the acquiescence of church officials and never conducted services which conflicted with those regularly scheduled by the local Methodist congregations. Knapp's Central Holiness League, in effect the Midwestern branch of the loosely federated General Holi-

This page: Martin Wells Knapp (1853-1901). Facing page: God's Bible School and Missionary Training Home, about 1902. Photographs from: Hills, Aaron Merritt, 1848-1935. A Hero of Faith and Prayer; or, Life of Rev. Martin Wells Knapp. Cincinnati: Mrs. M. W. Knapp, c1902; frontispiece; advertisement in back of book.

ness League, [29] fully concurred with the loyalists' determination to save the church, not to separate from it. Halfway measures served Knapp and his followers during the first years in Cincinnati. However, with the decision to put down roots for an all-out evangelistic thrust, after 1895 concern for churchly approbation faded. Now Knapp fretted under ecclesiastical controls and ever more determinedly pursued his own program, independent of church and association alike.

Discovering that his ministry offended sophisticated urban Methodists but effectively appealed to unchurched country people coming to Cincinnati, Knapp decided to orient his work to this group. Interested in Appalachian mountain folk, he conducted summer camp meetings at Beulah Heights near Flat Rock, Kentucky, and helped establish a school and orphanage there. In 1899 he opened the Revivalist Chapel in a rented storeroom in downtown Cincinnati and conducted evangelistic meetings every night in the fashion of a rescue mission. The next year Knapp purchased property in Mount Auburn (which he publicized as "The Mount of Blessings") and opened the God's Bible School and Missionary Training Home, combining training in the theory of evangelistic work with the discipline of the Victorian household. [30]

Mission work soon brought Knapp into conflict with the General Holiness League. Chafing under rules which forbade preaching on divine healing and the second coming of Christ in League-sponsored meetings, Knapp gradually withdrew. Finding the poor country people at Revivalist Chapel and the new converts who made up the student body

of God's Bible School and Missionary Training Home interested in healing for their bodies as well as salvation for
their souls, Knapp stressed both. Recognizing the iminent
return of Christ as a major incentive for repentance, he
used it to attract reluctant sinners to the mourner's bench.

To foster teaching on these subjects and to garner
support for missionary projects, in September 1897 Knapp
and about a dozen followers met in the parlor of his Mount
Auburn home and formed the International Holiness Union
and Prayer League. Committed to independent missionary
activity, conducted on the "faith" principle, the new organization retained most of the characteristics of the Holiness
League. Interdenominational in scope, the group included
George B. Kulp, a Methodist minister of the Michigan Conference; Seth C. Rees, an Indiana-born Quaker evangelist
then residing in Providence; Rees' son Byron, a student at
Brown University; C. W. Ruth, an evangelist from Indianapolis identified with the Holiness Christian Church; and W.
N. Hirst, Knapp's bookkeeper at the Revivalist Office.[31]
In its constitution the new organization stated it was not "an
ecclesiastical body, but a fraternal union of Christian believers." Intent on "publishing the gospel of holiness in the
slums and jungles and to all the world," Knapp and his
associates, while "not opposed to church organization," condemned "ecclesiastical popery" and supported "liberty of
conscience in all matters ... not sinful."[32] Despite protes-
tations to the contrary, the International Holiness Union
early assumed churchly features. The International Holiness
Union ordained workers, acquired property, and sponsored
independent missions, camp meetings, and revivals, activities which soon embroiled Knapp in a controversy and eventually resulted in his leaving the Methodist Episcopal Church.
In 1898 the Michigan Conference censured Knapp for "improper conduct and contumacy" in conducting a meeting for
the Chesapeake Holiness Union in Maryland without permis-
sion of local Methodist officials. Justifying his actions as
"Pentecostal aggressiveness," he repeated the performance
the next summer and won acquittal from the conference that
fall. In 1901 Knapp withdrew from the conference, but died
before he had a chance to discover the problems of a church-
less minister.[33]

By the turn of the century, associationism was fast
breaking down as a means of tying the holiness movement
to the church. The founders were being replaced by younger
men who in the face of official hostility prepared the way for

separations which during the next two decades moved thousands of Methodists into holiness sects. The independent
movement forced the loyalist minority to perpetuate itself
by independent institutions which carried the older program
forward with ever-decreasing financial resources and man-
power.

THE LOT IN CANAAN'S LAND (1906)

There is a lot in Canaan,
For ev'ry one today,
Who would be pure and holy,
And walk the narrow way.
God has reserved it for you,
The Bible tells us so,
So will you take possession
And into Canaan go.

[Refrain:] I possess my lot in Canaan, yes I do;
And I know that Jesus saves me, thro' and thro'
I feel so well, I love to tell,
How I love to live in Canaan's happy land.
I possess my lot in Canaan, yes I do;
And it keeps my soul aflaming, thro' and thro'
I know 'tis mine, I'm feeling fine,
Since I got my lot in Canaan's happy land.

The churches are not formal;
The service is not cold;
They love to pay the preacher,
Give God one tenth they hold;
They work in heat of summer;
Don't care what church they're in,
They preach a full salvation,
With freedom from all sin.

The lot has no tobacco,
No clubs, no cards, no ball;
All dwell in peace together,
With love for one and all;
They set no fads or fashions,
They pay all debts they owe;
The men vote prohibition;
Saloons, they say, must go.

We want you for our neighbor;
The people there are free,
The deed is freely given,
The lot is there for thee.
Quit fighting and complaining,
About this Holy way,
Cross over into Canaan,
And get your lot today.

W. E. Cissna
Arr. by Isaiah Guyman Martin
(1862-1957)

THE REUNION

Once out of the Methodist Episcopal Church, holiness leaders attempted to create a pure church, free from the machinations of ecclesiastical politicians and the formality and worldliness of lukewarm church members. Citing wealth as the chief factor in Methodism's failure to perpetuate her heritage, the new independents felt that the first sign of a revival of primitive Wesleyanism would be the evangelization of the poor. Practically every holiness group originating around the turn of the century claimed a ministry to the poor as justification for separation. Most of them backed their professions with evangelistic social activity. During their early years these groups sponsored many social agencies--rescue missions, orphanages, rescue homes, old people's homes, and Bible training schools--operation of which ultimately demonstrated the motivation and function of such work in the holiness movement. Armed with revival methods and the conviction that Christian perfection was an antidote to every social evil, holiness spokesmen launched their crusade.

Aware of the work of holiness evangelistic associations, at first the new independents thought they should make common cause with such ventures. Thanks to the existence of the International Holiness Union, for Martin Wells Knapp's followers this was not hard. Phineas Bresee faced a more complex situation. Forced to withdraw from the Southern California Conference in 1894, he at first joined forces with T. P. and Manie Ferguson at the Peniel Mission in Los Angeles. He found that neither the program nor the administration of this faith mission fitted his preconceptions. As editor of the Peniel Herald, Bresee proposed large changes in the mission's program. He projected a school for workers that would offer specialized training in the Biblical, musical and medical subjects; practice in "house-to-house visitation"; and experience in conducting Gospel meetings during the noon hour and in the evening every day. In addition he suggested

that the Peniel Hall provide regular church membership for
unchurched converts, even going so far as to print a doctrinal statement and requirements for membership. These
proposals never received the endorsement of the Fergusons,
however, and after a frustrating year Bresee again found
himself outside. [1]

Although Bresee refused to talk about it, friends said
he was unhappy at Peniel Hall because the Fergusons denied
him sufficient voice in administrative decisions and because
he felt his calling was to poor people with families, not the
"floating class." [2] As a result he decided that any future
project must be susceptible to his control. Informed of his
dismissal in 1895 during a tour of camp meeting evangelism
in the Midwest, upon his return Bresee immediately set
about making plans for an independent work. Freed from
worry about personal support by the devoted solicitude of
prosperous children, [3] he found supporters for the new project among people he had known in Methodist pastorates and
at the Peniel Mission. Together with Dr. J. P. Widney, a
physician-minister and former president of the University of
Southern California who had also been associated with the
Fergusons' work and several others, Bresee announced
services at the Red Men's Hall, 317 South Main Street, Los
Angeles, starting Sunday, October 6, 1895. [4]

The new venture succeeded immediately and just three
and one-half weeks after the initial service, 135 charter
members organized the Church of the Nazarene. Electing
Bresee and Widney to life tenure as joint pastors and superintendents, the congregation adopted a statement of doctrines
and purposes. In effect an outline of the program which
Bresee had developed for the Peniel Mission, the "Articles
of Faith and General Rules" declared that the Church of the
Nazarene would seek "the simplicity and the pentecostal
power of the primitive New Testament Church" through "the
conversion of sinners, the sanctification of believers and the
building up in holiness of those ... committed" to its care.
"In the neglected quarters of the cities" and other "waste
places, " the group proposed to save souls, care for the
poor and comfort the dying in "city missions, evangelistic
services" and "house-to-house visitation, " [5] a program ad-
mirably suited to the needs of homesick Midwesterners arriving in Southern California by the thousands. From the first
service Dr. Bresee pleaded for a return to "the old paths. " [6]
Leaders of Nazarene meetings encouraged congregational participation, feeling that services like those of the camp meeting

allowed for more spiritual freedom than did the conventional
services of the city churches.

Forced to re-locate twice during the first six months
of its existence (the first time because of the noise occasioned by the worship, the other because the owner was
demolishing the building), the Church of the Nazarene steadily
increased its membership. Moving from the Red Men's Hall
at the end of its first month, the group rented the old Good
Templars' Hall near the intersection of Spring and North
Main Street. The next spring the church contemplated rent-
ing a theatre for Sunday meetings but abandoned the idea as
too expensive. At this juncture, Pastor Bresee was riding
in his buggy one day when he came upon a large church edi-
fice under construction. Almost despairing, he bowed his
head and prayed: "Oh, Lord, there is plenty of money
seemingly for great churches out in this part of the city; I
would that Thou wouldst give me some money to make a
place for the Church of the Nazarene."[7] This experience
convinced Bresee that the congregation should erect a temporary building of its own. Since most of the members were
poor, the leaders secured a personal loan of $800 with which
to build a tabernacle on a leased lot at 526 Los Angeles
Street.[8]

Bresee believed that in order to relieve congregations
from excessive "financial burdens," "houses of worship should
be plain and cheap" and that "everything" about them should
say "welcome to the poor."[9] Accordingly, volunteers constructed a simple board tabernacle plain enough to make the
poor feel at home and big enough to hold the crowds. The
building witnessed such outbursts of religious ecstacy that
worshippers nicknamed it the Glory Barn. I. G. Martin
declared that "out from this center of revival fire and pentecostal glory poured forth streams of light and salvation to
the ends of the earth. For about seven years Dr. Bresee
kept" continual "revival fires burning in this primitive place
of worship, bringing" the "leading evangelists of the holiness
movement" to assist him in bringing this "revival" to an
ever heightened "tide of victory."[10] The experiences enjoyed
there became emblematic of feelings which holiness congregations felt they should normally expect in their services.
The tabernacle became a model holiness church building,
including in elemental simplicity all the physical features
necessary to the Methodist camp meeting tradition. Incorporating potentialities which holiness promoters believed
universally applicable, the tabernacle built on Los Angeles

Top: Church of the Nazarene (exterior view), 527 South Los Angeles Street, Los Angeles, erected in 1896. Bottom: The same, interior view. From: Girvin, Ernest Alexander, 1857– Phineas F. Bresee: A Prince in Israel; A Biography. Kansas City, Mo.: Pentecostal Nazarene Publishing House, 1916; opposite pp. 120, 136.

Street in 1896 and its commodious brick replacement built
at Sixth and Wall in 1903, represented an ideal toward which
numerous congregations in other parts of the country moved. [11]

Advertising itself as "a simple, primitive church" for
the common people, the Church of the Nazarene explicitly
sought "to discard all superfluous forms and ecclesiasticism."
"Not a mission, but a church with a mission," the tabernacle made its chief impact upon multitudes of newcomers
to Los Angeles who found home-like fellowship in its pre-
cincts. [12] Henry Clay Morrison, who held an eleven-day
meeting at the tabernacle in January 1899, felt that Bresee's
approach to urban evangelization was the most effective yet
devised. In marked contrast to most city churches where
"stiffness and coldness" froze out "the common people,"
services at the Church of the Nazarene were characterized
by "remarkable liberty" and the "people" regarded "a service
as a comparative failure if some soul" was "not saved."
Chiefly concerned with "the salvation of the masses of lost
men about them," the congregation seemed "perfectly satisfied with their" humble "place of worship." "Without doubt,"
Morrison observed, "the times are ripe in all our large
cities for just such churches as the Nazarene in Los Angeles. "[13]

Despite continual pronouncements about ministering to
the poor, the Los Angeles church attracted several well established people. In addition to Dr. Widney and members
of the Bresee family, the congregation included Gardner
Howland, retired paper manufacturer from Troy, New York
(also a member of Joseph Hillman's famous Troy Praying
Band and one of the founders of the Ocean Park Camp Meet-
ing), Dr. Michael Everley Whistler, an elderly physician;
Judge William S. Knott, a prominent attorney who with his
wife, Lucy, had followed Bresee from the First Methodist
Church (Lucy P. Knott became a well-known minister in the
Church of the Nazarene); and Mrs. Mary Jane Willard, an
Episcopalian sanctified at Peniel Hall, and her wealthy
Southern friend, Colonel Duncan. [14]

The new venture succeeded gloriously. Starting with
a charter membership of 135, the church increased so
rapidly that a few months after it was built the four hundred seat tabernacle had to be enlarged. Even after the
addition, worshippers had to arrive early to get seats. [15]
Continuing a practice he had previously followed in Methodist pastorates and at Peniel Hall, for revivals Bresee secured

This page: Phineas Franklin Bresee (1838-1915). Facing
page: Nazarene Tabernacle 6th and Wall Streets, Los
Angeles, erected in 1903.   Bresee was pastor here until
1911. From: Girvin, Phineas F. Bresee: A Prince in
Israel... (1916), frontispiece, and opposite p. 168.

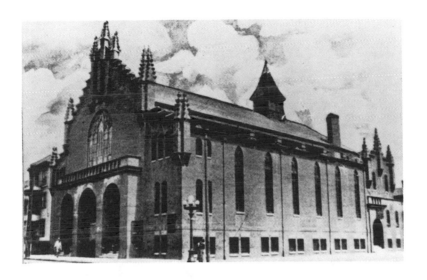

prominent Eastern and Midwestern evangelists and singers
including C. J. Fowler, president of the National Holiness
Association, Henry Clay Morrison, C. W. Ruth, and Will
Huff, evangelists who worked under National Association
auspices, Bud Robinson, a witty cowboy-preacher from
Texas who capitalized upon a lisp he was never fully able
to overcome, L. Milton Williams, one-time Salvation Army
officer, Seth C. Rees, Quaker independent early identified
with the International Holiness Union and Prayer League,
John T. Hatfield, commonly known as "The Hoosier Evangelist," and I. G. Martin and J. M. and M. J. Harris,
evangelistic singers from Illinois. These workers spread
praises of the Los Angeles experiment across the nation.[16]
Similarly, The Nazarene, a periodical started in July 1898
(re-named The Nazarene Messenger in 1900), conveyed the
month-to-month progress of the movement to a rapidly assembled national audience.[17]

The first years of the new century witnessed expansion not only in California, but in the Northwest and Midwest as well. In 1907 the church claimed 3827 members
in fifty-two churches, classes, and missions scattered from
Ohio and Michigan to the Pacific coast. Led by the First
Church in Los Angeles, the national organization concentrated
its efforts in urban areas. It was at work not only in Los
Angeles, its suburbs, and the S. F. Bay Area, but also in

Top: Seth Cook Rees (1854-1933). From: Rees, Paul Stromberg, 1900- . Seth Cook Rees, the Warrior-Saint. Indianapolis: Pilgrim Book Room, 1934; frontispiece. Bottom: Rest
Cottage, for unwed mothers, Pilot Point, Texas; founded 1903
by J. P. Roberts, inspired by a Rees sermon. (Now sponsored
by several districts of the Church of the Nazarene, this is one
of only two surviving homes promoted by Rees.) From: Moore,
Mark Reynolds, 1916- . Fifty Years...and Beyond; A History
of the Chicago Central District, Church of the Nazarene. Kankakee, Ill. : 1954; 126.

Portland, Seattle, Spokane, Boise and Salt Lake City in the
Northwest and Topeka, Columbus, Flint, Decatur and Chicago
in the Midwest. By 1906 it had work among Mexicans and
Chinese in Los Angeles and among Swedes in Chicago, had
assumed financial responsibility for Hope School for Girls in
Calcutta, India, and had established the Deets Pacific Bible
College at Los Angeles to train potential workers. [18]

While this wave of expansion and institutionalization
swept over the Church of the Nazarene in the West, a similar, though less pervasive tendency became apparent in the
activities of the International Holiness Union and Prayer
League in the Midwest. Founded as a loosely federated
evangelistic association, the International Holiness Union
promoted the individual evangelistic concerns and agencies
of its several members without attempting to control any of
them. For instance, Seth Cook Rees, who served as president of the International Holiness Union from 1897 to 1905,
promoted establishment of a string of homes for unwed
mothers from Rhode Island to California free from supervision by the Union. [19] Likewise, Martin Wells Knapp, an
officer and leading promoter of the Union, placed self-
perpetuating trustees in charge of God's Bible School and
Missionary Training Home and the Revivalist publishing
enterprises, effectively preventing their absorption by any
ecclesiastical body. [20] Such circumvention of church control
over particular institutions, however, did not alleviate pressure to make the International Holiness Union and Prayer
League into a Church rather than an interdenominational
association. And, as in the Church of the Nazarene, expansion and institutional development combined to promote
denominational order.

Known as the "Revivalist people" because of their
support of Knapp's school and of God's Revivalist, the first
members regarded themselves merely as supporters of aggressive missionary activity in the United States and abroad.
A local union was simply a band of members of the International Union who in fact usually sponsored a local mission
project. Although the constitution of the International Union
declared that it was "not an ecclesiastical body, but a fraternal union of Christian believers,"[21] successful mission
projects tended to develop into churches, a case in point
being Knapp's own Revivalist Chapel in Cincinnati. [22]

To keep abreast of its own organizational changes the
group changed its name twice during [continued on page 119]

Top: Deets Pacific Bible College, Los Angeles, established in 1902. Bottom: Bresee Memorial Administration Building, Pasadena College, California, erected in 1930. Pasadena College is the institutional descendant of Deets Pacific Bible College. Photographs from: Knott, James Proctor, 1886-1963. History of Pasadena College. Pasadena, Calif.: The College, 1960; opposite pp. 12 and 48.

Suburban camp meetings like this one (about 1906) at West Pullman, Illinois, did much to maintain the rural worship traditions among urban newcomers. Photographs from: Moore, Fifty Years ... and Beyond... (1954), 24.

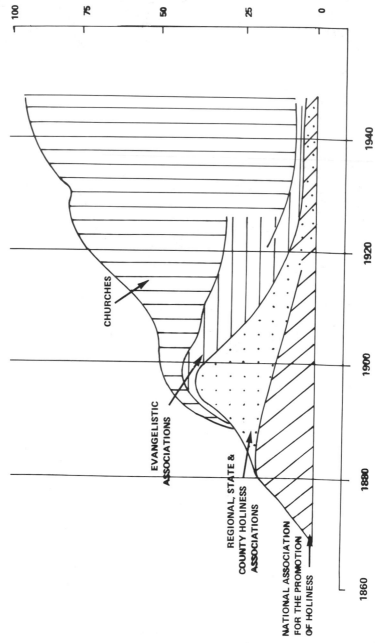

Figure 2. Proportional Growth of Holiness Organizations by Form, 1867–1947.

its first sixteen years. "In 1905, the International Holiness Union and Prayer League became the International Apostolic Holiness Union and Churches. The interdenominational features of the organization having largely ceased, in 1913 the name was changed to the International Apostolic Holiness Church."[23] In 1906 the Union reported 2774 members in seventy-four missions and churches in fourteen states. Scattered from Iowa and Kansas to Massachusetts and North Carolina, the group, which had branches in Cincinnati, Evansville, Grand Rapids and Battle Creek, was still largely rural. Committed to preaching the Gospel in the "slums and jungles," the Union was helping to support twenty-five missionaries in India, Japan, China and South Africa. In the homeland local affiliates in North Carolina, West Virginia, Kentucky and Oklahoma were busy evangelizing neglected areas of those states.[24]

In 1900 the holiness movement was well on its way to denominationalism. The new groups originated not from schism, but in response to social and geographical dislocation of the native white, rural middle class. The impetus for separate, pure churches originated not in rural areas from whence most of the adherents had recently come, but in cities, from whence it spread homeward to the countryside. Attached to organizational systems and evangelistic methods requiring little administration, holiness sects moved steadily toward denominational status.

THE HOME-COMING WEEK (1927)

Upon our journey here below
We meet with pain and loss;
Sometimes there is a crown of thorns,
Sometimes the heavy cross.
The dreary road to Calvary,
The bitter goad and sting,
But what's inside those gates of pearl
Will be worth everything.

> [Refrain:]   When we're inside the gates of pearl,
> We'll learn a lot of things,
> We'll have a harp that's made of gold,
> Perhaps a thousand strings;
> We'll sing and shout and dance about,
> The Lamb will dry our tears;
> We'll have a grand home-coming week,
> The first ten thousand years.

The shadows now begin to fall,
The time is drawing nigh,
When Christ our Lord shall come again
Like lightning from the sky.
And while we wait and suffer here,
Praise God, we'll shout and sing,
For one glimpse thro' those gates of pearl
Will be worth everything.

The precious blood of God's own Son
Has saved and sanctified
A wondrous people for His name
And they are called the bride.
Tho' here neglected and despised,
One day the Lord will bring
His chosen ones within the gates,
And that's worth everything.

Raymond Browning
(1874-1953)

11

HOME

The decision to organize churches rested on factors inherent in the origins of the American holiness movement. Since the holiness promotion depended on revivals and camp meetings, converts came from the sector of society most familiar with them. Least attracted by the new Wesleyanism were those groups (foreign immigrants, Jews, Catholics, Negroes and the establishment) unfamiliar with rural culture.[1]

Practical necessities and a common pattern of economic and social aspiration dictated organizational form. Wide-ranging evangelists, national periodicals, and missionary activity brought widely separated groups into contact, encouraging some to hope the whole movement might someday be one body. Although unity was never achieved, mergers gathered the overwhelming majority of holiness believers into two national churches.

In 1907 and 1908 merger brought the Church of the Nazarene, the Association of Pentecostal Churches of America, and the Holiness Church of Christ together in the Pentecostal Church of the Nazarene, a national body with 10,414 members and 228 congregations. Augmented in 1908 by members from the Holiness Association of Texas and the Pennsylvania Conference of the Holiness Christian Church; in 1911, from the People's Mission of Colorado and the Mississippi and Louisiana Conferences of the Methodist Protestant Church; and in 1915 by merger with the Pentecostal Mission of Tennessee and the Pentecostal Church of Scotland, the new church grew rapidly. In 1919 when it dropped "Pentecostal" from its name to disassociate itself from the "tongues" movement,[2] the Church of the Nazarene numbered 978 congregations and 34,928 members.[3]

A similar wave swept the International Apostolic Holiness Church into the stream of denominationalism. Merger in 1910 with the Holiness Christian [continued on page 125]

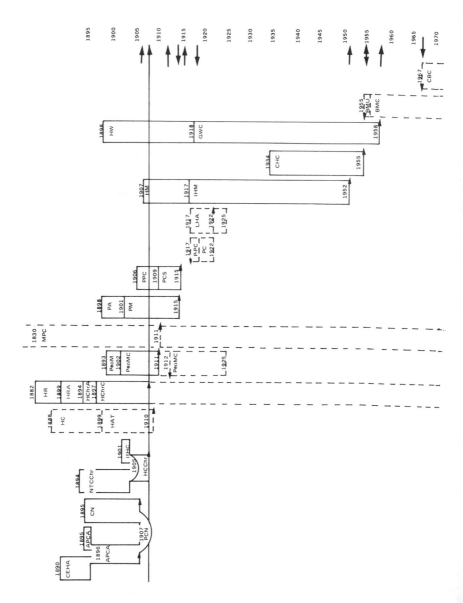

Figure 3. Predecessors of the Church of the Nazarene, 1882–
1908, and Formation of the Church of the Nazarene, 1907–1967
(Mergers, Additions and Withdrawals). For legend: see page
124.

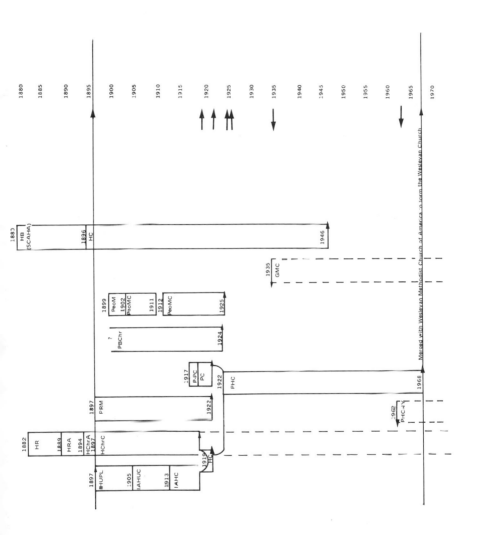

Figure 4. Predecessors of the Pilgrim Holiness Church, 1880-1922, and Formation of the Pilgrim Holiness Church, 1897-1968 (Mergers and Withdrawals). For legend: see next page.

LEGEND FOR FIGURES 3 AND 4

_____ body with which formal merger was effected; --------
body from which significant addition of members were received or into which a significant number of members withdrew; ⟶ addition or merger; ⟵ withdrawal.

APCA: Association of Pentecostal Churches of America.
BMC: Bible Missionary Church.
BMU: Bible Missionary Union.
CBC: Church of the Bible Covenant.
CEHA: Central Evangelical Holiness Association.
CHC: Calvary Holiness Church.
CN: Church of the Nazarene.
GMC: God's Missionary Church
GWC: Gospel Workers Church.
HAT: Holiness Association of Texas.
HB (SCAHA): Holiness Bands of the Southern California and Arizona Holiness Association.
HC: Holiness Church.
HCChr: Holiness Church of Christ.
HChrA: Holiness Christian Association.
HChrC: Holiness Christian Church.
HM: Holiness Mission.
HR: Heavenly Recruits.
HRA: Heavenly Recruit Association.
HW: Holiness Workers.
IAHC: International Apostolic Holiness Church.
IAHUC: International Apostolic Holiness Union and Churches.
IHC: International Holiness Church.
IHM: International Holiness Mission.
IHUPL: International Holiness Union and Prayer League.
ItHC: Independent Holiness Church.
LHA: Laymen's Holiness Association.
MPC: Methodist Protestant Church (La. & Miss. conferences)
NTCChr: New Testament Church of Christ.
PA: Pentecostal Alliance.
PBChr: Pentecostal Brethren in Christ.
PC: Pilgrim Church.
PCS: Pentecostal Church of Scotland.
PCN: Pentecostal Church of the Nazarene.
PeoM: People's Mission.
PeoMC: People's Mission Church.
PHC: Pilgrim Holiness Church.
PHCNY: Pilgrim Holiness Church of New York.
PM: Pentecostal Mission.
PPC: Parkhead Pentecostal Church.
P-PC: Pentecost-Pilgrim Church.
PRM: Pentecostal Rescue Mission.

Church and in 1922 with the Pilgrim Church of California
resulted in formation of the Pilgrim Holiness Church. Like
the Pentecostal Church of the Nazarene, the Pilgrim Holiness Church absorbed several smaller groups: the Pentecostal Rescue Mission centered in Binghamton, New York,
in 1922; the Pentecostal Brethren in Christ of Ohio in 1924;
and the People's Mission Church of Colorado in 1925. In
sharp contrast to the 5276 members and 170 churches the
International Apostolic Holiness Church had claimed ten
years earlier, in 1926 the Pilgrim Holiness Church reported
15,040 members in 441 congregations. [4]

Far-reaching organizational changes followed mergers.
Both groups provided for the election of general and district
superintendents to oversee the churches; to supervise missionary, educational and publishing enterprises; to preside
at legislative assemblies and ceremonies; to maintain discipline; and to inspire, counsel, and instruct the faithful. In
the early days of the united churches General Superintendents
P. F. Bresee, H. F. Reynolds and R. T. Williams in the
Church of the Nazarene, and George B. Kulp and Seth C.
Rees in the Pilgrim Holiness Church, brought to holiness
church administrative practices learned in other groups and
fired the new churches with zeal for institutional success.
Determined that their churches should flourish, they inordi-
nately valued numerical and financial gains but eschewed any
modification of the holiness evangelistic tradition. [5]

By 1930 the Church of the Nazarene and the Pilgrim
Holiness Church had both combined specialized administrative
boards into a unified one. Composed of clerical and lay
representatives from geographical areas, the General Board
had acted for the General Assembly in the interim between
general assemblies. Successful in largely eliminating financial competition between church agencies, it paved the way
for efficient administration by introducing bureaucratic methods used by business, government, and established religious
denominations. [6]

Although good housekeeping was important to people
recently gathered from particularist associations, it was not
the principal benefit which they sought from the new church
arrangements. Administration was rather the handmaiden of
nurture--the failure of which, even its friends said, was the
age-old weakness of the holiness movement. As one despairing loyalist put it, holiness workers were tired of "hatching
chickens for the hawks. "[7] As a consequence, they looked to

Top: Publishing House of the Pentecostal Church of the Nazarene, 2109 Troost Avenue, Kansas City, Missouri, occupied in 1912. For a few months the congregation of the city's church met here. Bottom: Nazarene Publishing House, Kansas City, occupied in 1926. From: Kansas City, Mo. First Church of the Nazarene. [Brochure] "30th Anniversary, March 1911-1941, First Church of the Nazarene, 41st and Harrison, Edwin E. Hale, pastor, Kansas City, Missouri" (1941).

the organized holiness church to provide instruction for converts and children which had been practically non-existent in
rescue missions and camp meetings. It was the desire for
a church home which set the movement on the course of upward social and economic mobility.

In the organized movement, middle-class propensities
were noticeable from the beginning. J. Proctor Knott recalled that in 1902 when the Church of the Nazarene in Los
Angeles decided to re-locate it chose a site "close to the
downtown area" "in a respectable middle-class neighborhood. "[8] When the Los Angeles newspapers said the building
was going to cost $50,000, Bresee dismissed the claim as
extravagant. He intimated it had been made by one unfamiliar with the work of the Church of the Nazarene, one who
did not realize that even if it were possible to do otherwise,
the congregation would put only such part of the "Lord's
money" into the building as was necessary to "accommodate
the multitudes" which attended the services. "People who
know this church, " the pastor declared, "know that its fideli-
ty to the poor has been such that it is without the necessary
means for even such a plain, commodious building. "[9] Nevertheless, the new building, which was brick veneer to meet
fire department regulations, cost $35,000, $15,000 more
than the first estimate. In 1907 the estimated value of the
building was $82,000. [10] In 1906 one-third of the Pente-
costal Church of the Nazarene and International Apostolic
Holiness Union congregations worshipped in rented halls
while ten years later only one-fifth occupied such quarters.
In this period these groups increased from 174 to 1037
congregations. [11]

Self-support seemed inevitably to signal abandonment
of mission work and desertion of downtown locations for
residential neighborhoods. Such at least was the case of
the John Three Sixteen Mission in Spokane, which, at the
close of a revival meeting conducted by C. W. Ruth in 1902,
was organized as a Church of the Nazarene. The mission
was started two years earlier during a tent meeting conducted by William H. Lee, founder of the People's Mission of
Colorado Springs. [12] It continued under the direction of the
Reverend Mrs. Elsie M. Wallace and her husband, DeLance
Wallace. Mr. Wallace, who at first worked at secular employment during the daytime and helped his wife in the mission at night, eventually became a minister also. Located
across the street from the Coeur d'Alene Theatre, mission
workers took advantage of the crowds gathered to see the

FIRST CHURCH TENT MEETING, 64TH AND EGGLESTON

I. G. MARTIN, PASTOR

Top: Tent at 62nd Street and Lexington Ave., Chicago, where the First Church of the Nazarene was organized, August 28, 1904. Bottom: Interior, at later location. Photographs from: Moore, Fifty Years ... and Beyond... (1954), 15, 24.

film previews and conducted street meetings in an attempt
to attract them to the mission instead.   The mission made
a large number of converts, many of them young people who
soon would marry and have families of their own.   Commenting in December 1904, Bresee said that although "like
all mission work" much of its clientele was "transient," the
Spokane mission was attracting whole families "more than
ever before." There were, he declared, "a fine class of
workers, especially among the young people."[13]   Poorly
equipped for ministering to families, the leaders began thinking about re-locating in a residential neighborhood.   Encouraged by Bresee, who presided at the first annual Northwest
District Assembly held at the mission hall in 1905, the
majority of the members voted in favor of buying property.
After complicated negotiations, they bought a lot and erected
a tabernacle-type church building. When, however, some who
had opposed abandoning mission work persisted, the majority
initiated disciplinary action and the mission faction withdrew.[14]

Estrangement on account of separation of church from
mission was rare, however, and volunteers from suburban
congregations continued to serve in independent missions
after official ties had been severed.[15]   A cooperative relationship usually prevailed.   Leonard Spangenberg, Nazarene
layman and an executive in the Babson statistical organization, attributed his membership in the Church of the Nazarene to a mission worker.   During World War I, Spangenberg's family moved from Plainfield, New Jersey, to Boston,
where his father became superintendent of an ordnance plant.
In Boston the family attended a "well-known" church.   Then
"one day, near the end of the war" Leonard's father was
scanning the church page of the newspaper when his eye fell
on an announcement of a Sunday afternoon service at the Old
Shawmut Mission.   Overcome with remorse for past sins,
Mr. Spangenberg decided "a mission was a good place for
any sinner to find help" and drove his family into the city
to the mission the next afternoon.   "Although ... dressed
much better than some of the poor wayfarers who frequent
missions, my father knew he needed Christ just as much as
they" and repented.   Immediately, the whole family began
attending the mission, actively participating in services every
Sunday.   Leonard recalled that at age twelve he learned to
play the trombone, a skill used in street meetings.   However,
"after attending ... for some time," the mission superintendent advised the Spangenbergs "to join some church."   Hearing
of their interest in "holiness," he [continued on page 133]

Facing page, top: South Side Pentecostal Mission (of the
First Church of the Nazarene, Chicago), which provided many
of the first members. Bottom: First building of the First
Church of the Nazarene, purchased by the congregation in
fall 1904. This page, top: Second building, a new church
constructed in 1911 on the site of the old one. Bottom:
Third building, occupied October 8, 1953. Four photographs
from: Moore, Fifty Years ... and Beyond... (1954), 22
(&22), 23(&23).

Top and Bottom: The holiness church's propensity toward becoming an extended family was nowhere more apparent than in the combination of evangelistic effort with recreational activity here illustrated by the band and the gospel team of the First Pentecostal Church of the Nazarene in Chicago about 1915. From: Moore, Fifty Years ... and Beyond... (1954), 24, 126.

recommended the Pentecostal Church of the Nazarene in
suburban Malden, a church the whole family joined.[16]

Although a few congregations continued to use "mission" in their names even after they moved to new locations,
the term's usefulness as a description for work among des-
titute, down-and-out people practically ended by the World
War. Describing themselves as poor, holiness people did
not regard their own action as a flight from needy people,
but as a step necessary to saving their own children and
conserving previous converts.

Intent on preserving holiness evangelistic usages,
when constructing buildings most holiness groups chose tabernacle-type structures. When they could secure a better
location or building by buying a church from another denomination, they did so even when such facilities provided a strange
setting for their camp meeting-style services. In 1915 the
First Pentecostal Church of the Nazarene of Kansas City,
Missouri, deserted the simple stucco tabernacle which it had
built two years earlier to move into a substantial rock church
building a few blocks away occupied previously by the Beacon
Hill Congregational Church. With this building the Kansas
City congregation inherited a pipe organ and stained glass
windows.[17]

Financing of buildings and support of full-time ministers in turn required recruitment of members from a more
stable portion of society than had missions. The church
program depended heavily on attracting men with jobs, families, and homes, people in fact who had a stake in middle-
class society.

The holiness method for creating solid church members
out of the rural newcomers sprang from theological roots and
flourished out of material necessity. Like the early Methodists, holiness people insisted that genuine spirituality issued
in right conduct. Consequently, as they organized churches
they early reinstated Methodist social prohibitions. The
faithful were to eschew pride in dress or behavior, specifi-
cally the wearing of jewelry and fashionable clothing, and to
tithe their income and to make additional offerings as the
program of the church required. The close-knit nature of
the holiness church community meant that rules were much
more often enforced by social pressure than by legal action.
The rules merely formulated convictions generally held by
holiness believers.[18]

Top: Church of the Nazarene, Youngstown, Ohio: the Old
Tabernacle. Bottom: The (new) Nazarene Tabernacle, ded-
icated June 11, 1939. From: Youngstown, Ohio. First
Church of the Nazarene. "Souvenir Dedication Booklet: The
Nazarene Tabernacle, 3310 Hudson Avenue, Youngstown,
Ohio" (1939).

Membership vows that explicitly excluded from the
holiness fraternity all who did not agree with its doctrinal
beliefs or behavioral standards, laid the foundation for
cultural as well as theological agreement among members.
Having achieved the basis of social cohesion, the holiness
church largely ignored the secular context in which it operated. Instead it concentrated on the salvation of individuals
who in conversion forsook the world to join the select company of the church. Despite pronouncements about ministering to the poor, holiness churches accepted no responsibility for outsiders beyond attempting to see them converted.
Instead holiness people meditated upon the quality of their
own fellowship and concentrated upon external expansion.
As a group the Pilgrim Holiness Church agreed with E. E.
Shelhamer, a well-known Free Methodist evangelist who
autographed his photograph "Yours for a clean rather than
a Big Work."[19] For many years they hewed rigidly to their
original standards, even at the expense of numerical and
financial increase. While not changing its rules, the Church
of the Nazarene reluctantly compromised standards and
reaped bountiful numerical and financial increases.[20]

Organized holiness did not promote social reform.
Generally concerned only with the needs of prospective converts; drinking, smoking, gambling, divorce, theater-going
and Sabbath observance received the bulk of the attention.[21]
Classifying themselves as poor even after they enjoyed moderate prosperity, holiness people faced genuinely impover-
ished people with moralism or apathy. Silently attributing
deprivation to sin, socially they favored the status quo. Few
supported either Alma White, founder of the Pillar of Fire
Church, who judged the Ku Klux Klan to be God's instrument
for preserving order,[22] or the Emmanual Association, splin-
ter of the Pilgrim Holiness Church, which rejected both
trade unionism and the military.[23] Representing majority
opinion, the Church of the Nazarene and the Pilgrim Holiness Church condemned secret societies but took no stand
on political, military or labor organizations. Both churches
maintained official contact with members in the armed services and supplied full quotas of military chaplains. Both
have been generally apathetic toward minorities and civil
rights.[24] Between 1906 and 1936 not one Negro congregation was reported by any of these groups.

At first holiness congregations were small, financial
obligations formidable and extinction a real threat. Prior
to 1936 the average holiness congregation consisted of about

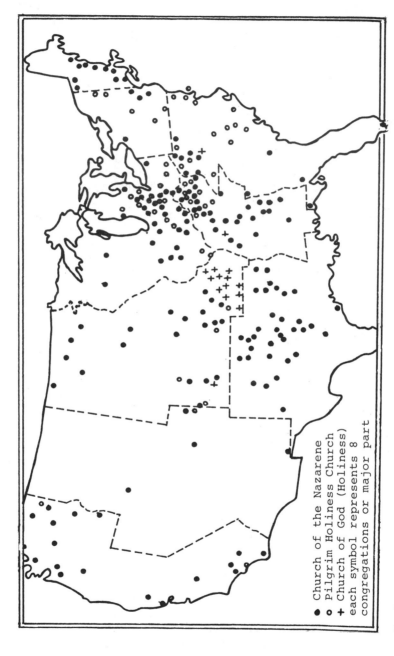

Figure 5. Locations of Congregations of Three Holiness Denominations, 1922-1925, by Geographical Regions.

● Church of the Nazarene
○ Pilgrim Holiness Church
+ Church of God (Holiness)
each symbol represents 8
congregations or major part

45 members.[25] As a consequence necessity often forced the
minister to take a second job.[26] Every member was enlisted as a worker and efforts to raise the pastor's salary,
buy a parsonage or meet the mortgage payment when due
became matters of common concern. Such involvement in
the administrative problems of the church helped members
deal with similar personal ones. Inadvertently the church
provided members with training in business and prepared
them for upward mobility.

The role of the holiness church in consolidating the
religious and secular goals of members was apparent in
changes which accompanied denominational organization.
Dependable support for institutional work had been one of
the reasons for church formation. Yet, while schools and
foreign missions flourished under denominational control,
social welfare agencies languished. Within twenty years of
assuming denominational form, holiness churches officially
abandoned welfare work. In 1923 the Church of the Nazarene
relinquished control of such institutions to local church units.
The only institution to survive under this arrangement was
Rest Cottage, a home for unmarried mothers at Pilot Point,
Texas.[27] By 1940 the Pilgrim Holiness Church was following a similar course.

Never deeply committed to the task of social amelio-
ration, denominational leaders largely left promotion to the
workers themselves. Under church control success depended
on individual administrators. As a consequence holiness
welfare institutions seldom outlived their original sponsors.
A case in point is the Voice of Canaan Mission and the
Beulah Rescue Home of St. Louis. Founded in 1907 by
Melvin F. Pratt, a Holiness Christian minister, and his
wife, the work prospered and in time the Pratts added the
Beulah Bible Training School to the program. In 1927 they
discontinued the mission and school and to remove the girls
from the temptations of city life moved the rescue home to
a farm near Terre Haute, Indiana. After a few years Mrs.
Pratt died and the home was closed.[28]

Abandonment of welfare activities issued from social
as well as administrative causes. Most of the people served
were newcomers from the country temporarily unable to cope
with city life. Only a minority of the girls rescued, for
instance, were professional prostitutes.[29] As public high
schools developed in rural areas, increasing numbers of
young people arrived with job skills. Better prepared ini-

This page: Camp meeting grounds often were chosen as locations for holiness schools, operation of which encouraged development of new towns. Here, during an Illinois camp meeting, Dr. Bresee auctions off lots in the village of Olivet, seat of the Illinois Holiness University. From: Moore, Fifty Years ... and Beyond... (1954), 119. Facing page, top: Tabernacle used by the Beulah Park Camp Meeting at Allentown, Pennsylvania. Facing page, center: Eastern Pilgrim College, Allentown, Pennsylvania, founded in 1921. Until 1954 it was called the Beulah Park Bible School. Bottom: In 1956 the camp meeting was discontinued at Eastern Pilgrim College and new grounds were purchased near Lehighton, Pennsylvania. Pictured is the tabernacle of the Bethany Camp located on these grounds.

tially, later newcomers located in residential areas. Ministering to this group, holiness churches experienced phenomenal
growth. From 1926 to 1936 holiness membership increased
nearly 32, 000 in cities of 25, 000 and over, [30] a gain exceed-
ing by one-fourth that of Methodist bodies which had twenty-
eight times as many members in these places. [31] No longer
in direct contact with slum dwellers and dissatisfied with
meager evangelistic returns of mission work, holiness denominations joined older church bodies in emphasizing programs which conformed to the aspirations of members.

Under denominational control education and missionary
enterprises thrived. Operating within a tradition inherited
from the holiness associations, church school administrators
borrowed practices from sources as disparate as the university, the Bible institute and the camp meeting. Several
established schools on camp meeting grounds and laid out
town sites near them. Following the Iowa Holiness Association which in 1906 established the Central Holiness University and the village of University Park adjacent to its camp
grounds at Oskaloosa, [32] school promoters developed Olivet,
a village south of Danville, Illinois; Bethany, a suburb of
Oklahoma City; and subdivisions of Pasadena and Nashville
as locations for colleges. In these places faculty, clergy
and townspeople collaborated in saving young people and
preparing them for church work. [33] When possible they
refused to license theatres or sellers of tobacco or alcohol.
The schedule included daily chapel and frequent prayer meetings. In addition there were several revival meetings during
the year and camp meeting immediately after commencement.
In 1921 trustess of the Olivet, Illinois, school recorded
"unalterable objection to permitting" students to leave campus before the end of camp meeting. [34]

Seldom equipped adequately to offer more than religious instruction, holiness schools had grandiose aspirations.
Recognized for the most part by neither accrediting agencies
nor graduate schools, some institutions called themselves
universities. By the 1920's, however, more realism characterized educational administration. While the Bible school
concept continued in force, a number of holiness schools
introduced liberal arts and pre-professional curricula and
sought regional accreditation. Replacing "university" with
"college" and "holiness" with the denominational title in
their names, they tied administration ever more closely to
the church. The movement toward sectarianism and respectability was in full sway. The history of Olivet Nazarene

Eventually many of the Methodist loyalists became virtual
independents.   Pictured is the Detroit Holiness Tabernacle,
about 1926.   No services were held on Sunday morning, but
Sunday school and worship services were conducted on Sunday afternoon, an evangelistic service on Sunday night, a
mid-week prayer meeting on Thursday night and an all day
meeting once a month.   From: Leaflet issued by Detroit
Holiness Tabernacle in 1926--in Florence Schleicher Teed
Papers, Michigan Historical Collections, University of
Michigan.

College illustrates the process.   Founded as a grammar
school by the Eastern Illinois Holiness Association, in 1912
the three-year-old Illinois Holiness University was taken
over by the Nazarenes.   In 1916 the name was changed to
Olivet University; six years later, to Olivet College.   When
fire destroyed the main building at Olivet in 1940, the school
moved to Bourbonnais, a suburb of Kankakee, Illinois.   At
that time "Nazarene" was inserted in the name.   The college
received state recognition for teacher-education in the 1940's
and regional accreditation in 1956.

        Foreign missionary programs also registered the
impact of denominational control.   At first church administration was indistinguishable from that of the Missionary
Society of the National Association for the Promotion of

Holiness[35] or other non-denominational agencies. Like independent groups, denominational boards insisted that candi-
dates feel a distinct call to missionary work and that conventional evangelistic methods be used in foreign areas.
Routines for selection were set up and medical examinations
initiated.   On the field institutional administration increasingly consumed time formerly devoted to free-lance evangelism.   Direct supervision from the homeland was introduced,
native self-support encouraged and leadership training begun.
Thanks to denominational administration, by 1930 the independence of holiness missionaries was a thing of the past.
To a large extent decisions of church officials had supplanted
spirit-guidance in holiness missionary administration.

    Although independent missions continued, few enjoyed
support as dependable as that of the denominational work.
In 1926 the Church of the Nazarene reported fifty-five missionaries, three hundred national workers and 3400 members
in Japan, China, India, Palestine, Africa and Central and
South America.   It was operating seventy-nine schools
serving 1740 student and eighteen hospitals and dispensaries
treating 21, 500 patients annually.   That year the Pilgrim
Holiness Church had sixty missionaries, 160 national workers
and 3660 members in India, Africa, the West Indies, Central
and South America and Alaska, and was helping support work
of the Oriental Missionary Society in Japan, China and
Korea. [36]

    By the 1930's a new day had dawned in the American
holiness movement.   Concern for the poor which the saints
once professed had largely been diverted to salvation for
their children.   Schools for training new converts now nurtured the already convinced.   "Faith" work once pursued
exuberantly in "slums and jungles" had been either abandoned
or institutionalized.   Yet in form the movement held tena-
ciously to its rural background.   Committed to the fortunes
of the lower middle class migrants which composed them,
holiness churches both followed and led their members to
the suburbs.   Contending for old-time Methodism, they
saved multitudes of rural newcomers from social disintegration and through churchmanship trained them in middle class
ways.

FORTY YEARS AGO: The Old Camp-Meeting Times (1914)

I wish I were a boy again
In the old camp-meeting times,
To hear old-fashioned people
Sing their hallelujah rhymes,
And see the mourners at the bench,
The pilgrims kneeling round,
Awaiting for the Holy Ghost
To show the Savior found.

    [Refrain:] Forty years ago! Forty years ago!
    I wish I were a boy again,
    As in the long ago;
    Bless God for old camp-meeting times,
    Forty years ago.

I'd like to be in church once more
In old revival years,
Among the folks who still believe
God listens with both ears;
With those who sang the loudest songs
Or prayed the longest prayers,
I'd go back with a willing heart
Could I once more be there.

I'd like to see the preacher's face
Above that bench again,
A-shining through his happy tears,
Like sunshine after rain,
And hear his "Glory be to God,"
His wonderful "AMEN,"
When half a dozen anxious souls
Were truly born again.

O for one day of those past years,
And of that day one hour
When good old Mother So-and-so
Was shouting with the power;
And men and women laughed and cried
As she danced down the aisle,
A-shaking hands and blessing all
In old camp-meeting style.

                Bushrod Shedden Taylor
                  (1849-1936)

REFERENCES AND NOTES
to Chapters 1-11

CHAPTER 1

1.1 John Wesley, "Minutes of Several Conversations between the Rev. Mr. Wesley and Others from the Year 1744, to the Year 1789," in his Works (14 vols., Grand Rapids, Mich.: Zondervan, 1958), VIII, 300. The edition used is a photo-offset reprint of the authorized edition of 1872 published by the Wesleyan Conference Office, London.

1.2 William Edward Hartpole Lecky, A History of England in the Eighteenth Century (8 vols., New York: D. Appleton, 1878-1890), II, 691-692. See also William Henry Pitchett, Wesley and His Century (London: Smith, Elder & Co., 1906), passim.

1.3 Wesley, "A Plain Account of Christian Perfection, as Believed and Taught by the Reverend Mr. Wesley, from the year 1725, to the year 1777," in his Works, XI, 371.

1.4 Wesley, "Sermon CXVI, Causes of the Inefficacy of Christianity," in his Works, VII, 289-290.

1.5 The History of American Methodism (3 vols., New York: Abingdon Press, 1964), I, 187, 600.

1.6 Leander Lycurgus Hamline, "Bishop Hamline's Recommendation," in George Peck, The Scripture Doctrine of Christian Perfection Stated and Defended (New York: Lane and Tippett, 1845), vii-ix.

1.7 See Wade Crawford Barclay, To Reform the Nation (History of Methodist Missions: Early American Methodism, 1769-1844, vol. 2), (New York: Board of Missions and Church Extension, 1950), 388.

1.8 John Leland Peters, Christian Perfection and American Methodism (New York: Abingdon Press, 1956), 101-102, 109, 114-115. See biographical sketch in Matthew Simpson, Cyclopaedia of Methodism, Embracing Sketches of Its Rise, Progress, and Present Condition, with Biographical Notices and Numerous Illustrations, 4th rev. ed. (Philadelphia: Louis H. Everts, 1881), 993.

1.9 Timothy Lawrence Smith, Revivalism and Social Reform in Mid-Nineteenth Century America (New York: Abingdon Press,

145

1957), 105, 113, 119-121, and 173. See also biographical sketches
of Phoebe and W. C. Palmer, in Matthew Simpson, Cyclopaedia of
Methodism, 691-692; in Ernest Wall, "I commend unto you Phoebe,"
Religion in Life, XXVI (Summer 1957), 396-408; and in Stephen Olin
Garrison, Forty Witnesses, Covering the Whole Range of Christian
Experience, introduction by Bishop C. D. Foss (New York: Hunt &
Eaton; Cincinnati: Cranston & Stowe, 1888). From early contact
with believers from non-Methodist communions, the holiness move-
ment received several long-lived and much used books, particularly
Hannah Whitall Smith, The Christian's Secret of a Happy Life, of
which over 2,000,000 copies had been sold by 1952, and Thomas C.
Upham, Principles of the Interior; or, Hidden Life (1843), the only
title by a non-Methodist author included in a series of "abridged
Holiness Classics" issued by a major holiness publisher in the 1940's.
Upham's Life and Religious Opinions and Experience of Madame de
La Mothe Guyon (1847) continued to be issued, read, and revered by
holiness advocates well into the twentieth century. According to
Ronald Knox, an English Roman Catholic, Upham read his own nine-
teenth-century evangelical and perfectionist ideas into Madame Guyon.
See Ronald Arbothnott Knox, Enthusiasm; A Chapter in the History
of Religion, with Special Reference to the XVII and XVIII Centuries
(New York: Oxford University Press, 1961), 235-238.

1.10 Smith, Revivalism and Social Reform, 124.

1.11 Among the hundreds of tracts issued from the Palmers'
New York offices was one by Harriet Beecher Stowe, entitled
Primitive Christian Experience. --Peters, Christian Perfection
and American Methodism, 110.

1.12 Phoebe Palmer, Four Years in the Old World; Compris-
ing the Travels, Incidents, and Evangelistic Labors of Dr. and Mrs.
Palmer in England, Ireland, Scotland and Wales (New York: Foster
& Palmer, 1867).

1.13 See Frank J. Metcalf, American Writers and Compilers
of Sacred Music (New York: Russell & Russell, 1925), 323-325; and
Robert Guy McCutchan, Our Hymnody; A Manual of the Methodist
Hymnal, 2d ed. (New York: Abingdon Press, 1937), 279-280.

1.14 Mrs. Joseph F. Knapp provided the music for her
mother's "The Cleansing Wave." This appears to be the only instance of collaboration between mother and daughter. In reference
to Charles Wesley and Mrs. Joseph F. Knapp see McCutcheon, Our
Hymnody, 386, 279-280.

1.15 Romans 12:1-2a.

1.16 Phoebe Palmer, The Way of Holiness, with Notes by
the Way; Being a Narrative of Religious Experience, Resulting from
a Determination to be a Bible Christian (New York: G. Lane & C.
B. Tippett, 1845), 33.

1.17 Garrison, Forty Witnesses, 100ff, 283ff, and (Mrs.) Clara McLeister, Men and Women of Deep Piety, ed. and published by Rev. E. E. Shelhamer (Syracuse, N.Y.: Wesleyan Methodist Publishing Association, 1920), 236ff.

1.18 For a description of the holiness-evangelical alliance in the 1840's and 1850's see Smith, Revivalism and Social Reform, 103-147.

CHAPTER 2

2.1 Edmund S. Janes, "Introduction" (1851), in Randolph S. Foster, Christian Purity; or, The Heritage of Faith (New York: Phillips & Hunt, 1869), 13.

2.2 Methodist preachers and officials of the mid-nineteenth century figure prominently in any list of standard holiness doctrinal works: R. S. Foster, Christian Purity (1851); Jesse Peck, The Central Idea of Christianity (1857); George Peck, The Scripture Doctrine of Christian Perfection Stated and Defended (1842); Asbury Lowrey, Possibilities of Grace (1884); John A. Wood, Perfect Love (1862).

2.3 Jesse T. Peck, The Central Idea of Christianity (Boston: Henry V. Degen, 1858), 326.

2.4 Foster, Christian Purity, 6.

2.5 Declaring that Methodists were "convinced" as much as ever of the "great evil of slavery," the 1844 Discipline declared, nevertheless, that Methodist officials could hold slaves where the laws forbade emancipation or where the "liberated" slave would be denied freedom anyway. Methodist Episcopal Church, Doctrines and Discipline (New York: G. Lane & C. B. Tippett, 1844), 202-203.

2.6 Quoted in Ira Ford McLeister, History of the Wesleyan Methodist Church of America, rev. [i.e., 3d] ed. by Roy Stephen Nicholson (Marion, Ind.: Wesley Press, 1959), 28.

2.7 Ibid., 35-37.

2.8 Hunter Dickinson Farish, The Circuit Rider Dismounts; A Social History of Southern Methodism, 1865-1900 (Richmond, Va.: Dietz Press, 1938), 16-17; William Warren Sweet, Methodism in American History, revision of 1953 (New York: Abingdon Press, 1954), 253.

2.9 Judges 13:4, 5.

2.10 Benjamin Titus Roberts, Why Another Sect; Containing a Review by Bishop Simpson and Others on the Free Methodist Church (Rochester, N.Y.: "The Earnest Christian" publishing house, 1879), 186.

2.11   Quoted in Leslie Ray Marston, From Age to Age a
Living Witness; A Historical Interpretation of Free Methodism's
First Century (Winona Lake, Ind.: Light and Life Press, 1960),
573-578.

2.12   Roberts, Why Another Sect, 186, 209.

2.13   Marston, From Age to Age a Living Witness, 234.

2.14   Robert Donald Clark, The Life of Matthew Simpson (New
York: Macmillan, 1956), 154.

2.15   Quoted in Roberts, Why Another Sect, 111.   Joseph Mc-
Creery, expelled from the Genesee Conference along with Roberts in
1858, describe the church in terms markedly resembling Peck's:
"Some of the younger boys have taken my mother, the Methodist
Church, in her old age, painted her face and curled her hair, hooped
her, and flounced her, and jeweled her, and fixed her up, until we
could hardly" distinguish "her from a woman of the world.   Now
when I have taken the old lady and washed her face, and straight-
ened out her hair, and dressed her up in modest apparel, so that
she looks like herself again, they make a great hue and cry, and
call it abusing mother." Quoted in Roberts, 141-142.

2.16   Clark, The Life of Matthew Simpson, 276.

2.17   Ibid., 192.

2.18   Methodist Episcopal Church, Doctrines and Discipline,
1856 (Cincinnati: Swormstedt & Poe, 1858), 173.

2.19   See Harris Elwood Starr, "John Swanel Inskip," in
Dictionary of American Biography (22 vols., New York: G. Scrib-
ner's Sons, 1927-1957), IX, 490-491; and William McDonald and
John E. Searles, The Life of Rev. John S. Inskip (Boston: McDonald
& Gill, 1885).

2.20   Books Mrs. Hamline recommended included: The Life
of Hester Ann Rogers, the Life of Carvosso, the Life of Mrs. Mary
Fletcher, John Wesley's Sermons on Christian Perfection, and Mrs.
Palmer's paper, Guide to Holiness.   These, along with Jesse T.
Peck's Central Idea of Christianity, with which she was already ac-
quainted, gave Frances a good theoretical grasp of contemporary
Wesleyan teaching.

2.21   Stephen Olin Garrison, Forty Witnesses, Covering the
Whole Range of Christian Experience; introduction by Bishop C. D.
Foss (New York: Hunt & Eaton; Cincinnati: Cranston & Stowe, 1888),
91, 94-95, 97.

2.22   Ibid., 97-98.

2.23   Simpson, Cyclopaedia of Methodism, 368.

2.24   Garrison, Forty Witnesses, 96.

2.25   Ibid., 103-104.   Watson joined the South Carolina Conference of the Wesleyan Methodist Connection in 1896, where he
retained his membership until his death in 1924.   McLeister, History of the Wesleyan Methodist Church of America, 460.

2.26   James Wesley Horne, a graduate of Wesleyan University
and a future holiness evangelist, served from 1853 to 1858 as principal of the Monrovia Academy in Liberia under the Methodist Episcopal Church.   --Matthew Simpson, Cyclopaedia of Methodism, 455,
1015.   After the war began, another future evangelist, Alfred Cookman, briefly toyed with the idea of Negro colonization, but quickly
abandoned it as, at the time, unprovidential.   See William McDonald,
Life Sketches of Rev. Alfred Cookman (Cincinnati: Freedmen's Aid
and Southern Education Society, 1900), 101-102.

2.27   On leave from Trinity Church, Philadelphia, Alfred
Cookman served under the Christian Commission with the Army of
the Potomac during 1864.   --Henry Bascom Ridgaway, The Life of
the Rev. Alfred Cookman; With Some Account of His Father, the
Rev. George Grimston Cookman, with an introduction by the Rev.
R. S. Foster (New York: Nelson & Phillips; Cincinnati: Hitchcock &
Walden, 1874), 258-274.   During the first fourteen months of the
war, Inskip served as chaplain of the 14th New York Militia.   --Har-
ris Elwood Starr, "John Swanel Inskip," in Dictionary of American
Biography, V, 490.   For a brief time at the beginning of the war,
Gilbert Haven was chaplain of the 8th Massachusetts regiment.
--Simpson, Cyclopaedia of Methodism, 434.   Lucius C. Matlack, a
Wesleyan Methodist who was re-admitted to the Philadelphia Conference of the Methodist Episcopal Church in 1867, served as chaplain
of the 17th Illinois Cavalry.   --Simpson, Cyclopaedia of Methodism,
569.

2.28   Harrison D. Brown, Personal Memories of the Early
Ministry of Dr. Phineas F. Bresee (Seattle: 1930), 25.

2.29   Simpson's Cyclopaedia of Methodism mentions J. W.
Horne, L. R. Dunn, Alfred Cookman, William McDonald, John S.
Inskip, and G. C. M. Roberts.   Simpson singles out Alfred Cookman as having held prominent pulpits.   G. C. M. Roberts, a Baltimore physician, served voluntarily in clerical posts.   For a long
time he was military chaplain in Baltimore.

2.30   From 1859 to 1863, Walter and Phoebe Palmer were
evangelizing in Great Britain.   See Phoebe Palmer and Walter Clark
Palmer, Four Years in the Old World; Comprising the Travels, Incidents, and Evangelistic Labors of Dr. and Mrs. Palmer in England,
Ireland, Scotland and Wales (New York: Foster & Palmer, 1867).
From 1860 to 1862, Andrew Longacre was assistant to Dr. McClin-
tock at the American Chapel in Paris.   In 1856 William Taylor returned from California, where he had pioneered Methodist work in
the San Francisco Bay area.   Taylor spent five years evangelizing in

the Eastern states and Canada, then in 1862 departed for Australia
by way of Europe. During the war years, he labored with marked
success in Australia, Tasmania, and Ceylon. Taylor, an intimate
of Bishop Simpson, preached at Genesee Conference at the height of
the "Nazarite" troubles. --Timothy Lawrence Smith, Revivalism
and Social Reform in Mid-Nineteenth-Century America (New York:
Abingdon Press, 1957), 132. See also William Taylor, Story of My
Life; An Account of What I Have Thought and Said and Done in My
Ministry of More Than Fifty-Three Years in Christian Lands and
Among the Heathens, ed. by John Clark Ridpath (New York: Hunt
and Eaton, 1896). His chaplaincy completed, in 1862 Gilbert Haven
visited western Europe, Egypt, Palestine, and Greece. --Simpson,
Cyclopaedia of Methodism, 434-435, 990, 1004.

2.31   Clark, The Life of Matthew Simpson, p. 231.

2.32   Elected bishop in 1872, Gilbert Haven spent most of the
remainder of his life working for Negro betterment in Africa and
the Southern states. One of the Freedmen's Aid Society institutions,
the Haven Normal School, Waynesborough, Georgia, probably was
named for him. Alfred Cookman was honored in the naming of
Cookman Institute, Jacksonville, Florida. --Simpson, Cyclopaedia
of Methodism, 256, 381.

2.33   McDonald, Life Sketches of Rev. Alfred Cookman, 99-
100.

2.34   Simpson, Cyclopaedia of Methodism, 568-569; 922-924.
Although the Wesleyan Methodists did not include a doctrinal statement on Christian perfection in their Discipline until the 1890's, the
group from its beginnings had leaned toward perfectionism. After the
slavery issue was settled and large numbers returned to the mother
church, the remaining Wesleyan Methodists tended more and more
toward ultraist piety and practically ceased to grow. --McLeister,
History of the Wesleyan Methodist Church of America, 86-89, 449-
471.

2.35   "The Rev. W. B. Osborn," Christian Advocate (New
York), vol. 9 (Sept. 18, 1902), 1489.

2.36   Delbert Roy Rose, A Theology of Christian Experience
(Wilmore, Ky.: The Seminary Press, 1958), 63.

CHAPTER 3

3.1   Charles Albert Johnson, The Frontier Camp Meeting:
Religion's Harvest Time (Dallas: Southern Methodist University Press,
1955), passim.

3.2   [James Porter] An Essay on Camp-Meetings (New York:
Lane & Scott, 1849), 80-81.

3.3 Methodist Church (United States), The Methodist Hymnal (Baltimore: Methodist Book Concern, 1939), 503.

3.4 Alexander McLean and J. W. Eaton, eds., Penuel; or, Face to Face with God (New York: W. C. Palmer, Jr., 1869), 4.

3.5 Ibid., 7-9, 11.

3.6 In 1830, the United States had only one city of more than 100,000 population (New York, with 202,589), while in 1870 it had twelve, with a combined population of 4,129,989. --U.S. Bureau of the Census, Historical Statistics of the United States, Colonial Times to 1957; prepared by the Bureau of the Census with the cooperation of the Social Science Research Council (Washington, D.C.: Government Printing Office, 1960), 14.

3.7 Notice the nostalgia in [George Hughes] Evenings with Grandfather Braddock, a Veteran Itinerant; Showing His Labors, Joys, and Triumphs in the Methodist Itinerancy, Being an Antidote to "My Grandfather Braddock," Advocating True Reform, and Unmasking Pretended Reformers in the Methodist Episcopal Church, by Rev. Frank F. Fairfield [pseud.], with an introduction by Rev. Theophilus T. Trueman [pseud.], also a preface by Rev. Henry H. Hopeful [pseud.] (Philadelphia: Published for the Author by Perkinpine & Higgins, 1859), passim.

3.8 McLean and Eaton, Penuel, 9.

3.9 Delbert Roy Rose, A Theology of Christian Experience (Wilmore, Ky.: The Seminary Press, 1958), 36.

3.10 McLean and Eaton, Penuel, 0-10.

3.11 Lucy Reed Drake Osborn, Pioneer Days at Ocean Grove (New York: Printed for the author by the Methodist Book Concern, n.d.).

3.12 McLean and Eaton, Penuel, 16-17.

3.13 Ibid., 12.

3.14 Ibid., 19.

3.15 Ibid., xv.

3.16 Ibid., 149-150.

3.17 Rose, A Theology of Christian Experience, 37.

3.18 McLean and Eaton, Penuel, 158.

3.19 Adam Wallace, ed., A Modern Pentecost; Embracing a Record of the Sixteenth National Camp-Meeting for the Promotion of

Holiness, Held at Landisville, Pa., July 23d to August 1st, 1873
(Philadelphia: Methodist Home Journal Publishing House, 1873), 199-
202.

3.20   Rose, A Theology of Christian Experience, 37. It did
not incorporate until 1899.

3.21   Robert Guy McCutchan, Our Hymnody; A Manual of the
Methodist Hymnal, 2d ed. (New York: Abingdon Press, 1937), 174-
175, 286-287.

3.22   William McDonald and John E. Searles, The Life of
Rev. John S. Inskip (Chicago: Christian Witness Co., 1885), 224ff.

3.23   Rose, A Theology of Christian Experience, 43-44.

3.24   In 1891 the name was changed to the Christian Witness.

3.25   Rose, A Theology of Christian Experience, 46-47.

3.26   In 1876 the Methodist Home Journal was re-named the
Christian Standard.

3.27   Rose, A Theology of Christian Experience, 46-47. See
Washington C. DePauw's biography in Matthew Simpson, Cyclopaedia
of Methodism, Embracing Sketches of Its Rise, Progress, and
Present Condition, with Biographical Notices and Numerous Illustra-
tions, 4th rev. ed. (Philadelphia: Louis H. Everts, 1881), 287-289.
Michael F. O'Brien's "A Nineteenth Century Hoosier Business Man:
Washington Charles DePauw" (Unpublished B.A. thesis, DePauw
University, 1966) makes no mention of DePauw's connection with
the holiness movement or its publishing interests.

3.28   McDonald and Searles, The Life of Rev. John S. Inskip,
333.

CHAPTER 4

4.1   Beulah, which literally means "married," was the name
given to Palestine after the Exile by the writer of Isaiah to cele-
brate its being re-peopled and restored to God's favor (Isaiah 62:4).
Land of Beulah: "In Bunyan's Pilgrim's Progress, a land of rest
and quiet, lying on the hither side of the River of Death" (Webster).
In Wesleyan perfectionist terminology, it was a synonym for the
Land of Canaan. It represented the sinless life as well as heaven.
The Land of Beulah could also refer to physical camp meeting
grounds, a place where one first experienced perfect love. See
Thomas Cook, New Testament Holiness (London: Epworth Press,
1902), 82-87. The symbolic connection between camp meeting
grounds and the spiritual Promised Land is apparent in chapter
headings ("Entering Canaan" and "Established in Canaan") chosen

by John F. Grimes for his book on the camp meeting. See John Franklin Grimes, The Romance of the American Camp Meeting; Golden Jubilee Etchings of the Lancaster Assembly and Camp Meeting, 1872-1922, Illustrative of the Camp Meeting As an American Institution (Cincinnati: Printed for the Semi-Centennial Commission by the Caxton Press, 1922), passim.

4.2 Simpson, Cyclopaedia of Methodism, 162.

4.3 Ibid., 992.

4.4 Ibid., 992-993.

4.5 George Hughes, Days of Power in the Forest Temple; A Review of the Wonderful Work of God at Fourteen National Camp Meetings, from 1867 to 1872 (Boston: John Bent & Co., 1873), passim.

4.6 Simpson, Cyclopaedia of Methodism, 162.

4.7 Mrs. W. B. Osborn listed the following camp and re-sorts as having been inspired by "Ocean Grove's financial and spiritual success": Asbury Park, Ocean Park, Ocean Beach, Pitman Grove, Sea Grove (near Camp May), Mount Tabor, and Atlantic Highlands, New Jersey; Sea Cliff, and Shelter Island, New York; Wesley Park (Niagara Falls), and Thousand Islands in the St. Lawrence River, Ontario, Canada; Lake Bluffs, Illinois; Chester Heights, Pennsylvania; Rehoboth, Delaware; Arlington Heights, Florida; and Ocean Park, Washington; as well as Queenscliff, Australia and Lanowli, India. --Lucy Reed Drake Osborn, Pioneer Days of Ocean Grove (New York: Printed for the Author by the Methodist Book Concern, n.d.), 21. National Camp Meetings were held at a number of these places in the 1870's and 1880's. See The Double Cure; or, Echoes from National Camp-Meetings (Boston: Christian Witness Co., 1894), p. 7.

4.8 Osborn, Pioneer Days of Ocean Grove, 7.

4.9 Ibid., 9.

4.10 The seven ministers were Ruliff V. Lawrence, George Hughes, John S. Inskip, William H. Boole, Benjamin M. Adams, Alfred Cookman, and Adam Wallace. See frontispiece in Alexander McLean and J. W. Eaton, eds., Penuel; or, Face to Face with God (New York: W. C. Palmer, Publisher, 1869).

4.11 See text of charter in Ocean Grove Camp Meeting Association of the Methodist Episcopal Church. Ocean Grove, Its Origin and Progress, As Shown in the Annual Reports Presented by the President, to which are added other papers of interest, including list of lot-holders, charter, by-laws, &c., &c. (Ocean Grove, N. J.: 1874), 86.

4.12   Ibid.

4.13   Simpson, Cyclopaedia of Methodism, 673.

4.14   Morris S. Daniels, The Story of Ocean Grove, Related in the Year of Its Golden Jubilee... [with] Illustrations from His Private Collection of Original Photographs (New York: Methodist Book Concern, 1919), 35.

4.15   Ocean Grove Camp Meeting Association of the Methodist Episcopal Church, Service by the Sea; Ninth Annual Report of the President... (Ocean Grove, N.J.: 1878), 23.

4.16   Daniels, The Story of Ocean Grove, 35.

4.17   Ibid., 34-35.

4.18   Ocean Grove Camp Meeting of the Methodist Episcopal Church, City by the Sea; Fifth Annual Report of the President... (Ocean Grove, N.J.: 1847), 24-25.

CHAPTER 5

5.1   Proceedings of Holiness Conferences, held at Cincinnati, November 26th, 1877, and at New York, December 17th, 1877. (Philadelphia: National Publishing Association for the Promotion of Holiness, 1878?), 20.

5.2   For a succinct summary of the role of the Exodus and Beulah land analogies in theological discussion see James Blaine Chapman, The Terminology of Holiness (Kansas City, Mo.: Beacon Hill Press, 1947), 87-89 and 91. One of the first song books issued by the National Association betrayed by title its indebtedness to John Bunyan. See William McDonald and Lewis Hartsough, eds., Beulah Songs: A Choice Collection of Popular Hymns and Music, New and Old, Especially Adapted to Camp Meetings, Prayer and Conference Meetings, Family Worship and All Other Assemblies Where Jesus Is Praised (Philadelphia: National Publishing Association for the Promotion of Holiness, 1879).

5.3   Haldor Lillenas, Modern Gospel Song Stories, introduction by Wm. M. Runyan (Kansas City, Mo.: Lillenas Publishing Co., 1952), 75. Charles Ives, a product of this era and environment, used Stites' "Beulah Land" in his Symphonies nos. 2 and 4 and the Violin Sonata no. 3.

5.4   For a biographical sketch of Mrs. Wittenmeyer, see Matthew Simpson, Cyclopaedia of Methodism Embracing Sketches of Its Rise, Progress, and Present Condition, with Biographical Notices and Numerous Illustrations, 4th rev. ed. (Philadelphia: Louis H. Everts, 1881), 960-961.

5. 5   Lillenas, Modern Gospel Song Stories, 17.

5. 6   Salem here referred to the New Jerusalem, heaven.   See Psalm 76:2.

5. 7   For a biographical sketch of William Hunter who in 1876 was appointed to the hymnal revision committee of the Methodist Episcopal Church see Simpson, Cyclopaedia of Methodism, 459.

5. 8   See Daniel 3 and Matthew 11:29-30.

5. 9   See Revelation 2:17b.

5. 10   For biographical data concerning J. M. Harris, see Lillenas, Modern Gospel Song Stories, 65.

5. 11   See Isaiah 35:8.

5. 12   For full exposition of the Exodus analogy, see Martin Wells Knapp, Out of Egypt into Canaan; or, Lessons in Spiritual Geography (Boston: McDonald, Gill & Co.; Albion, Mich.: Revivalist Pub. Co., 1889).

5. 13   See Exodus 12-13.

5. 14   See Numbers 13-14; Joshua 3, 14.

5. 15   Lillenas, Modern Gospel Song Stories, 64-65.

5. 16   Mrs. Morris, gospel song writer from Ohio, was sanctified after attending Mountain Lake Park, Maryland, Camp Meeting. --Ibid., 11.   See also obituary, New York Times, July 24, 1929; and Mary Ethel Wiess, Singing at Her Work; A Biography of Mrs. C. H. Morris (Kansas City, Mo.: Nazarene Publishing House, n.d.).

5. 17   Haldor Lillenas, Down Melody Lane; An Autobiography. (Kansas City, Mo.: Beacon Hill Press, 1953).

CHAPTER 6

6. 1   For a list of meetings held through 1893 see The Double Cure; or, Echoes from National Camp-Meetings (Boston: Christian Witness Co., 1894).

6. 2   By 1871 Inskip and McDonald seem to have accepted "supernumerary" relations to the New York East and New England Conferences respectively.   In 1905 Charles J. Fowler was "located" by the New Hampshire Conference.   In Methodist parlance inherited from an era when ministers' salaries were so meager that they were scarcely sufficient to maintain even a single man, "location" implied retirement from the traveling ministry because of marriage

and its accompanying temporal responsibilities, hence, retirement from the ministry altogether. A "supernumerary" relationship, on the other hand, consisted of relief from regular pastoral duties to pursue other religious work: missionary, evangelistic, educational, or administrative activities, and allowed the supernumerated to retain ministerial relationship in the conference. For actions concerning Fowler, see: Methodist Episcopal Church. Conferences. New Hampshire, Minutes (Spring 1905), 83. For circumstances surrounding the supernumerated status of Inskip and McDonald, see Rose, A Theology of Christian Experience (Wilmore, Ky.: The Seminary Press, 1958), 43-44. For evidence of their continued relationships to Methodist annual conferences, see: Methodist Episcopal Church. Conferences. New York East, Minutes (Spring 1884), 49, 58, and 94; and also --. --. New England, Minutes (Spring 1902), 83 and 106; and Minutes (1905), 436.

6.3 See Proceedings of Holiness Conferences, Held at Cincinnati, November 26th, 1877, and at New York, December 17th, 1877 (Philadelphia: National Publishing Association for the Promotion of Holiness, 1878?).

6.4 Ibid., 85, 87.

6.5 Charles Brougher Jernigan, Pioneer Days of the Holiness Movement in the Southwest (Kansas City, Mo.: Pentecostal Nazarene Publishing House, 1919), 19. The Texas Holiness Association is not to be confused with the Holiness Association of Texas, a later organization.

6.6 Rose, A Theology of Christian Experience, 51.

6.7 Clarence Eugene Cowen, A History of the Church of God (Holiness)... (Overland Park, Kan.: Herald and Banner Press, 1949), 18. The Southwestern Holiness Association was organized at the National Camp Meeting held at Bismark Grove, near Lawrence, Kansas, in June 1879.

6.8 Jernigan, Pioneer Days of the Holiness Movement in the Southwest, 25.

6.9 Not until 1894, when the National Association dropped "Camp-Meeting" from its name and became the National Association for the Promotion of Holiness, did it begin admitting members of all evangelical denominations to full membership. Incorporating in 1899, the National Association did not start promoting the organization of state, county, and local holiness associations as auxiliaries of the National until 1907. See Rose, A Theology of Christian Experience, 48.

6.10 In 1873, only William T. Perkins and William Nast, both of Cincinnati, out of a total membership of twenty-one, were listed from places west of the Appalachians. By 1894, twenty of the forty-four members were from western places. See Adam Wallace, ed., A Modern Pentecost; Embracing a Record of the Sixteenth National Camp-Meeting for the Promotion of Holiness, Held at Landisville, Pa., July 23d to August 1st, 1873 (Philadelphia: Methodist Home Journal Publishing House, 1873); and The Double Cure.

6.11 Jesse Truesdell Peck, The Central Idea of Christianity (Boston: Henry V. Degen, 1858), 326; In 1872 Peck urged the General Conference of the Methodist Episcopal Church to revise the church's doctrinal statement so as to commit it completely to entire sanctification as a second work of grace. See Timothy Lawrence Smith, Called unto Holiness; The Story of the Nazarenes: The Formative Years (Kansas City, Mo.: Nazarene Publishing House, 1962), 19.

6.12 By coincidence he preached during the exciting 1859 Genessee conference session when Benjamin Titus Roberts and J. M. McCreery, leaders of the so-called "Nazarites," were expelled from the Methodist ministry. --Timothy Lawrence Smith, Revivalism and Social Reform in Mid-Nineteenth-Century America (New York: Abingdon Press, 1957), 132.

6.13 Simpson, Cyclopaedia of Methodism, 1004.

6.14 Wade Crawford Barclay, Widening Horizons, 1845-95 (History of Methodist Missions; part 2: The Methodist Episcopal Church, 1845-1939), (New York: The Board of Missions of The Methodist Church, 1957), 174, 179.

6.15 See advertisement on back cover of William McDonald [et al.], eds., Songs of Joy and Gladness (Boston: McDonald, Gill & Co., 1885); and also see Byron S. Lamson, Venture! The Frontiers of Free Methodism (Winona Lake, Ind.: Light and Life Press, 1960), 57.

6.16 Amanda Smith, An Autobiography; The Story of the Lord's Dealings with Mrs. Amanda Smith, the Colored Evangelist, containing an account of her life work of faith, and her travels in America, England, Ireland, Scotland, India and Africa, as an independent missionary, with an introduction by Bishop Thoburn, of India (Chicago: Meyer & Bros., 1893); reprinted, Noblesville, Ind.: J. Edwin Newby, 1962), 68, 75.

6.17 "The Rev. W. B. Osborn," Christian Advocate (New York), LXXVII September 18, 1902, 1489.

6.18 Smith, Autobiography, 282-285.

6.19 "The Rev. W. B. Osborn," op. cit., 1489.

6.20 The site of a National Camp Meeting in 1886. See The Double Cure.

6. 21 "The Rev. W. B. Osborn," op. cit., 1489.

6. 22 The National Camp Meeting Association limited its
formal membership to Methodists until 1894, when age and death
was swiftly depleting the ranks of militant perfectionism in the
church.   That year the average age of the forty clerical and seven
lay members of the National Association was 54. 5 years, the medi-
an age, 61 years.   For changes in the structure of the Association
see Rose, A Theology of Christian Experience, 48.

6. 23 For the Western Union Holiness Convention, held at
Jacksonville, Illinois, in 1880, see John Leland Peters, Christian
Perfection and American Methodism (New York: Abingdon Press,
1956), 136.   For the General Holiness Assembly, held in the Park
Avenue Methodist Episcopal Church, Chicago in May 1885, see Ibid.,
137-138; and Isaiah Reid, quoted in Rose, A Theology of Christian
Experience, 49; and the Michigan Holiness Record, III (June 1885),
9-12, and III (July 1885, 17-18); and Aaron Merritt Hills, Scriptur-
al Holiness and Keswick Teaching Compared (Manchester, Eng.:
Star Hall Publishing Co., 1900), 29, quoted in Peters, Christian
Perfection and American Methodism, 162.   For the General Holi-
ness Assembly, held in the First Methodist Episcopal Church,
Chicago, May 1901, see the official report of the proceedings,
Echoes of the General Holiness Assembly Held in Chicago, May
3-13, 1901, ed. by S. B. Shaw (Chicago: S. B. Shaw, 1901); and
Timothy Lawrence Smith, Called unto Holiness, 126-128.

6. 24 J. W. Caughlan, quoted in Cowen, A History of the
Church of God (Holiness), 19.

6. 25 George Hughes' address upon taking the chair, quoted
in Michigan Holiness Record, III (June 1885), 9.

6. 26 B. A. Washburn, "To the General Assembly, Chicago,
May 20, 1885, " The Good Way, VIII (May 23, 1885), quoted in
Cowen, A History of the Church of God (Holiness), 24-25.

6. 27 Michigan Holiness Record, III (June 1885), 9.

6. 28 Simpson, Cyclopaedia of Methodism, 552.

6. 29 James Newbury Fitzgerald, elected bishop in 1888 after
eight years as denominational secretary of the Missionary Society,
was the son of Mrs. Osee Fitzgerald of Newark, New Jersey.   In
her endorsement of the calling of the General Holiness Assembly
in 1901, the bishop's mother claimed that for over forty years she
had been the leader of holiness meetings.   Her son, likewise, took
charge of the holiness meetings at Ocean Grove during the last few
years before his death in 1907.   See Who Was Who in America,
1897-1942 (Chicago, Marquis Who's Who, 1943), 403; and Echoes of
the General Holiness Assembly Held in Chicago, May 3-13, 1901,
14; and also Morris S. Daniels, The Story of Ocean Grove, Related

in the Year of its Golden Jubilee... (New York, Methodist Book Concern, 1919).

6.30 Phoebe, daughter of Walter and Phoebe Palmer and composer of the music for gospel songs written by her mother and Fanny Crosby, married Joseph Fairchild Knapp, a wealthy business man in 1885. Faithful to her parents' vision, Mrs. Knapp was for many years an active participant in the camp meetings at Ocean Grove. When at her husband's death she fell heir to an estate yielding a yearly income of over $50,000, she used her wealth subsidizing religious projects. It was probably her beneficence which enabled the Guide to Holiness to continue until 1901. See biography of Joseph Fairchild Knapp in National Cyclopaedia of American Biography; and Robert Guy McCutchan, Our Hymnody; A Manual of the Methodist Hymnal, 2d ed. (New York: Abingdon Press, 1937), 279-280.

6.31 Maury E. Redford, The Rise of the Church of the Nazarene (Kansas City, Mo.: Nazarene Publishing House, 1948), 38. For numerous statements by individual Methodist bishops, professors, and ministers, see John Allen Wood, Perfect Love; or, Plain Things for Those Who Need Them, Concerning the Doctrine, Experience, Profession and Practice of Christian Holiness, rev. and enl. ed. (Boston: Published by the author, 1880; reprinted, Chicago: W. B. Rose, 1909), passim. Though sharing with its Northern counterpart the Wesleyan perfectionist tradition, the Methodist Episcopal Church, South, was more reluctant explicitly to commit itself to the doctrine. Its Discipline carried no statement signed by the bishops claiming the teaching on perfect love as the Methodist's peculiar possession. Furthermore, the Southern church voiced its criticism of holiness associations and promotion earlier and more distinctly than the Northern church did.

6.32 While considerations of unity within the movement undoubtedly lay behind the decision to ban millennial discussion from National Camp Meetings, it was also true that most National evangelists were postmillennialists, most regional leaders premillennialists. Commenting on Martin Wells Knapp's use of pictures in illustrating the first resurrection, National evangelist George W. Wilson declared that the Western leader's pictures "would be amusing" if they "were not ridiculous." See George Washington Wilson, The Sign of Thy Coming; or, Premillennialism, Unscriptural and Unreasonable, with an introduction by Rev. W. X. Ninde (Boston: Christian Witness Co., 1899), 363.

6.33 See Cowen, A History of the Church of God (Holiness), 26-29 and passim. The classic apology for this theory of the New Testament Church is John P. Brooks, The Divine Church; A Treatise on the Origin, Constitution, Order, and Ordinances of the Church, Being a Vindication of the New Testament Ecclesia, and an Exposure of the Anti-scriptural Character of the Modern Church or Sect (Columbia, Mo.: Herald Publishing House, Printers and

Binders, 1891) (Reprinted: El Dorado Springs, Mo.: Witt Printing
Co., 1960).

6.34   See Timothy Lawrence Smith, Called Unto Holiness, 31-
33; and Josephine M. Washburn, History and Reminiscences of Holiness Church Work in Southern California and Arizona (South Pasadena, Calif.: Record Press, 1912?), passim; and also Pilgrim Holiness Church, Manual (Indianapolis: 1946), 12.   In his pamphlet entitled The New Testament Church, George M. Teel, a Holiness
Church leader, declared that his group recognized "other bodies"
neither as constituting "the true church nor as branches of it."
--Quoted in Elmer Talmage Clark, The Small Sects in America,
rev. ed. (New York: Abingdon Press, 1949), 114.

6.35   See Brooks, The Divine Church, 281-282; also see
Michigan Holiness Record, VII (September-October 1889) through
VIII (May-June 1890).   Shaw was a principal instigator of the Gen-
eral Holiness Assembly of 1885 as well as the one in 1901.

6.36   See Handley C. Mullen, "Some Facts about the Origin
of the Reformed Baptist Church," The King's Highway; an Advocate
of Scriptural Holiness, XXXVIII (July 15, 1957), 6; (August 15,
1957), 6; (August 31, 1957), 6, 8; and (September 16, 1957), 3, 6;
and Reformed Baptist Church, Manual, 1958 (Sussex, N.B., Can.:
1958); and "The Reformed Baptists," The Wesleyan Methodist,
CXXIV (July 6, 1966), 5; and also Timothy Lawrence Smith, Called
Unto Holiness, 75-76.

6.37   The Mennonite Brethren had become Methodistic well
before the end of the nineteenth century.   They were the first group
in the Mennonite tradition to conduct camp meetings, beginning as
early as 1878.   During merger negotiations with the Missionary
Church Association in 1947, they changed their name to the United
Missionary Church, thereby making nomenclature adhere more closely to reality.   --See Clark, The Small Sects in America, 70-71; and
Frank Spencer Mead, Handbook of Denominations in the United States,
2d rev. ed. (New York: Abingdon Press, 1961), 223-224; and also
Everek Richard Storms, History of the United Missionary Church
(Elkhart, Ind.: Bethel Publishing Co., 1958), passim.

6.38   See John W. V. Smith, Truth Marches on; A Brief
Study of the History of the Church of God Reformation Movement
(Anderson, Ind.: Warner Press, 1951), passim; and Cowen, A His-
tory of the Church of God (Holiness), 15, 155; and Clark, The Small
Sects in America, 80-81; and also U.S. Bureau of the Census, Re-
ligious Bodies: 1926 (Washington, D.C.: Government Printing Office,
1929), II, 367-369.   Daniel Sidney Warner's church theory was ex-
plained in his The Church of God; or, What Is the Church and What
Is Not (Moundsville, W. Va.: Gospel Trumpet Co., 1920?; reprinted,
Anderson, Ind.: Gospel Trumpet Co., n.d.).

6.39   For a general summary see Timothy Lawrence Smith,

Called unto Holiness, 22; and Dougan Clark and Joseph H. Smith, David B. Updegraff and His Work (Cincinnati: Pub. for Joseph H. Smith by M. W. Knapp, Revivalist Office, 1895). For the liberal viewpoint see Elizabeth Gray Vining, Friend of Life; The Biography of Rufus M. Jones (Philadelphia: J. B. Lippincott Co.), 80-81 and 118-119. For the evangelicals' views see J. Edwin Newby, Teachings of Evangelical Friends, As Gleaned from George Fox's Journal and Friends Disciplines; Messages Given at Central Yearly Meeting, 1952 (n.p., n.p., 1952).

CHAPTER 7

7.1 Vivian Adelbert Dake, quoted in Byron S. Lamson, Venture! the Frontiers of Free Methodism (Winona Lake, Ind.: Light and Life Press, 1960), 132-133.

7.2 Arthur M. Schlesinger claimed that in the 1880's Midwestern cities attracted so many country people into their environs as "to threaten many rural districts with paralysis." Though western settlement accounted for part of the losses, urban migration was a strong factor in population losses in "central Missouri ... the eastern half of Iowa, northern and western Illinois, central and southwestern Indiana, southern Michigan and central and southern Ohio.... Yet during the same decade every Middle Western state gained substantially in total number of inhabitants." --Arthur Meier Schlesinger, The Rise of the City, 1878-1898 (New York: Macmillan, 1933), 67.

7.3 Quoted in William Warren Sweet, Methodism in American History, revision of 1953 (New York: Abingdon Press, 1961), 343.

7.4 Beverly Carradine, The Sanctified Life (Cincinnati: Office of the Revivalist, 1897), 213.

7.5 See Lura Ann Mains, Mizpah: Autobiographical Sketches (Grand Rapids, Mich.: Hansen & Reymders, 1892), 67-68, 71-72.

7.6 See Walter Edwards Houghton, The Victorian Frame of Mind (New Haven: Pub. for Wellesley College by Yale University Press, 1957), passim.

7.7 See Michigan Holiness Record, VI (September–October 1889), 18; and VI (March-April 1890), 45.

7.8 See U.S. Bureau of the Census, Religious Bodies: 1906 (2 vols., Washington, D.C.: Government Printing Office, 1910), II, 284-285; and Elmer Talmage Clark, The Small Sects in America, rev. ed. (New York: Abingdon Press, 1949), 77. For a Free Methodist account of the exodus of Dake's followers, see Leslie Ray Marston, From Age to Age a Living Witness; A Historical Interpretation of Free Methodism's First Century (Winona Lake, Ind.: Light and Life Press, 1960), 434-436; and also Lamson, Venture! The Frontiers of Free Methodism, 129-135. For the union with the Wesleyans, see Ira Ford McLeister, History of the Wesleyan Methodist Church of America, rev. ed. by Roy Stephen Nicholson (Marion, Ind.: Wesley Press, 1959), 503.

7.9 Hephzibah, meaning "my delight is in her," is a synonym for Jerusalem and is used along with the "Land of Beulah" in Isaiah 62:4.

7.10 See U.S. Bureau of the Census, Religious Bodies: 1906, II, 282-283; and Frank Spencer Mead, Handbook of Denominations in the United States, 2d rev. ed. (New York: Abingdon Press, 1961), 104-105; and McLeister, History of the Wesleyan Methodist Church of America, 275, 329, 331, 446-446; and also Paul W. Worcester, The Master Key; The Story of the Hephzibah Faith Missionary Association (Kansas City, Mo.: Printed for the Author by the Nazarene Publishing House, 1966), passim.

7.11 See U.S. Bureau of the Census, Religious Bodies: 1906, II, 283; and Mead, Handbook of Denominations in the United States, 105, 223-224; and The Missionary Church. "Minutes of the Merging General Conference ... March 12-16, 1969, Detroit, Michigan" (mimeographed) and Constitution Proposed As Basis for Union of the Missionary Church Association and the United Missionary Church (n.p., n.p., 1968).

7.12 See Clarence Eugene Cowen, A History of the Church of God (Holiness) (Overland Park, Kan.: Herald and Banner Press, 1949), 42-46; and Charles Brougher Jernigan, Pioneer Days of the Holiness Movement in the Southwest (Kansas City, Mo.: Pentecostal Nazarene Publishing House, 1919; reprinted, Bethany, Okla.: Arnett Publishing Co., 1964), 151-154; and Charles Allen McConnell, The Potter's Vessel; My Life Story As Told to My Children at Their Request (Kansas City, Mo.: Beacon Hill Press, 1946), 50; and also Mead, Handbook of Denominations in the United States, 107-108.

7.13 Forrest B. Whisler, "Reminiscenses of Evangelistic Enterprises in Home and Foreign Lands," Church Herald and Holiness Banner, LXXXV (December 24, 1964), 5, 15; LXXXVI (January 7, 1965), 5, 7.

7.14 Jernigan, Pioneer Days of the Holiness Movement in the Southwest, 138-145.

7.15 U.S. Bureau of the Census, Religious Bodies, 1906, II, 286.

7.16 Ibid., II, 281; and Timothy Lawrence Smith, Called unto Holiness; The Story of the Nazarenes: The Formative Years. (Kansas City, Mo.: Nazarene Publishing House, 1962), 128; and

Clark, The Small Sects in America, 77-78; and also Mead, Handbook of Denominations in the United States, 105.

7.17 For discussion of Finney's methods, see William Gerald McLoughlin, Modern Revivalism: Charles Grandison Finney to Billy Graham (New York: Ronald Press Co., 1959), passim; and Bernard Allen Weisberger, They Gathered at the River; The Story of the Great Revivalists and Their Impact upon Religion in America (Boston: Little, Brown and Co., 1958), passim.

7.18 The Newton Mission was probably run by George Newton, editor of the Pacific Herald of Holiness, official organ of the Pacific Coast Holiness Association. Methodist Episcopal Church records show that Newton withdrew from the California Conference in 1876. See Methodist Episcopal Church. Conferences. California, Minutes, 1876, 116. The Pacific Coast Holiness Association became the nucleus of the Salvation Army on the West Coast. See Herbert Andrew Wisbey, Soldiers without Swords; A History of the Salvation Army in the United States (New York: Macmillan, 1955), 69-73.

7.19 See Manie Payne Ferguson, T. P. Ferguson; The Love Slave of Jesus Christ and His People and Founder of Peniel Missions (Los Angeles? n.d.), passim.

7.20 Manie Payne Ferguson, "Peniel Missionary Work," in Leander Lycurgus Pickett (comp.), Faith Tonic, 1 and 2 Combined; Being a Series of Articles by Different Writers Exemplifying God's Dealings with Those Who Trust Him (Louisville, Ky.: Pentecostal Publishing Co., n.d.), 3-4.

7.21 Ibid., 4-6.

7.22 Ibid., 6.

7.23 Ibid., 17. See Timothy Lawrence Smith, Called unto Holiness, 49, for identification of Studd as the donor.

7.24 Ferguson, in Pickett, Faith Tonic, 18-19.

7.25 Ibid., 6-7.

7.26 Mrs. Ferguson wrote many gospel songs which were collected and published under the title Echoes from Beulah. "Blessed Quietness," her most noted contribution has been included in most twentieth-century holiness song books. Also the Methodists included it in their popular Cokesbury Worship Hymnal which was first issued in 1938. For background on Manie Payne Ferguson's song writing activity, see Haldor Lillenas, Modern Gospel Song Stories (Kansas City, Mo.: Lillenas Publishing Co., 1952), 66-67. Norway-born Lillenas, who later became noted in holiness circles for his own activities as song writer and music editor, recalled the circumstances surrounding his conversion in a Peniel Mission: "The street meeting had come to an end. The lady in charge of the service announced a meeting to follow in the little Peniel Mission 'on Fifth Street just above Commercial.' I followed the little company into the unpretentious hall in Astoria, Oregon" and was saved. Haldor Lillenas, Down Melody Lane; An Autobiography (Kansas City, Mo.: Beacon Hill Press, 1953), 19.

7.27 See Ferguson, T. P. Ferguson, 27; and also Clark, The Small Sects in America, 79.

7.28 Ferguson, in Pickett, Faith Tonic, 20-29.

7.29 Ibid., 28.

CHAPTER 8

8.1 For an excellent account of late nineteenth-century physical and demographic rearrangement in Boston, see Sam Bass Warner, Jr., Streetcar Suburbs; The Process of Growth in Boston, 1870-1900 (Cambridge, Mass.: Harvard University Press and the Massachusetts Institute of Technology Press, 1962), passim.

8.2 Randolph Sinks Foster, quoted in John P. Brooks, The Divine Church; A Treatise on the Origin, Constitution, Order, and Ordinances of the Church, Being a Vindication of the New Testament Ecclesia and an Exposure of the Anti-Scriptural Character of the Modern Church of Sect (Columbia, Mo.: Herald Publishing House, Printers and Binders, 1891; reprinted, El Dorado Springs, Mo.: Witt Printing Co., 1960), 274.

8.3 For a succinct statement of conditions faced by newly arrived rural immigrants, see Arthur Meier Schlesinger, The Rise of the City, 1878-1898 (New York: Macmillan, 1933), 330-336. For an account of the growing formality of Methodist worship during this period, see The History of American Methodism (3 vols., New York: Abingdon Press, 1964), II, 629-636; and William Ketcham Anderson, ed., Methodism (Cincinnati: Methodist Publishing House, 1947). Anderson claimed that the divided chancel, essential to liturgical worship, was first introduced in Methodist church construction in 1902.

8.4 Josiah Strong, The New Era; or, The Coming Kingdom (New York: Baker & Taylor, 1893), 200-201.

8.5 Prostitutes came from a wide variety of backgrounds; "newcomers to the city, starved for companionship and lacking the ... restraining influence of neighborhood opinion"; "shopgirls" and "housemaids eager for the pretty clothes and good times which ... meager wages denied them"; some were "the hapless victims ... of ... youthful surroundings in the slums, while still others were ...

of feeble mentality." --Schlesinger, The Rise of the City, 1878-1898, 157-158. For personal histories, given in Seth Cook Rees, Miracles in the Slums; or, Thrilling Stories of Those Rescued from the Cesspools of Iniquity, and Touching Incidents in the Lives of the Unfortunate (Chicago: Seth C. Rees, 1905), see Appendix IV.

8.6 Missions sponsored by Methodists provided the nucleus for independent holiness churches in Lynn and Haverhill, Mass.; Providence; Washington, D.C.; East Liverpool, Ohio; Minneapolis; St. Louis; Little Rock; Omaha; Colorado Springs, Colo.; and Spokane. In 1895 Isaiah Reid, long-time leader in the Iowa Holiness Association, said that the mission sponsored by the First Methodist Episcopal Church, South, of St. Louis, had developed into "the natural rallying center for the holiness movement" in that city. Later he declared, "In many of the city churches the holiness evangelist has no standing room. In the mission he has." --See Timothy Lawrence Smith, Called unto Holiness; The Story of the Nazarenes: The Formative Years (Kansas City, Mo.: Nazarene Publishing House, 1962), 48-49.
Although between 1884 and 1895, holiness men held pastoral appointments in some of American Methodism's largest churches, holiness preaching was the exception rather than the rule. B. F. Haynes served the McKendree Church in Nashville, the headquarters church of the Southern church; Beverly Carradine pastored the St. Charles Avenue Church in New Orleans and the First Methodist Episcopal Church, South, in St. Louis; Samual Ashton Keen (d. 1895) once ministered to the aristocratic Roberts Park Methodist Episcopal Church in Indianapolis; and P. F. Bresee served Los Angeles' First Methodist Episcopal Church. Bresee, who was appointed to the Los Angeles church after long ministerial service in Iowa, did not claim to be in an experience of entire sanctification at the time of his appointment. There, for the first time in his career, the church had an aggressive holiness group which was undoubtedly a factor in Bresee's claiming perfect love during his tenure there. --See Timothy Lawrence Smith, Called unto Holiness, 96-97; and Donald Paul Brickley, Man of the Morning; The Life and Work of Phineas F. Bresee (Kansas City, Mo.: Nazarene Publishing House, 1960), 86-94; and also Ernest Alexander Girvin, Phineas F. Bresee; A Prince in Israel; A Biography (Kansas City, Mo.: Pentecostal Nazarene Publishing House, 1916), 81-85.

8.7 Ulla Earl Harding, Is the Young Man Safe? (Georgetown, Ill. [Silent Evangel Press, Indianapolis]: 1911), 31-32.

8.8 See accounts of converts carrying the revival back to their home communities, in Josephine M. Washburn, History and Reminiscenses of Holiness Church Work in Southern California and Arizona (South Pasadena, Calif.: Record Press, 1912?), passim.

8.9 During the years following 1897 in rural areas of eastern Texas, faith workers preached in camp meetings and schoolhouse

revivals during the summer months and conducted rescue missions
in various towns during the winters. --See "City Mission and Slum
Work, " in Charles Brougher Jernigan, Pioneer Days of the Holiness Movement in the Southwest (Kansas City, Mo.: Pentecostal
Nazarene Publishing House, 1919), 138-145.

8.10 Called the old man of sin, carnality, the carnal mind,
and the flesh.

8.11 Hebrews 13:12.

8.12 Theological vocabulary is ably treated in James Blaine
Chapman, The Terminology of Holiness (Kansas City, Mo.: Beacon
Hill Press, 1947), passim.

8.13 Milton Lorenzo Haney, The Inheritance Restored; or,
Plain Truths on Bible Holiness, 4th ed., rev. and enl. (Chicago:
Christian Witness Co., 1897), 213.

8.14 Carnality was inherent depravity which remained in the
believer's heart after conversion, finally to be removed "root and
branch" at the time an individual experienced entire sanctification.

8.15 See Charles Allen McConnell, The Potter's Vessel; My
Life Story As Told to My Children at Their Request (Kansas City,
Mo.: Beacon Hill Press, 1946), 35.

8.16 See Milton Lorenzo Haney, Pentecostal Possibilities; or,
Story of My Life; An Autobiography (Chicago: Christian Witness Co.,
1906), 252-253. Holiness promoters, from the early days of the
movement onward, compiled books of testimonies which illustrated
their belief that individual experience must validate formal theology.
Books of this type included: Holiness Miscellany, Essays [of] Dr.
Adam Clarke and Richard Watson; Experiences of Bishop Foster,
Rev. George Peck, D.D., Rev. Alfred Cookman, Rev. J. A. Wood,
Rev. E. M. Levy, D.D., D. Steele, D.D. (Philadelphia: National
Publishing Association for the Promotion of Holiness, 1882); Stephen
Olin Garrison, Forty Witnesses, Covering the Whole Range of Chris-
tian Experience, introduction by Bishop C. D. Foss (New York:
Hunt & Eaton, 1888); James Gilchrist Lawson, Deeper Experiences
of Famous Christians Gleaned from Their Biographies, Autobiog-
raphies and Writings (Anderson, Ind.: Warner Press, 1911); L. M.
Campbell, A Cloud of Witnesses (Kansas City, Mo.: Pentecostal
Nazarene Publishing House, 1915; re-issued under title, Witnesses
to the Doctrine of Holiness); Mrs. Clara McLeister, Men and Women
of Deep Piety, ed. and pub. by Rev. E. E. Shelhamer (Syracuse,
N.Y.: Wesleyan Methodist Publishing Association, 1920); Harry
Edward Jessop, Foundations of Doctrine in Scripture and Experience; A Student's Handbook on Holiness (Chicago: Chicago Evangelistic Institute, 1938); Bernie Smith, Flames of Living Fire; Testimonies to the Experience of Entire Sanctification (Kansas City, Mo.:
Beacon Hill Press, 1950); and Holiness in Doctrine and Experience;

A Source Book of Quotable Material: Testimonies, Experiences, Definitions, Illustrations, comp. anonymously by "A fellow servant of the master" (Kansas City, Mo.: Beacon Hill Press, 1951).

8.17 Jeremiah 6:16.

8.18 For a fuller explanation of doctrinal significance, see Stephen Solomon White, Eradication, Defined, Explained, Authenticated (Studies in holiness, no. 2) (Kansas City, Mo.: Beacon Hill Press, 1954), passim.

8.19 Haney, The Inheritance Restored; or, Plain Truths on Bible Holiness, 233-234. Haney devotes a whole chapter (228-236) to the dress of the sanctified.

8.20 Titus 2:11-14.

8.21 The same writer blamed the decimation of the songbird population on slaughter of birds for their feathers. See "Victim of Senseless Fashion," Pentecostal Herald, II (August 11, 1897), 6.

8.22 See Pilgrim Holiness Church, Manual, 1946 (Indianapolis: Pilgrim Publishing House, 1946), 52; and Emmanuel Association, Guidebook, of 1961 (Colorado Springs, Colo.: Emmanual Association, 1961), 12-13.

8.23 William Erastus Arnold, [no title], Pentecostal Herald, XI (February 1, 1899), 1.

8.24 See Beverly Carradine, "The Choir," in Pastoral Sketches (Chicago: Christian Witness Co., 1896), 74-89.

8.25 For an extensive critique of the state of the church, especially in relation to the new theology, see Leander Whitcomb Munhall, Breakers! Methodism Adrift (New York: Charles C. Cook, 1913), passim.

8.26 Carradine, Pastoral sketches, 90.

CHAPTER 9

9.1 "Letters from the Folk," The Pentecostal Advocate, May 14, 1908.

9.2 For a fuller account of the Central Evangelical Holiness Association, see Timothy Lawrence Smith, Called unto Holiness; The Story of the Nazarenes: The Formative Years (Kansas City, Mo.: Nazarene Publishing House, 1962), 54-59. From 1879 to 1886 John A. Wood, prominent National Association evangelist, served as pastor of one of these independent churches, the Free Evangelical

Church of North Attleboro, Massachusetts. --See John Allen Wood, Autobiography (Chicago: Christian Witness Co., 1904).

9.3 In 1895 the Brooklyn work consisted of only three congregations: the Utica Avenue Pentecostal Tabernacle, founded in January 1894, and the Bedford Avenue Pentecostal Tabernacle and the Emmanuel Pentecostal Tabernacle, both founded in 1895. --See Church of the Nazarene, Manual, 1952 (Kansas City, Mo.: Nazarene Publishing House, 1952), 15-17; and also Smith, Called unto Holiness, 66-70.

9.4 See Smith, Called unto Holiness, 229; and "A Brief History of the Holiness Christian Church," Holiness Christian Messenger, VI (August 1943), 4; and Pilgrim Holiness Church, "The Days of Our Pilgrimage; A Brief Historical Sketch of the Pilgrim Holiness Church, revised to General Conference, 1962" (mimeographed) (Indianapolis, Ind.: 1962), 2; and Pilgrim Holiness Church, Manual, 1946 (Indianapolis, Ind.: Pilgrim Publishing House, 1946), 9. See also under Heavenly Recruit Church, in U.S. Bureau of the Census, Religious Bodies: 1906 (2 vols., Washington, D.C.: Government Printing Office, 1910), II, 286.

9.5 See Pilgrim Holiness Church, Manual, 1946, 10; and James Herbert Bossard, The Churches of Allentown; A Study in Statistics (Allentown, Pa.: Jacks, the Printer, 1918).

9.6 Nashville, Tenn. First Church of the Nazarene, [Brochure for] Homecoming Day, March 22, 1953, in Celebration of our 55th Anniversary, 1898-1953 (Nashville, Tenn.: 1953).

9.7 Quoted in William Warren Sweet, Methodism in American History, revision of 1953 (New York: Abingdon Press, 1961), 343.

9.8 See Smith, Called unto Holiness, 54-57.

9.9 Ibid., 57, 59-60.

9.10 The name changes which have marked the history of this periodical (still published) point to trends in the holiness movement. --See Percival A. Wesche, Henry Clay Morrison: Crusader, Saint (Berne, Ind.: Herald Press, 1963), 51-64.

9.11 Quoted in Wesche, Henry Clay Morrison: Crusader, Saint, 83-84.

9.12 See Methodist Episcopal Church, South, Discipline, 1894 (Nashville, Tenn.: Publishing House of the M.E. Church, South, 1894), 60, 63; and Wesche, Henry Clay Morrison: Crusader, Saint, 82-92.

9.13 Morrison's tabernacle in Louisville was, of course, a branch of the Holiness Union. --See Wesche, Henry Clay Morrison:

Crusader, Saint, 77-78, 90-92, 195; and also U.S. Bureau of the Census, Religious Bodies, 1906 (2 vols., Washington, D.C.: Government Printing Office, 1910), II, 315.

9.14   Subsequently, Morrison was elected as a delegate to six General Conferences of the Methodist Episcopal Church, South, and asked to speak to the entire conference assembled or part of it each time.   In 1921, he was sent as a representative of the Southern church to the Ecumenical Methodist Conference in London, and was many times invited as speaker to annual conferences of the Methodist Episcopal Church as well as the Methodist Episcopal Church, South.   --See Wesche, Henry Clay Morrison: Crusader, Saint, 197, 199; and also Who Was Who in America, 1943-1950 (Chicago: Marquis Who's Who, 1951), 385.

9.15   See Ernest Alexander Girvin, Phineas F. Bresee: A Prince in Israel; A Biography (Kansas City, Mo.: Pentecostal Nazarene Publishing House, 1916), 23-78.

9.16   Ibid., 80.

9.17   Ibid., 80-96; and Donald Paul Brickley, Man of the Morning; The Life and Work of Phineas F. Bresee (Kansas City, Mo.: Nazarene Publishing House, 1960), 94-111.

9.18   Girvin, Phineas F. Bresee: A Prince in Israel, 81-82.

9.19   Ibid., 82-83.

9.20   Ibid., 59-62.

9.21   See description of Bresee's Pasadena pastorate in Ibid., 85-89; and Brickley, Man of the Morning, 96-106.

9.22   Girvin, Phineas F. Bresee: A Prince in Israel, 91-101; and Brickley, Man of the Morning, 107-120.

9.23   Aaron Merritt Hills, A Hero of Faith and Prayer; or, Life of Rev. Martin Wells Knapp (Cincinnati: Mrs. M. W. Knapp, 1902), 22-59.   Jared Knapp, Martin's father, long served as a Methodist class leader.   Martin Wells Knapp located at his own request in 1886, was readmitted to a supernumerary relationship in 1892, and finally withdrew from the Michigan Conference and from the church in 1901.   --See Methodist Episcopal Church. Conferences. Michigan, Minutes (Lansing: 1877-1901).

9.24   Lloyd Raymond Day, "A History of God's Bible School in Cincinnati, 1900-1949" (unpublished M.Ed. thesis, University of Cincinnati, 1949), 13-14.   Before Knapp went to Cincinnati, he was already having Cranston & Stowe print many of his books.

9.25   Workers for this meeting were Edgar Levy, a Baptist

minister from Philadelphia; John Thompson, who personally owned
the Mountain Lake Park Camp Meeting grounds in Maryland; and
Beverly Carradine, who by 1895 was pastor of the First Methodist
Episcopal Church, South, of St. Louis. In 1894 Thompson and
Carradine were listed as National Association members.

9.26 Day, "A History of God's Bible School in Cincinnati,
1900-1949," 16-17.

9.27 Ibid., 17, 20.

9.28 Methodist Episcopal Church. Conferences. Michigan,
Minutes ... 1894, 386.

9.29 Outside of New England where the parent organization,
the General Holiness League, had been organized in 1891 to counter-
act the independency of the Central Evangelical Holiness Association,
Knapp's Central Holiness League was the only holiness association
having the "league" idea as a principle of organization. --See
Smith, Called unto Holiness, 59-60.

9.30 Day, "A History of God's Bible School in Cincinnati,
1900-1949," 18-19, 25-33, 71.

9.31 In 1898 Kulp, then pastor of the Second Street Methodist Episcopal Church of Grand Rapids, was still prominent enough
in Michigan Methodism to be included in a conference sermon anthology. --See George B. Kulp, "The Damnation Army, Its Victims
and Sponsors," in C. S. Eastman, ed., The Methodist Episcopal
Pulpit; A Volume of Sermons by Ministers of the Michigan Conference of the M. E. Church in Michigan, with an introduction by the
Rev. Joseph F. Berry, D.D. (Monroe, Mich.: Sermon Printing
House, 1898), 242-255; and Methodist Episcopal Church. Conferences.
Michigan, Minutes ... 1898, 260. After evangelizing several years
with his father and writing several religious books including one entitled Trumpet Calls to the Unsaved, Byron Rees went on to Harvard
for graduate study. From 1904 until his death in 1920, he taught
at Williams College. The compiler of an early anthology of American literature, Rees seems to have rapidly lost his religious fervor
after going to Harvard. --See biographical sketch in Who Was Who
in America, 1897-1942 (Chicago: Marquis Who's Who, 1943), 1018.
In 1900 Hirst went as a missionary to Africa under the sponsorship
of the International Holiness Union. --See Martin Wells Knapp,
Pentecostal Letters, selected from the correspondence (Cincinnati:
Office of God's Revivalist, 1902), 11-12.

9.32 See International Holiness Union and Prayer League,
Constitution and By-Laws (Cincinnati: 1897); and Pilgrim Holiness
Church, "The Days of Our Pilgrimage," 1-2; and also U.S. Bureau
of the Census, Religious Bodies, 1906, II, 317.

9.33 See Martin Wells Knapp, Pentecostal Aggressiveness;

or, Why I Conducted the Meetings of the Chesapeak Holiness Union at Bowens, Maryland (Cincinnati: M. W. Knapp, 1899?), passim; and Methodist Episcopal Church. Conference. Michigan, Minutes ... 1899, 428.

CHAPTER 10

10.1 See Donald Paul Brickley, Man of the Morning; The Life and Work of Phineas F. Bresee (Kansas City, Mo.: Nazarene Publishing House, 1960), 121-131; and Harrison D. Brown, Personal Memories of the Early Ministry of Dr. Phineas F. Bresee: Character Study (Seattle: 1930), 32; and also Ernest Alexander Girvin, Phineas F. Bresee: A Prince in Israel; A Biography (Kansas City, Mo.: Pentecostal Nazarene Publishing House, 1916), 102-103.

10.2 See Isaiah Guyman Martin, Dr. P. F. Bresee and the Church He Founded (Kansas City, Mo.: Printed for I. G. Martin, Mansfield, Ill., by the Nazarene Publishing House, 1937), 11; and Timothy Lawrence Smith, Called unto Holiness: The Story of the Nazarenes: The Formative Years, (Kansas City, Mo.: Nazarene Publishing House, 1962), 49-51, 107-108.

10.3 Bresee received pay for preaching and undoubtedly met most ordinary expenses, although his son Paul, who was a physician, and his other children, several of whom operated a going furniture and undertaking business known as Bresee Brothers, were ever ready to stand behind their father in any emergency. --See Brickley, Man of the Morning, 103-104, 106-107 and 114-115; also Los Angeles city directories, 1896-1922. Paul's wife, Ada, was one of her father-in-law's most devoted followers. --Girvin, Phineas F. Bresee: A Prince in Israel, 372, 444.

10.4 Brickley, Man of the Morning, 133.

10.5 Ibid., 137-138.

10.6 Jeremiah 6:16.

10.7 See Girvin, Phineas F. Bresee: A Prince in Israel, 106.

10.8 Ibid., 103-107; and Brickley, Man of the Morning, 132-139. Dependence on Spirit-guidance in decision making long continued as a prominent feature in holiness church administration.

10.9 Quoted in Martin, Dr. P. F. Bresee and the Church He Founded, 17.

10.10 Ibid., 14.

10.11 Nearly forty years later, Martin declared that every

"normal Nazarene church should be like this first one--in a con-
stant spirit of revival from year to year." Ibid.

10.12 Advertising brochure issued by the Church of the Nazarene, Los Angeles, 1895, quoted in Smith, Called unto Holiness,
111. The Church of the Nazarene tabernacle was regarded as being
so novel, in fact, that it was pointed out as one of the city's tour-
ist attractions. --See Girvin, Phineas F. Bresee: A Prince in
Israel, 108-109.

10.13 Morrison's account appeared as an editorial in the
Pentecostal Herald, XI (January 25, 1899), 8. He said he would
ever remember this meeting as "one of the green spots" of his
ministry. "Remarkable liberty exists ... yet we saw nothing of-
fensive to good sanctified taste."

10.14 See Girvin, Phineas F. Bresee: A Prince in Israel,
112-116 and 114-151. An article in the Midland Methodist, quoted
in the Nazarene Messenger, June 12, 1902, claimed that although
"lawyers, doctors, scientists, businessmen: men and women of
education and refinement" had been gathered into the Church of the
Nazarene in Los Angeles, the church was "emphatically" dedicated
to giving "Salvation" "to the poor." --Quoted in Brickley, Man of
the Morning, 160.

10.15 Girvin, Phineas F. Bresee: A Prince in Israel, 162.

10.16 See Ibid., 112; and also Smith, Called unto Holiness,
passim.

10.17 See Girvin, Phineas F. Bresee: A Prince in Israel,
117-120; for a thorough treatment of the history of the paper, see
Brickley, Man of the Morning, 180-188. The enthusiastic, expan-
sionist character which the church assumed during these formative
years disappointed Bresee's partner, Joseph Widney, who apparently
expected a new mission rather than a new church. From 1899 to
1911 he again ministered in the Methodist Episcopal Church, then
until his death in 1938 toyed with other religious movements quite
unlike holiness. --See Brickley, Man of the Morning, 139-145; and
Smith, Called unto Holiness, 120. The biographical sketch of Widney by Glenn S. Dumke in the Dictionary of American Biography,
XXII, 715-716, omits his connection with the Church of the Nazarene.

10.18 See "Numerical and Financial Statistics--1907" in the
Proceedings of the First General Assembly of the Pentecostal Church
of the Nazarene (Los Angeles: Nazarene Publishing Co., 1907); and
Russell Victor DeLong and Mendell Taylor, Fifty Years of Nazarene
Missions (Kansas City, Mo.: Beacon Hill Press, 1955), II, 18-21;
and also Smith, Called unto Holiness, 137-139, 250-251.

10.19 Rees played some part in establishing and/or securing support for rescue homes in Providence; Greensboro and Asheville, North Carolina; Columbus; Cincinnati; Chicago; Kansas City; Pilot Point, Texas; and Oakland, California.

10.20 Lloyd Raymond Day, "A History of God's Bible School in Cincinnati, 1900-1949" (unpublished M.Ed. thesis, University of Cincinnati, 1949), 32-33, 47-48, 73, 83-84, passim. Trusteeship of this property has remained a thorny problem through the present. During his lifetime Knapp acted as sole trustee.

10.21 International Holiness Union and Prayer League. Constitution and By-Laws (Cincinnati: 1897).

10.22 Day, "A History of God's Bible School in Cincinnati, 1900-1949," 18 and 25.

10.23 See Pilgrim Holiness Church, "The days of our Pilgrimage; A Brief Historical Sketch of the Pilgrim Holiness Church, revised to General Conference, 1962," (mimeographed), (Indianapolis: 1962), 3.

10.24 U.S. Bureau of the Census, Religious Bodies: 1906, (Washington, D.C.: Government Printing Office, 1910), II, 317-319.

CHAPTER 11

11.1 A statistical study comparing holiness church membership in cities of over 25,000 in 1926 and 1936 with other religious, nationality and racial groups in relation to geographical, economic, residential and vocational characteristics showed differences between the holiness groups and Roman Catholics, Negroes, and people of foreign birth and parentage. See Appendix V.

11.2 Accomplished in response to memorials from thirty-five of the thirty-seven district assemblies of the church, the name change was part of an attempt by holiness groups to deny relationship between entire sanctification and glossolalia. They believed the modern "tongues" movement to be unscriptural and not to be equated with Pentecost. --See Acts 2:1-13; also Alma Bridwell White, Demons and Tongues (Bound Brook, N.J.: Pentecostal Union, 1910); and Benjamin Franklin Neely, The Bible Versus the Tongues Theory, rev. ed. (Kansas City, Mo.: Nazarene Publishing House, ca. 1925). Between 1917 and 1925 every holiness group with "Pentecost" or "Pentecostal" remaining in its name deleted it. The Pentecost-Pilgrim Church, formed in 1917, discontinued using Pentecost and became known as the Pilgrim Church. In 1917 the Pentecostal Union, organized in 1901, was re-named the Pillar of Fire Church. Established as a body separate from the Free Methodist Church in 1898, the Pentecost Bands of the World became the Missionary Bands of the World in 1925.

11. 3 See Figure 3, entitled, "Predecessors of the Church of
the Nazarene, 1882-1908, and Formation of the Church of the Naza-
rene, 1907-1967 (Mergers, Additions and Withdrawals). " Also see
Harold William Reed, "The Growth of a Contemporary Sect-type
Institution As Reflected in the Development of the Church of the
Nazarene" (unpublished Th. D. dissertation, Graduate School of Re-
ligion, University of Southern California, 1943), 270-271, 277; and
see Kenneth Shelby Armstrong, "The Church of the Nazarene: A
Study of an Institutionalized Sect" (unpublished Th. D. dissertation,
Iliff School of Theology, 1958), partially published in his Face to
Face with the Church of the Nazarene, (Boulder, Colo.: 1958); and
see Timothy Lawrence Smith, Called unto Holiness: The Story of
the Nazarenes: The Formative Years (Kansas City, Mo.: Nazarene
Publishing House, 1962), passim. Also see U. S. Bureau of the
Census, Religious Bodies: 1906 (Washington, D. C.: Government
Printing Office, 1910), II, 503-506, passim; Religious Bodies: 1916
(Washington, D. C.: Government Printing Office, 1919), II, 536-539,
passim; Religious Bodies: 1926 (Washington, D. C.: Government
Printing Office, 1929-1930), II, 383-393, passim; and Religious
Bodies: 1936 (Washington, D. C.: Government Printing Office, 1941),
II, passim. The Church of the Nazarene claimed:

Churches	Members	Sunday School Scholars	Year
100	6, 657	5, 039	1907
228	10, 413	6, 756	1908
470	20, 501	17, 800	1911
792	31, 600	35, 961	1915
867	32, 259	40, 575	1916
978	34, 928	50, 397	1919
1, 304	50, 631	97, 174	1923
1, 444	63, 558	109, 237	1926
1, 700	74, 057	128, 998	1928
1, 963	102, 018	202, 908	1932
2, 335	136, 371	270, 531	1936
2, 728	169, 443	343, 146	1940
4, 849	342, 032	719, 026	1963

11. 4 See Figure 4, entitled "Formation of Pilgrim Holiness
Church". Also see "Part I, Historical Statement" in Pilgrim Holi-
ness Church, Manual, 1966 (Indianapolis: Pilgrim Publishing House,
1966), 11-16 particularly sec. 2, par. 1-20; and Pilgrim Holiness
Church, "The Days of Our Pilgrimage; A Brief Historical Sketch of
the Pilgrim Holiness Church, revised to General Conference, 1962"
(mimeographed) (Indianapolis: 1962); and also Chester Wilkins, "A
Review of the Recently Proposed Union of the Wesleyan Methodist
Church and the Pilgrim Holiness Church" (unpublished M. A. thesis,
Butler University, 1960), 10-11. Also see U. S. Bureau of the
Census, Religious Bodies, 1906, II, 317-319, passim; Religious
Bodies, 1916, II, 315-318, passim; Religious Bodies, 1926, II, 1098-
1104; and Religious Bodies, 1936, III, passim. The Pilgrim Holi-
ness Church claimed:

Churches	Members	Sunday School Scholars	Year
74	2,774	3,276	1906
169	5,276	7,923	1916
441	15,040	23,467	1926
510	20,124	48,884	1936
1,035	33,709	99,235	1962

11.5 For Bresee's previous administrative record, see
Ernest Alexander Girvin, Phineas F. Bresee: A Prince in Israel;
A Biography (Kansas City, Mo.: Pentecostal Nazarene Publishing
House, 1916), 92-101; and Donald Paul Brickley, Man of the Morn-
ing; The Life and Work of Phineas F. Bresee (Kansas City, Mo.:
Nazarene Publishing House, 1960), 107-120. For Reynolds' record,
see Amy N. Hinshaw, In Labors Abundant; A Biography of H. F.
Reynolds, D. D. (Kansas City, Mo.: Nazarene Publishing House,
1938); and Smith, Called unto Holiness, 60-61, 68, 77-80, passim;
and also Mendell Taylor and Russell Victor DeLong, Fifty Years of
Nazarene Missions (Kansas City, Mo.: Beacon Hill Press, 1952-
1958), II, 14-18, passim. For Williams' record, see Gideon Brooks
Williamson, Roy T. Williams, Servant of God (Kansas City, Mo.:
Nazarene Publishing House, 1947); and Smith, Called unto Holiness,
337-340, passim. For Kulp's, see Pilgrim Holiness Church, Man-
ual, 1966, 12, par. 9-10; and U. S. Work Projects Administration,
Inventory of the Church Archives of Michigan: Pilgrim Holiness
Church, Michigan District, prepared by the Michigan Historical
Records Survey Project, Division of Community Service Programs,
Work Projects Administration (Detroit, Michigan, Historical Records
Survey Project, 1942), 2-3, passim; and "Condolence Committee
Report," in Pilgrim Holiness Church. General Conference, Owosso,
Mich., 1942, Minutes (Indianapolis: 1942), 64; and also Methodist
Episcopal Church. Conferences. Michigan, Minutes of the Michigan
Annual Conference, 37-63 sessions, 1882-1898. For Rees', see
Paul Stromberg Rees, Seth Cook Rees, the Warrior-Saint (Indianap-
olis: Pilgrim Book Room, 1934), abbreviated as The Life of Seth
Cook Rees (Indianapolis: Pilgrim Publishing House, 1964); and Pil-
grim Holiness Church, Manual, 1966, 11, 13-14 sec. 2, par. 1-5,
14-17, 21-22; and also Smith, Called unto Holiness, 272-287, 289-
291, passim.

11.6 See Taylor and DeLong, Fifty Years of Nazarene Mis-
sions, 9-60, passim, for an account of administrative structural
changes on missionary activity. See Smith, Called unto Holiness,
322-341, passim, for the Church of the Nazarene. See Pilgrim
Holiness Church, Manual, 1966, 14 sec. 2, par. 22; and Chester
Wilkins, "A Review of the Recently Proposed Union of the Wesleyan
Methodist Church and the Pilgrim Holiness Church," 12-42, for the
Pilgrim Holiness Church.

11.7 Title of an editorial by J. G. Morrison in the Holiness
Layman on the eve of Morrison's abandonment of associationism in

1922. Troubled by an Association member who had fallen under the "spell" of Aimee Semple McPherson, Morrison joined the Church of the Nazarene and influenced about a thousand other Methodists in the Dakotas and surrounding states to do likewise. --See Smith, Called unto Holiness, 312; for a full account of the Laymen's Holiness Association's development and activities, see 298-315. For the Methodist reaction, see Methodist Church (United States). Conferences. North Dakota. Historical Society, History of the Methodist Church in North Dakota and Dakota Territory (Nashville, Tenn.: 1960), 52-61, 94, 113, 117.

11. 8 James Proctor Knott, History of Pasadena College (Pasadena, Calif.: Pasadena College, 1960), 13.

11. 9 P. F. Bresee, quoted in Brickley, Man of the Morning, 159.

11. 10 "Numerical and Financial Statistics--1907, " in: Pentecostal Church of the Nazarene. General Assembly, Chicago, 1907, Proceedings (Los Angeles: Nazarene Publishing Co., 1907).

11. 11 In considering these figures one must remember that in the streetcar era empty store buildings at car stops in residential neighborhoods were often used for church purposes.

11. 12 Lee, whose uncle, Jason Lee, had pioneered Methodist work in the Northwest, founded the People's Mission in 1899. Aimed at ministering to miners and others in the "neglected" classes, the mission rendered a large number of social services. By 1906 it was running a "workingmen's home, a free reading room, an employment agency ... and a rescue home" and maintaining "a large store of supplies for relief of the poor." Eventually it established branches in neighboring places. In 1911 the People's Mission joined the Pentecostal Church of the Nazarene, but withdrew the next year after an administrative misunderstanding. In 1925, six years after William H. Lee died, his followers joined the Pilgrim Holiness Church. --See Smith, Called unto Holiness, 230-232.

11. 13 Quoted in Girvin, Phineas F. Bresee: A Prince in Israel, 243.

11. 14 Church of the Nazarene. Northwest District, Fiftieth Anniversary Book, Compiled in Commemoration of Fifty Years of Progress--1904-1954 (n. p., 1954), passim.

11. 15 Holiness congregations in all parts of the country owe their existence to rescue missions which preceded them. Holiness work in Haverhill and Lynn, Massachusetts; Binghamton, New York; Philadelphia and Allentown; Cleveland and Cincinnati; Nashville; Chicago and Peoria; St. Louis; Little Rock; Oklahoma City; Omaha; Denver and Colorado Springs; Phoenix; and Los Angeles originated in missions. In other places no tie existed although most of the members had previously attended missions.

11. 16   See "The Sanctification of Dr. Leonard Spangenberg, " in Bernie Smith, ed., Flames of Living Fire; Testimonies to the Experience of Entire Sanctification (Kansas City, Mo. : Beacon Hill Press, 1950), 104-107.

11. 17   See brochures issued by the church relating to celebration of its thirtieth and fiftieth anniversaries in 1941 and 1961. Three general assemblies were held in this building.   In 1912 Kansas City became the denominational headquarters.

11. 18   See Church of the Nazarene, Manual, 1948 (Kansas City, Mo.: Nazarene Pub. House, 1948), II, Church Constitution, part II, V, "The General Rules, " pp. 33-36, and VII, Ritual, chap. II, "The Reception of Church Members," pp. 224-226.   And see Pilgrim Holiness Church, Manual, 1946 (Indianapolis: Pilgrim Pub. House, 1946), part III, Government, sections 28-29, "Reception of Members, " pp. 29-30, and section 30-32, "Church Covenant, " pp. 30-33, and sections 63-67, "Special Rules, " pp. 48-52.

11. 19   See portrait used as frontispiece in Elmer Ellsworth Shelhamer, Sixty Years of Thorns and Roses (Cincinnati: God's Bible School and Missionary Training Home, 1930).   Shelhamer's daughter, Evangeline, married Walter L. Burbrook, a Pilgrim minister who later became general superintendent of the Pilgrim Holiness Church.

11. 20   The Church of the Nazarene never exchanged its original rules for less demanding ones.   It did, however, liberalize popular interpretation of what some required as styles changed, especially in the area of dress.   The time came when wedding rings which many had regarded as jewelry in the early days were generally worn.   (Its official ritual for the marriage ceremony includes no provision for exchange of rings.)   Also, while the stricture against attendance at commercial movie houses was never changed, the church did not forbid ownership of television sets by members. In 1950 it adopted official advice concerning use of television.   --See Church of the Nazarene, Manual, 1956 (Kansas City, Mo. : Nazarene Publishing House, 1956).

11. 21   The limited scope of holiness social concern may be seen in the responsibilities delegated to the Committee of Public Morals created by the Church of the Nazarene in 1944.   Re-named the Committee on Christian Action in 1964, its function remained essentially the same.   --See Church of the Nazarene, Manual: History, Constitution, Government, Ritual, 1948 (Kansas City, Mo. : Nazarene Publishing House, 1948), 291, par. 574; and see Church of the Nazarene. General Assembly, Portland, Ore. , 1964, Journal (Kansas City, Mo. : 1964), 91, par. 365-366, and 143-144 concerning Memorials SC406-407.

11. 22   Elmer Talmage Clark, The Small Sects in America, rev. ed. (New York: Abingdon Press, 1949), 79.

11. 23   Emmanual Association, Guidebook, ed. of 1961
(Colorado Springs, Colo.: 1961), 12-14.

11. 24   In relation to military service the Pilgrim Holiness
Church and the Ohio Yearly Meeting of Friends Church support the
individual conscience.   --See Pilgrim Holiness Church, Manual,
1946 (Indianapolis: Pilgrim Publishing House, 1946), 52, sect. 76;
and Ohio Yearly Meeting of Friends Church. Canton, Ohio, 1965,
Minutes (Damascus, Ohio: 1965), 53-54; and Church of the Nazarene.
General Assembly, Portland, Ore., 1964, Journal (Kansas City,
Mo.: 1964), 141-142, concerning Memorials SC401 and SC411.   Also
see Gideon Brooks Williamson, "Meritocracy," Herald of Holiness,
LII (July 22, 1964); and F. O. Parr, "Perfect Love and Race
Hatred" (mimeographed), (Bourbonnais, Ill.: 1964), a Nazarene
sociology professor's analysis of second and third generation holi-
ness young people's attitude toward race.

11. 25   At ten-year intervals from 1906 to 1936 the average
for ten holiness groups was 45. 5 members per church.   In 1906
nine groups averaged 49 members; in 1916, 37 members.   In 1926
eight groups averaged 42 members; in 1936, 58 members.

11. 26   Of the 1326 clergy reported by six holiness groups in
1916, 645 had supplemental occupations.

11. 27   See Maury E. Redford, The Rise of the Church of the
Nazarene (Kansas City, Mo.: Nazarene Publishing House, 1948),
197-220.

11. 28   See William H. Pratt, God Amid the Shadows; Thrilling
Sketches from the Lives of Rev. and Mrs. Melvin Pratt, Well-
Known Spiritual Leaders and Founders of Missions and Homes for
Penitent, Erring Girls (Indianapolis, n. d.), passim.

11. 29   See personal histories in Appendix IV.

11. 30   See Appendix VI.

11. 31   While increasing by over 110, 000 in cities of 25, 000
and over, Methodist membership as a whole decreased by 1, 040, 000
between 1926 and 1936.

11. 32   After denominational churches were formed, independent
holiness schools continued to receive the support of Methodist loyalists.

11. 33   A fictionalized account of Pasadena College in the
1920's is given in Hannah Smith, For Heaven's Sake (Boston: Little,
Brown, 1949).   The school is controlled by the Church of the Nazarene.

11. 34   Olivet University. Board of Trustees, "Minutes,"
May 27, 1921.

11. 35   Founded in 1910 the society was later known as the
National Holiness Missionary Society and the World Gospel Mission.
For its history, see William Walter Cary, Story of the National
Holiness Missionary Society (Chicago: National Holiness Missionary
Society, 1940); and Laura Trachsel, Kindled Fires in Africa (Marion,
Ind. : World Gospel Mission, 1960), Kindled Fires in Asia (Marion,
Ind. : World Gospel Mission, 1960), and Kindled Fires in Latin
America (Marion, Ind. : World Gospel Mission, 1961).

11. 36   See U. S. Bureau of the Census, Religious Bodies:
1926, II, 393, 1104.

Appendices

Lasting Effects of the Camp Meeting
on the Church

Michigan District Assembly, Church of the Nazarene, held at Indian Lake near Vicksburg, Michigan, about 1944. General Superintendent R. T. Williams, presiding. This page: Williams preaching. The five photographs on this and next two pages, from:
Williamson, Gideon Brooks, 1898- . Roy T. Williams, Servant
of God. Kansas City, Mo.: Nazarene Publishing House, 1947; opposite p. 120.

181

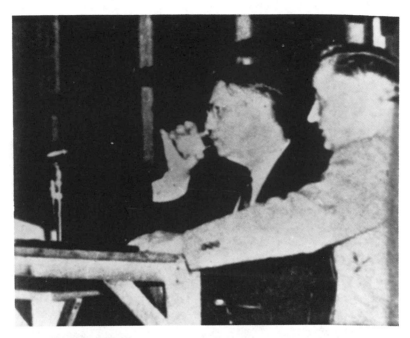

Top: Williams taking a break; bottom: baptizing a minister's child.

Top: Williams officiating at ordination; bottom: signing ministerial credentials.

APPENDIX II

National Holiness Camp Meeting Sites, 1867-1924

1867: Vineland, New Jersey

1868: Manheim, Pennsylvania

1869: Round Lake (near Saratoga Springs), New York

1870: Des Plaines, Illinois; Oakington (near Baltimore), Maryland; Hamilton, Massachusetts

1871: Sacramento, California (tabernacle meeting); San Francisco, California (tabernacle meeting); Santa Clara, California (tabernacle meeting); Salt Lake City, Utah (tabernacle meeting); Indianapolis, Indiana (tabernacle meeting); Round Lake (near Saratoga Springs), New York; Urbana, Ohio

1872: Williamsville (near Springfield), Illinois; Richmond, Maine; Oaks Corners (near Geneva), New York; Sea Cliff, New York; Urbana, Ohio; Knoxville, Tennessee.

1873: Cedar Rapids, Iowa; Baltimore, Maryland (tabernacle meeting); Landisville (near Philadelphia), Pennsylvania Knoxville, Tennessee; Moundsville, West Virginia

1874: Washington, D. C. (tabernacle meeting); Joliet, Illinois; Old Orchard, Maine; Baltimore, Maryland (tabernacle meeting); Sterling, Massachusetts

1875: Washington, D. C. (tabernacle meeting); Cedar Rapids, Iowa; Old Orchard, Maine; Newburgh, New York; Urbana, Ohio; Fernwood, Pennsylvania

1876: Old Orchard, Maine; Bennett (near Lincoln), Nebraska; Newburgh, New York; Shelter Island, New York; Loveland (near Cincinnati), Ohio; Milwaukee, Wisconsin

1877: Clear Lake (near Mason City), Iowa; Framingham, Massachusetts; Chester Heights (near Philadelphia), Pennsylvania

1878: Clear Lake (near Mason City), Iowa; Epping (near Portsmouth), New Hampshire; New Castle, Pennsylvania

1879: Lawrence, Kansas; Summit Grove (near Baltimore), Maryland; Douglas, Massachusetts; Bennett (near Lincoln), Nebraska; Urbana, Ohio; New Castle, Pennsylvania; Sewickley (near Pittsburgh), Pennsylvania

1880: Round Lake (near Saratoga Springs), New York

1881: Warsaw, Indiana; Round Lake (near Saratoga Springs), New York

1882: Lincoln, Nebraska; Round Lake (near Saratoga Springs), New York

1883: Old Orchard, Maine; Pitman Grove, New Jersey

1884: Old Orchard, Maine; Lansing, Michigan; Pitman Grove, New Jersey

1885: Augusta, Georgia; Jacksonville, Illinois; Warsaw, Indiana; Old Orchard, Maine; Lansing, Michigan; Red Rock (near Minneapolis), Minnesota; Ocean City, New Jersey

1886: Murdock (near Decatur), Illinois; Clear Lake (near Mason City), Iowa; Joanna Heights (near Reading and Pottstown), Pennsylvania; Wesley Park (Niagara Falls), Ontario, Canada

1887: Pitman Grove, N. J.

1888: Mount Tabor (near Dover and Morristown), New Jersey

1889: Beulah Park (Santa Cruz or Oakland), California; Des Plaines, Illinois; Old Orchard, Maine

1890: Camden (near Dover), Delaware; Decatur, Illinois

1891: Linwood Park (near Cincinnati), Ohio; Northfield, Vermont

1892: Des Plaines, Illinois; Des Moines, Iowa; Linwood Park (near Cincinnati), Ohio; Ogden, Utah

1893: Long Beach, California; Des Plaines, Illinois; Hackley Park (Muskegon), Michigan

1894: Decatur, Illinois; Silver Heights (near New Albany), Indiana

1895: Silver Heights (near New Albany), Indiana; Decatur, Illinois

1896: New Albany, Indiana; Storm Lake, Iowa

1897: Valley Camp (near Pittsburgh), Pennsylvania; New Albany, Indiana; Des Plaines, Illinois; Greenville, Illinois

1898:   New Albany, Indiana; Hollow Rock (near Toronto), Ohio

1899:   Summit Grove (near York), Pennsylvania; New Albany, Indiana; Denton, Texas

1900:   Summit Grove (near York), Pennsylvania; New Albany, Indiana; Acton (near Indianapolis), Ind.; Denton, Texas

1901:   Greenwood (near Indianapolis), Indiana; New Albany, Indiana

1902:   Des Moines, Iowa; Douglas (near Worcester), Massachusetts; New Albany, Indiana

1903:   Des Moines, Iowa; Douglas (near Worcester), Massachusetts; New Albany, Indiana; Denton, Texas

1904:   Des Moines, Iowa; Lincoln, Nebraska; Springfield, Illinois; New Albany, Indiana; Old Orchard, Maine

1905:   Des Moines, Iowa; Lincoln, Nebraska; Ferndale (near Bellingham), Washington; Portland, Oregon; Old Orchard, Maine

1906:   Des Moines, Iowa; West Pullman (near Chicago), Illinois; Old Orchard, Maine

1907:   Oskaloosa, Iowa; Old Orchard, Maine

1908:   Oskaloosa, Iowa; Old Orchard, Maine

1909:   Oskaloosa, Iowa; West Pullman (near Chicago), Illinois; Lincoln, Nebraska; Old Orchard, Maine

1910:   University Park (near Oskaloosa), Iowa; Lincoln, Nebraska; Old Orchard, Maine

1911:   University Park (near Oskaloosa), Iowa; Old Orchard, Maine

1912:   University Park (near Oskaloosa), Iowa; Lincoln, Nebraska; Robinson (near Houlton), Maine; Mooers, Clinton County, New York; Old Orchard, Maine

1913:   University Park (near Oskaloosa), Iowa; Lincoln (near Mitchell), South Dakota; Riverside (near Chicago), Illinois; Gordon, Sheridan County, Nebraska; Mooers, Clinton County, New York; Old Orchard, Maine

1914:   University Park (near Oskaloosa), Iowa; Mooers, Clinton County, New York; Wichita, Kansas Old Orchard, Maine

1915:   University Park (near Oskaloosa), Iowa; Mooers, Clinton County, New York; Old Orchard, Maine

1916: University Park (near Oskaloosa), Iowa; Mooers, Clinton County, New York; Old Orchard, Maine; Mount Vernon, Virginia

1917: University Park (near Oskaloosa), Iowa; Lincoln, Nebraska; Mooers, Clinton County, New York; Old Orchard Maine; Mount Vernon, Virginia

1918: University Park (near Oskaloosa), Iowa; Lincoln, Nebraska; Mooers, Clinton County, New York; Old Orchard, Maine

1919: University Park (near Oskaloosa), Iowa; Lincoln, Nebraska; Old Orchard, Maine; Mooers, Clinton County, New York

1920: University Park (near Oskaloosa), Iowa; Old Orchard, Maine; Mooers, Clinton County, New York

1921: University Park (near Oskaloosa), Iowa; Lincoln, Nebraska; Bloomingdale, Essex County (near Saranac Lake), New York; Old Orchard, Maine

1922: University Park (near Oskaloosa), Iowa; Old Orchard, Maine; Mooers, Clinton County, New York; Bloomingdale, Essex County (near Saranac Lake), New York; Richland, Oswego County (near Pulaski and Syracuse), New York

1923: University Park (near Oskaloosa), Iowa; Old Orchard, Maine; Scottsville, Harrison County, Texas (near Marshall, Texas and Shreveport, Louisiana); Mooers, Clinton County, New York; Bloomingdale, Essex County (near Saranac Lake), New York; Richland, Oswego County (near Pulaski and Syracuse), New York

1924: University Park (near Oskaloosa), Iowa; Old Orchard, Maine; Mooers, Clinton County, New York; Bloomingdale, Essex County (near Saranac Lake), New York; Mount Vernon, Virginia; Richland, Oswego County (near Pulaski and Syracuse), New York

APPENDIX III

Presidents of the Christian Holiness Association
(with church affiliation)

1867-1884   John S. Inskip (Methodist Episcopal Church)

1884-1892   William McDonald (Methodist Episcopal Church)

1892-1919   C. J. Fowler (Methodist Episcopal Church)

1920-1921   Will Huff (Methodist Episcopal Church)

1921-1925   George Kunz (Methodist Episcopal Church)

1925-1928   Joseph H. Smith (Methodist Episcopal Church)

1928-1942   C. W. Butler (Methodist Episcopal Church)

1942-1946   C. I. Armstrong (Wesleyan Methodist Church)

1946-1950   H. M. Couchenour (Methodist Church)

1950-1955   Paul F. Elliott (Pilgrim Holiness Church)

1955-1959   Myron F. Boyd (Free Methodist Church)

1959-1960   Morton Dorsey (Churches of Christ in Christian Union)

1960-1964   Kenneth E. Geiger (United Missionary Church)

1964-1968   Paul L. Kindschi (Wesleyan Methodist Church)

1968-1972   Myron F. Boyd (Free Methodist Church)

1972-1974   Henry A. Ginder (Brethren in Christ Church)

1974-   B. Edgar Johnson (Church of the Nazarene)

APPENDIX IV

Summary Histories of People Helped
by Holiness Rescue Homes

as reported by Seth Cook Rees in <u>Miracles in the
Slums; or, Thrilling Stories of those Rescued from
the Cesspools of Iniquity, and Touching Incidents
in the Lives of the Unfortunate</u> (Chicago, 1905).

LITTLE ELLA: Born to irreligious parents in rural Iowa, she had
no moral training. An early drinker, she also early became a
drunkard. At age fifteen she went to Chicago where she posed as
a cab driver's wife. Sold as a prostitute for $5.00, she soon be-
came ill and went to a public hospital. While there she came into
contact with rescue workers who succeeded in getting her saved and
sanctified. Rees himself placed Ella in Bible school after discovering that she was "called" to be a missionary in China. Later she
became a Quaker and started preaching.

MABEL and ORIGENE: Mabel was of French-German extraction,
and Origene of French-Spanish descent. Both were raised Catholic.
Mabel went to school until age fourteen and left home at fifteen.
Origene was educated for the priesthood, spending ten years in a
convent and three years as a priest. After being put on bread and
water "for speaking to women," Origene ran away and met Mabel.
They tried to marry, but since the priest charged too much, they
lived together without marriage. Origene became a sailor, and
Mabel took to drink. A missionary found Mabel in a "barrel" house,
and she went to Rest Cottage. Later, her "fiery preaching" converted Origene. Mabel was saved from rum and tobacco, Origene
from tobacco. They were married by the matron at the rescue
home.

"ONE of our best girls": A real Christian, she was saved and
sanctified at age eleven, but joined a "dead, formal church." She
early "got into trouble," disgracing herself and her family. Through
the <u>Revivalist</u>, she learned of the rescue homes and wrote asking to
be admitted. She was saved, sanctified, and eventually returned
home.

MAY JENSEN: Motherless at two, she was adopted by a Danish
family and robbed of her purity by her adopted father at age thirteen.

Becoming a waitress, she took to drink, and spent several terms
in the workhouse. After four years of sinful life, she was found
by a missionary during her second hospital confinement. Taken to
Rest Cottage, she was saved and sanctified. Desperately ill upon
her arrival, she soon died. Her funeral was held at Rest Cottage.

MABEL: Born in an Illinois country home to pious Methodist
parents, she was ruined before she was sixteen while buggy riding
at night. She went to the Rest Cottage in Chicago and was saved.

BERTHA and ESTHER, twins: Probably born in Arkansas, they
were orphaned and adopted by a sixty-year-old man who ruined both
before they were thirteen. They were put on a train at Ozark, Arkansas, bound for Denton, Texas. Cold, thinly clad, and penniless,
they were found by a holy woman and taken to Rest Cottage, Pilot
Point, Texas. Both were saved.

SALOON-keeper's daughter: This girl could not remember when she
did not drink. As a youth she became a drunkard, started smoking,
and was imprisoned many times, including one five-month term in
the workhouse. In the three months before her rescue, she without
any visible means of support paid one hundred twenty dollars in fines.
After approximately seven years of sinful life, she was saved and
sanctified. She returned stolen money and jewelry. After leaving
Rest Cottage, she married.

MYRTLE: Her father was a Christian minister who died when she
was four years old. From ages eight to thirteen, she lived with
her sister because of her mother's poverty. At thirteen she started
working as a nurse. However, in 1903, while visiting a relative in
Texas, an honored member of the YMCA, crazed by drink, ruined
her. She, rescued through the efforts of a male missionary in
Texarkana, went to Rest Cottage at Pilot Point, Texas. There she
was saved, and sanctified. Her baby died.

JULIA: Born in Springfield, Illinois to a drunken father, at age
thirteen or fourteen Julia was forced to do washing and ironing to
support herself. Poverty forced her into sin. She inherited an alcoholic appetite from her father, started smoking and became a high
class prostitute. At age twenty-five, she married a brute. After
fifteen years of sinful life, she was saved at Hope Cottage, Cincinnati, and gave up morphine, rum, and tobacco.

LITTLE MAY: Born in a small, Southern town to Christian parents,
May was ruined in Cincinnati under the guise of marriage. After
two or three months of sinful life, workers from Hope Cottage found
her and soon returned her to her parents.

ORPHA: She was born in an Ohio Village to a wicked father and a
godly, praying mother. When she was fifteen, her mother died.
Going to Cincinnati, she fell prey to a professional procurer who
promised her a nice home and clothes. She was sold for two dollars

plus expenses and went lower and lower until rescued by slum missionaries.   Later, she became a slum missionary and an ordained deaconess.

DICIE, the sporting madam: Although Dicie had a Christian mother, she became a drunkard, cigarette fiend, and user of morphine, cocaine, and other drugs.   When missionaries visited her house, she allowed them to pray and gave up drugs for a time.   After a relapse, she became a patient in a rescue home, where she was saved.   As a result she went home to mother and later became a slum missionary herself.

MARGARET, the barrel-house sport: Born in Owen's Sound, Ontario, she was forced by her drunken father into domestic service. She proved a good worker but was seduced after being drugged, and her drunken father turned her out.   She started drinking and smoking and spent six months in the worst houses.   In jail, she was given a Bible and hymn book.   When released a missionary took her six hundred miles to a Chicago rest home (Rest Cottage).   Although she backslid twice, she eventually became stable enough to become a missionary.

HALLIE, an artless girl: Born in a Virginia country village, she was ruined by a married church member while she was taking cows to pasture.   When she was fifteen, Hallie was converted in a rescue home and became a missionary.

CHASE HALL, a bummy bum: Chase came from a southern Ohio family which was religious but had no salvation.   Leaving home at thirteen, he went to Cincinnati, married, and had children.   Then he took to drink.   He went to Trinity Methodist Episcopal Church seeking help but found the preacher delivering travel lectures.   He had his first contact with workers at a street meeting in Chicago. He was ready to commit suicide when he found a card (dropped by a missionary) inviting him to a rescue mission.   After several years in sin, he was saved at the penitent form in the mission.   He got a job on the railroad but refused to work on Sunday and was laid off. Next he was employed in a cooper shop but was dismissed when he refused to make wine barrels.   Finally, he became a janitor at the University of North Dakota.

LILLIE, a friendless girl: Born in Indiana, her mother died when she was four.   Her father was a drinker and gambler who lost several good homes as the result of gambling.   Her stepmother disliked Lillie because she looked like her mother.   She went to work and sent money home, but the mayor's son whom she met at a dance ruined her.   She worked in a minister's family, but the minister made advances   Going to Chicago, she was jailed as a vagrant.   The jail matron called rescue workers from Rest Cottage. As a result Lillie was saved, went to Bible School, and was ordained a deaconess in the International Apostolic Holiness Union.

MISS M___ :   Everything indicated she was from the better walks of
life.   At nineteen she was put in jail for grand larceny.   Mission
workers found her there and the head missionary pleaded for her
release.   The missionary "preached Jesus until they were glad to
give her the girl, to get rid of her. "   Miss M___ made amends,
went to Bible School, attended a deaconess training school in Washington, D. C. , and became a missionary in the New York City slums.

BERNIE: From an aristocratic Southern family, she ignored the
preachings of her religious mother and became an infidel.   A school
teacher for five years, she spurned offers of marriage because she
wanted to be a professional woman.   However, her health failed,
and the doctor prescribed marriage.   After trying suicide, she decided to have a man without marriage.   As a result, she only experienced despair until she heard of the rescue home through a
holiness paper and went to Chicago.   There, she was saved, sanctified, became assistant matron of the Home.

LULU L___ , or from drunkenness to womanhood: An Ohio girl,
Lulu was orphaned at eight.   Having no formal education, she was
ruined at seventeen with a promise of marriage.   She then went to
Cincinnati where she lived two years in open shame.   A regular
attendant at "public picnics, theaters, " and dances, she eventually
became a drunkard, public character, and manager of a house of
ill-repute.   After twelve years of sin, she went to Hope Cottage in
Cincinnati and abandoned rum and tobacco.

LUCY: A Chicagoan, she was from a Christian home and had a
guarded childhood.   At age fifteen, while looking for employment,
she was lured by a girls wanted ad.   She was ruined by her employer who turned out to be a bartender and was put in a Negro
sporting house.   She escaped, and when tried in court for running
away from home, she testified against her violators.   Just as she
was about to be sentenced to five and a quarter years in reform
school, the missionaries from Rest Cottage secured her release.
After a sinful life of one or two weeks, she was converted and returned to her home.   Soon she began teaching a Sunday School class
of nineteen scholars.

LITTLE H___ :   Her Godless parents (her father a drunkard, her
mother a moderate drinker) made home a miniature hell.   Before
she was fourteen, her virtue was gone and she had been taken to
men's rooms and forced to drink.   She worked at housework, but
resorted with another girl to thievery.   Then, she found Rest Cottage and confessed all but thieving.   When she was arrested and put
in jail, the missionaries secured her release.   Finally, she was
sanctified and went to Bible School in order to prepare to become
a slum missionary.

B___ :   A Virginian, she was orphaned as a small child and ruined
by a relative when she was twenty-one.   She drifted on in sin.
Finding a rescue home, she was saved.   As a result she returned

the stolen things and confessed to the wife of a man with whom she had lived in sin.

PEARL, a marvelous transformation: Pearl arrived at a rescue home on a wintry night with babe in arms. Since she was an inveterate liar, Rees hesitated to send her to Bible School. Later her roommate declared, "I have never heard an unkind word fall from her lips."

DELLA: Born in Alabama to Methodist parents who lacked salvation, she was ruined at fourteen by a married man who claimed he was single and promised to marry her. Afterward, she was put in a house of prostitution where she claimed the girls were drugged and forced into shameful life. Della herself was liquor-drugged. When Brother B___, an Alabama holiness preacher, and a missionary held a meeting in the house, her sister converted but soon died. The Sunday after her sister's funeral, Della converted and went to Hope Cottage in Cincinnati for shelter. After five years of sinful life, she gave up drink and tobacco and never expressed any desire to return to her former life.

CARL: A German immigrant, Carl came to the United States at age twenty-two. He was a machinist earning eighteen dollars a week. Then when a miserable strike put him out of work, he became a bartender in a saloon where he was encouraged to steal from helpless customers. After missionaries Dicie and Anna came into his saloon to preach, he hired a substitute and went to the mission. There he fell at the altar and was saved. He never went back to the saloon but got another machinist job. Afterward he was sanctified.

FANNY, the notorious high-life sport: She was born in Cincinnati in 1869 while her father was in jail. Because of family trouble, she was put in a children's home. Although her father was a whiskey dealer and professional gambler, Fanny supported the family by taking in washing. At seventeen, she married a railroad man who suggested she go into prostitution to supplement the family income. As a result she opened a high-class house. She became an excessive drinker, and eventually lost everything. Finally, she reached bottom, begging whiskey in a low-class saloon. There, she was rescued by Orpha, now a missionary, who herself had come from such a life. Fanny was taken to the Rescue Home and was saved.

LULA, a strange story: Born in New York City, Lula's mother died when she was four. Her father proved to be an infidel. At age fifteen she went to work as a nurse. Later she worked as a housekeeper. Finally, she got a job as a traveling agent for a humane society. In a Chicago park, she met a man who by promises of marriage led her into sin. He kept putting off marriage. While in a hospital having her baby she heard of the Rescue Home. Her sinful life was very brief. After she was saved, she gave up worldly dress.

MARGARET ROLLER: An Irish Catholic immigrant, Margaret lived
in Pawtucket, Rhode Island, with her husband and six children. She
became a drunkard, and her husband refused to live with her any
longer. Homeless and intoxicated, she went to a Protestant church
in Providence. The brethren there took her to Rest Cottage where
she was saved and sanctified. Soon re-united with her family, she
moved with them to Providence and established a home where at the
family altar her "little ones ... knelt in a row, devout" as saints.

CHRISTINE, a broken-hearted girl: Born in Wisconsin to Christian
parents, at age twelve Christine lost her mother and left home because of her step-mother. As a saleslady in Milwaukee and Chicago, she was active in the churchwork: the Epworth League,
church entertainments, and attendance promotion. In addition she
sang in a popular quartet. Occasionally, she drank wine until at
one party, a drug was placed in her glass, and she was forever
hopelessly ruined. In Cook County Hospital, she learned of the rescue home. There, although her baby died, she was saved. Called
to be a slum missionary, she went to Bible school for training.

APPENDIX V

Eight Tables: Relative Growth of Holiness and Other Religious Bodies

Introduction

The following eight tables indicate relative growth trends of the Holiness bodies and parallel relative growth of other religious bodies and demographic groups in places of 25,000 population and over. Comparisons appear for cities and suburban areas (Tables 1 and 2), geographical regions (Tables 3 and 4), cities and suburban areas by income characteristics (Tables 5 and 6), and cities and suburban areas by economic specialties (Tables 7 and 8). A plus sign (+) indicates that the rate of membership growth of the group in question was significantly faster (p < .05) by chi-square analysis) than the growth of the group as a whole in places of 25,000 population and over. A minus sign (-) indicates a statistically significant slower rate of growth as compared with the group as a whole in places of 25,000 population and over, or even a numerical decrease in population within the category. NS indicates no statistically significant deviation from the total group growth rate.

Technical assistance for this study was given by Robert Jones and William Miller, students at the University of Michigan. Equipment was made available through the courtesy of the Computing Center of the University of Michigan. Urban and economic categories were taken from Otis Dudley Duncan and Albert J. Reiss, Jr., Social Characteristics of Urban and Rural Communities, 1950 (New York: Wiley, 1956).

Table 1. Relative Growth of Holiness Churches and Parallel Growth of Other Religious Groups in Cities and Suburban Areas of 25,000 Population and Over, 1926-1936.

	Holiness	Holiness Methodist*	Methodist†	Roman Catholic
Central Cities	-	-	-	-
Suburban Areas	-	+	+	+
Independent Cities	+	+	+	+

*Free Methodist, Wesleyan Methodist
†Methodist Episcopal, Methodist Episcopal, South, Methodist Protestant

195

Table 2. Relative Growth of Holiness Churches and Parallel General Population Growth by Demographic Groups in Cities and Suburban Areas of 25,000 Population and Over, 1926-1936.

	Holiness	Native White	Colored	Foreign Born	Foreign Mixed Parentage	Total U. S. Population
Central Cities	-	-	-	-	-	-
Suburban Areas	-	+	+	+	+	+
Independent Cities	-	NS	NS	NS	NS	NS

Table 3. Relative Growth of Holiness Churches and Parallel Growth of Other Religious Groups in Different Geographical Regions, 1926-1936.

	Holiness	Holiness Methodists	Methodist	Roman Catholic
New England	-	-	-	-
Middle Atlantic	-	-	-	-
East North Central	+	-	+	+
West North Central	-	-	+	-
South Atlantic	+	+	+	+
East South Central	+	-	+	+
West South Central	+	-	+	+
Mountain	-	-	-	+
Pacific Coast	-	+	+	+

Table 4. Relative Growth of Holiness Churches and Parallel General Population Growth by Demographic Groups in Different Geographical Regions, 1926-1936.

	Holiness	Native White	Colored	Foreign Born	Foreign Mixed Parentage	Total U. S. Population
New England	-	-	-	-	-	-
Middle Atlantic	-	-	+	+	-	-
East North Central	+	+	+	+	+	+
West North Central	-	-	-	-	-	-
South Atlantic	+	-	-	-	-	-
East South Central	+	+	-	-	-	-
West South Central	+	+	+	-	-	+
Mountain	-	-	+	-	-	-
Pacific Coast	-	+	+	+	+	+

Table 5.   Relative Growth of Holiness Churches and Parallel Growth of Other Religious Groups in Different Urban Income Areas, 1926-1936.

	Holiness	Holiness Methodist	Methodist	Roman Catholic
High Income Areas	+	-	+	+
Medium Income Areas	-	+	-	-
Low Income Areas	-	-	+	+

Table 6.   Relative Growth of Holiness Churches and Parallel General Population Growth by Demographic Groups in Different Urban Income Areas, 1926-1936.

	Holiness	Native White	Colored	Foreign Born	Foreign Mixed Parentage	Total U. S. Population
High Income Areas	+	+	+	+	+	+
Middle Income Areas	-	-	+	-	-	-
Low Income Areas	-	+	-	-	-	+

Table 7.   Relative Growth of Holiness Churches and Parallel Growth of Other Religious Groups in Cities of 25,000 Population and Over by Economic Specialties, 1926-1936.

	Holiness	Holiness Methodist	Methodist	Roman Catholic
High (20%) Manufacturing	+	+	+	-
Medium Manufacturing	-	-	+	-
Low (20%) Manufacturing	-	+	+	+
Wholesale Trade Centers	-	-	-	-
Retail Trade Centers	+		+	+
Trade Centers	-	-	+	+
Maintenance Trade Centers	+	+	+	+

(Table 7, continued)

	Holiness	Holiness Methodist	Methodist	Roman Catholic
Education Centers	-	-	+	+
Public Administration Centers	+	+	+	+
Transportation Centers	+	+	-	+
Entertainment and Recreation Centers	-	-	-	-

Table 8. Relative Growth of Holiness Churches and Parallel General Population Growth by Demographic Groups in Cities of 25,000 Population and Over by Economic Specialties, 1926-1936.

	Holiness	Native White	Colored	Foreign Born	Foreign, Mixed Parentage	Total U.S. Population
High (20%) Manufacturing	+	+	+	+	+	+
Medium Manufacturing	-	-	-	+	-	-
Low (20%) Manufacturing	-	+	+	-	+	+
Wholesale Trade Centers	-	-	+	+	+	-
Retail Trade Centers	+	+	+	+	+	+
Trade Centers	-	-	-	-	-	-
Maintenance Trade Centers	+	+	+	-	+	+
Education Centers	-	+	-	-	+	+
Public Administration Centers	+	-	-	-	-	+
Transportation Centers	+	-	-	-	-	-
Entertainment and Recreation Centers	-	+	+	+	+	+

APPENDIX VI

Three Tables: Holiness and Other Church Membership in Cities

Table 9.   Urban Extent of Church Membership in 1926 and 1936: Percentage in Cities of 25,000 Population and Over.

1926

	Total	Omitting New York	Omitting New York Boston Philadelphia Baltimore Charleston
United States Population	37. 29	31. 95	28. 76
Roman Catholics	58. 52	49. 20	43. 94
Holiness (grouped)	30. 91	30. 23	29. 93
Nazarene	31. 78	30. 94	30. 63
Pilgrim Holiness	24. 49	24. 49	24. 49
Holiness Methodist (grouped)	18. 90	18. 71	18. 61
Methodist (grouped)	22. 81	21. 99	20. 25

1936

	Total	Omitting New York	Omitting New York Boston Philadelphia Baltimore Charleston
United States Population	40. 01	34. 37	31. 44
Roman Catholics	58. 69	50. 90	45. 74
Holiness (grouped)	34. 91	34. 52	34. 25
Nazarene	35. 52	35. 15	34. 90
Pilgrim Holiness	32. 57	32. 47	32. 47
Holiness Methodist (grouped)	24. 15	24. 03	23. 75
Methodist (grouped)	28. 90	26. 77	25. 05

Table 10:   Growth of Holiness Membership, 1906-1936, in Rural Areas and in Cities of Various Sizes.

	1906	1916	1926	1936
In places of				
Less than 2, 500			32, 866	51, 663
	8, 301	31, 274		
2, 500-25, 000			27, 052	56, 356
25, 000-50, 000	603	2, 384	7, 513	13, 739
50, 000-100, 000	844	1, 054	6, 322	11, 513
100, 000-250, 000	572	2, 235	4, 349	14, 219
250, 000-500, 000	2, 514	2, 187	3, 512	8, 309
500, 000-1, 000, 000	0	150	3, 098	2, 456
Over 1, 000, 000	970	1, 391	1, 501	4, 247
Total no. of				
Holiness Members	13, 804	42, 675	86, 248	166, 339
In places of				
25, 000 and over	5, 503	9, 401*	26, 352	58, 108

*Data incomplete and only partially specified

Table 11:   Growth of Holiness Membership, 1906-1936, Expressed As a Ratio of Holiness Members to the General Population in Rural Areas and in Cities of Various Sizes.

	1906	1916	1926	1936
In places of				
Less than 2, 500			1:160, 000	1:106, 000
	1:145, 000	1:48, 000		
2, 500-25, 000			1:67, 000	1:37, 000
25, 000-50, 000	1:566, 000	1:191, 000	1:92, 000	1:50, 000
50, 000-100, 000	1:408, 000	1:448, 000	1:93, 000	1:50, 000
100, 000-250, 000	1:709, 000	1:254, 000	1:162, 000	1:69, 000
250, 000-500, 000	1:135, 000	1:194, 000	1:178, 000	1:56, 000
500, 000-1, 000, 000	0	1:3, 079, 000	1:770, 000	1:295, 000

(Table 12.) Holiness Church Membership, 1906-1936,
by State and Region (total in cities of 25, 000 population
and over in parentheses)

United States Totals		Nazarenes		Pilgrims		Others **	
1906	13,804 (5,503)	6,657	(4,158)	2,774	(62)	4,373	(1,283)
1916	42,675 (9,401)*	32,259	(8,863)	5,276	(344)*	5,140	(194)*
1926	86,248 (26,352)	63,558	(19,890)	15,040	(3,673)	7,650	(2,789)
1936	166,339 (58,108)	136,227	(47,700)	20,124	(6,511)	9,988	(3,897)

New England Totals		Nazarenes		Pilgrims		Others	
1906	1,484 (809)	1,399	(764)	40		45	(45)
1916	2,300 (1,327)	2,300	(1,327)	....		....	
1926	2,460 (1,486)	2,426	(1,452)	....		34	(34)
1936	4,377 (2,295)	4,264	(2,182)	24	(24)	89	(89)

Maine							
1906	94	94		....		....	
1916	297 (23)	297	(23)	....		....	
1926	409 (59)	409	(59)	....		....	
1936	923 (90)	923	(90)	....		....	

New Hampshire							
1906	53 (27)	53	(27)	....		....	
1916	171 (50)	171	(50)	....		....	
1926	68	68		....		....	
1936	193 (52)	193	(52)	....		....	

Vermont							
1906	112	112		....		....	
1916	132	132		....		....	
1926	118	118		....		....	
1936	186	186		....		....	

Massachusetts							
1906	1,011 (687)	926	(642)	40		45	(45)
1916	1,319 (1,060)	1,319	(1,000)	....		....	
1926	1,470 (1,239)	1,438	(1,207)	....		32	(32)
1936	2,207 (1,734)	2,167	(1,694)	24	(24)	16	(16)

Rhode Island							
1906	133 (95)	133	(95)	....		....	
1916	198 (130)	198	(130)	....		....	
1926	139 (126)	137	(124)	....		2	(2)
1936	346 (293)	313	(260)	....		33	(33)

*Data probably incomplete
**Heavenly Recruit Church, Hephzibah Faith Missionary Association,
Holiness Church, Metropolitan Church Association, Missionary
Bands of the World, Missionary Church Association, Peniel Mis-
sions, Pillar of Fire
....Data not reported

	Totals		Nazarenes		Pilgrims		Others	
Connecticut								
1906	81		81		••••		••••	
1916	183	(64)	183	(64)	••••		••••	
1926	256	(98)	256	(98)	••••		••••	
1936	522	(241)	482	(201)	••••		••••	
Middle Atlantic								
1906	1,177	(591)	937	(591)	184		56	
1916	3,270	(966)	1,962	(966)	420		888	
1926	5,693	(1,759)	2,646	(929)	1,461	(321)	1,586	(509)
1936	12,980	(3,756)	7,213	(2,413)	5,040	(840)	2,727	(503)
New York								
1906	539	(335)	539	(335)	••••		••••	
1916	1,101	(714)	1,011	(714)	35		55	
1926	1,742	(872)	1,150	(659)	486	(132)	106	(81)
1936	3,096	(1,541)	1,948	(1,062)	911	(336)	237	(143)
New Jersey								
1906	96		20		20		56	
1916	635	(25)	93	(25)	••••		542	
1926	969	(96)	156	(26)	68		745	(70)
1936	2,347	(309)	425	(122)	152	(41)	1,770	(146)
Pennsylvania								
1906	542	(256)	378	(256)	164		••••	
1916	1,534	(227)	858	(227)	385		291	
1926	2,982	(791)	1,340	(244)	907	(189)	735	(358)
1936	7,537	(1,907)	4,840	(1,229)	1,977	(464)	720	(214)
East North Central								
1906	5,147	(1,261)	951	(571)	1,300	(62)	2,896	(628)
1916	9,326	(2,292)	5,183	(2,063)	1,941	(135)*	2,202	(94)*
1926	25,909	(9,947)	15,931	(6,477)	7,207	(2,205)	2,771	(1265)
1936	52,656	(22,294)	40,260	(16,990)	8,899	(3,623)	3,497	(1681)
Ohio								
1906	785	(28)	13		412	(28)	360	
1916	2,605	(347)	1,418	(347)	750		437	
1926	7,600	(2,660)	4,990	(1,780)	1,941	(591)	669	(289)
1936	18,817	(7,352)	14,984	(5,474)	2,950	(1,491)	883	(387)
Indiana								
1906	2,194	(452)	141		370	(19)	1,683	(433)
1916	2,412	(485)	1,141	(391)	539		732	(94)
1926	9,974	(3,297)	5,302	(1,911)	3,653	(961)	1,019	(425)
1936	17,311	(4,901)	12,277	(3,257)	3,670	(993)	1,364	(651)

Illinois

	Totals		Nazarenes		Pilgrims		Others	
1906	1,062	(681)	797	(571)	....		265	(110)
1916	1,906	(942)	1,756	(942)	....		150	
1926	4,005	(1,850)	3,463	(1,677)	348		194	(173)
1936	7,571	(2,824)	6,706	(2,505)	357		508	(319)

Michigan

	Totals		Nazarenes		Pilgrims		Others	
1906	710	(30)	....		513	(15)	192	(15)
1916	1,844	(445)	746	(310)	619	(135)	479	
1926	3,421	(1,972)	1,767	(997)	1,265	(653)	389	(322)
1936	7,915	(4,638)	5,560	(3,220)	1,922	(1,139)	433	(279)

Wisconsin

	Totals		Nazarenes		Pilgrims		Others	
1906	396	(70)	....		....		396	(70)
1916	554	(73)	122	(73)	33		399	
1926	909	(168)	409	(112)	....		500	(56)
1936	1,042	(347)	733	(302)	....		309	(45)

West North Central

	Totals		Nazarenes		Pilgrims		Others	
1906	636	(34)	142	(34)	106		388	
1916	4,413	(534)	3,940	(534)	105		368	
1926	10,219	(2,206)	8,422	(1,920)	993	(89)	804	(197)
1936	18,114	(4,659)	15,911	(4,334)	1,391	(275)	812	(50)

Minnesota

	Totals		Nazarenes		Pilgrims		Others	
1906	20		....		....		20	
1916	18		13		....		5	
1926	539	(191)	468	(172)	....		71	(19)
1936	962	(262)	949	(249)	....		13	(13)

Iowa

	Totals		Nazarenes		Pilgrims		Others	
1906	221		23		55		143	
1916	944	(96)	765	(96)	....		179	
1926	1,797	(463)	1,350	(408)	....		447	(55)
1936	2,786	(1,011)	2,568	(1,011)	19		199	

Missouri

	Totals		Nazarenes		Pilgrims		Others	
1906	46		....		....		46	
1916	903	(242)	903	(242)	....		....	
1926	2,130	(838)	1,986	(744)	139	(89)	5	(5)
1936	4,433	(1,445)	4,108	(1,297)	316	(139)	9	(9)

North Dakota

	Totals		Nazarenes		Pilgrims		Others	
1906	....		....		....		....	
1916	201		201		....		....	
1926	857		857		....		....	
1936	1,072	(42)	1,072	(42)	....		....	

South Dakota Totals		Nazarenes		Pilgrims		Others	
1906	....	....		....		....	
1916	112	112		....		....	
1926	463 (31)	463 (31)		....		....	
1936	605 (20)	462 (20)		....		143	

Nebraska							
1906	87	....		....		87	
1916	587 (75)	556 (75)		....		31	
1926	1,125 (211)	823 (161)		252		50	(50)
1936	1,767 (288)	1,319 (260)		151		297	(28)

Kansas							
1906	262 (34)	119 (34)		51		92	
1916	1,648 (121)	1,390 (121)		105		153	
1926	3,308 (472)	2,475 (404)		602		231	(68)
1936	6,489 (1,591)	5,433 (1,455)		905	(136)	151	

South Atlantic							
1906	1,243 (166)	248 (166)		995		....	
1916	3,058 (363)	887 (154)		2,149	(209)	22	
1926	5,323 (1,342)	1,976 (883)		3,214	(353)	133	(106)
1936	12,741 (4,492)	8,119 (3,447)		4,371	(818)	251	(227)

Delaware							
1906	168	....		168		....	
1916	77	47		30		....	
1926	371	63		308		....	
1936	583	182 (47)		401		583	(47)

Maryland							
1906	488	82		406		....	
1916	657 (40)	217 (40)		440		....	
1926	769 (186)	294 (166)		455		20	(20)
1936	1,684 (406)	1,003 (406)		681		....	

District of Columbia							
1906	166 (166)	166 (166)		....		....	
1916	44 (44)	44 (44)		....		....	
1926	100 (100)	100 (100)		....		....	
1936	270 (270)	210 (210)		....		60	(60)

Virginia							
1906	....	....		....		....	
1916	436 (168)	135 (70)		301	(98)	....	
1926	727 (333)	268 (197)		459	(136)	....	
1936	1,591 (565)	806 (456)		722	(46)	63	(63)

West Virginia

	Totals		Nazarenes		Pilgrims		Others	
1906	82		••••		82		••••	
1916	466	(111)	98		368	(111)	••••	
1926	774	(195)	352	(25)	422	(170)	••••	
1936	3,082	(666)	2,483	(639)	599	(27)	••••	

North Carolina

	Totals		Nazarenes		Pilgrims		Others	
1906	339		••••		339		••••	
1916	1,010		••••		1,010		••••	
1926	1,687	(140)	117	(93)	1,570	(47)	••••	
1936	2,435	(1,056)	467	(311)	1,968	(745)	••••	

South Carolina

	Totals		Nazarenes		Pilgrims		Others	
1906	••••		••••		••••		••••	
1916	••••		••••		••••		••••	
1926	16		16		••••		••••	
1936	213	(36)	213	(36)	••••		••••	

Georgia

	Totals		Nazarenes		Pilgrims		Others	
1906	••••		••••		••••		••••	
1916	230		230		••••		••••	
1926	448	(89)	442	(83)	••••		6	(6)
1936	1,246	(586)	1,246	(586)	••••		••••	

Florida

	Totals		Nazarenes		Pilgrims		Others	
1906	••••		••••		••••		••••	
1916	138		116		••••		22	
1926	431	(299)	324	(219)	••••		107	(80)
1936	1,637	(717)	1,509	(613)	••••		128	(104)

East South Central

	Totals		Nazarenes		Pilgrims		Others	
1906	172		••••		142		30	
1916	4,461	(594)	3,453	(594)	463		545	
1926	6,720	(1,492)	5,527	(1,379)	954	(81)	239	(32)
1936	12,839	(4,354)	11,612	(4,135)	987	(219)	240	

Kentucky

	Totals		Nazarenes		Pilgrims		Others	
1906	142		••••		142		••••	
1916	1,563	(163)	728	(163)	463		372	
1926	2,373	(443)	1,405	(366)	954	(63)	14	(14)
1936	4,243	(1,325)	3,412	(1,117)	831	(208)	••••	

Tennessee

	Totals		Nazarenes		Pilgrims		Others	
1906	30		••••		••••		30	
1916	2,075	(412)	1,903	(412)	••••		173	
1926	2,821	(984)	2,596	(966)	••••		225	(18)
1936	5,793	(2,753)	5,416	(2,742)	137	(11)	240	

Alabama

	Totals		Nazarenes		Pilgrims	Others
1906	....		....		....	....
1916	589	(19)	589	(19)	....	....
1926	1,299	(47)	1,299	(47)	....	....
1936	2,385	(258)	2,366	(258)	19	....

Mississippi

1906	....		....		....	....
1916	233		233		....	....
1926	227		227		....	....
1936	418	(18)	418	(18)	....	....

West South Central

1906	74		47		7	20
1916	8,542	(540)	8,479	(540)	63	....
1926	13,148	(1,781)	13,045	(1,781)	103	....
1936	24,918	(5,787)	24,696	(5,787)	222	....

Arkansas

1906	....		....		....	....
1916	1,613	(76)	1,613	(76)	....	....
1926	2,024	(309)	2,024	(309)	....	....
1936	3,963	(874)	3,931	(874)	32	....

Louisiana

1906	....		....		....	....
1916	214	(60)	214	(60)	....	....
1926	471	(131)	471	(131)	....	....
1936	1,142	(447)	1,127	(447)	15	....

Oklahoma

1906	7		....		7	....
1916	2,894	(52)	2,831	(52)	63	....
1926	5,697	(408)	5,594	(408)	103	....
1936	11,119	(1,321)	10,992	(1,321)	127	....

Texas

1906	67		47		....	20
1916	3,821	(352)	3,821	(352)	....	....
1926	4,956	(933)	4,956	(933)	....	....
1936	8,694	(3,145)	8,646	(3,145)	48	....

Mountain

1906	317	(187)	80		....		237	(187)
1916	1,126	(216)	926	(116)	100		100	(100)
1926	5,310	(1,385)	4,221	(700)	504	(170)	585	(515)
1936	9,761	(2,683)	8,171	(1,625)	580	(222)	1,010	(836)

Montana

	Totals		Nazarenes		Pilgrims		Others	
1906	....		....		....		....	
1916	69		69		....		....	
1926	202		202		....		....	
1936	386		386		....		....	

Idaho

	Totals		Nazarenes		Pilgrims		Others	
1906	30		30		....		....	
1916	425		325		100		....	
1926	1,435		1,342		93		....	
1936	2,712		2,570		142		....	

Wyoming

	Totals		Nazarenes		Pilgrims		Others	
1906	....		....		....		....	
1916	....		....		....		....	
1926	83		68		15		....	
1936	370		370		....		....	

Colorado

	Totals		Nazarenes		Pilgrims		Others	
1906	237	(187)	50		....		237	(187)
1916	470	(216)	370	(116)	....		100	(100)
1926	2,586	(1,080)	1,728	(518)	384	(158)	474	(404)
1936	4,289	(1,920)	3,061	(1,082)	370	(154)	858	(684)

New Mexico

	Totals		Nazarenes		Pilgrims		Others	
1906	....		....		....		....	
1916	69		69		....		....	
1926	450		450		....		....	
1936	832	(101)	832	(101)	....		....	

Arizona

	Totals		Nazarenes		Pilgrims		Others	
1906	50		....		....		50	
1916	93		93		....		....	
1926	522	(273)	399	(150)	12	(12)	111	(111)
1936	1,089	(620)	894	(425)	68	(68)	127	(127)

Utah

	Totals		Nazarenes		Pilgrims		Others	
1906	....		....		....		....	
1916	....		....		....		....	
1926	32	(32)	32	(32)	....		....	
1936	42	(42)	17	(17)	....		25	(25)

Nevada

	Totals		Nazarenes		Pilgrims		Others	
1906	....		....		....		....	
1916	....		....		....		....	
1926	....		....		....		....	
1936	41		41		....		....	

Pacific

	Totals		Nazarenes		Pilgrims		Others	
1906	3,646	(2,455)	2,853	(2,032)	....		793	(423)
1916	5,813	(2,569)	5,129	(2,569)	35		649	
1926	11,174	(4,954)	9,364	(4,369)	604	(454)	1,206	(131)
1936	17,712	(7,787)	15,981	(6,787)	610	(489)	1,121	(511)

Washington

1906	355	(221)	285	(171)	....		70	(50)
1916	1,011	(294)	976	(294)	35		....	
1926	1,832	(548)	1,742	(540)	9		81	(8)
1936	3,380	(945)	3,317	(898)	51	(35)	12	(12)

Oregon

1906	275	(150)	135	(75)	....		140	(75)
1916	773	(283)	773	(283)	....		....	
1926	1,533	(500)	1,507	(500)	26		....	
1936	2,831	(1,065)	2,793	(1,065)	38		....	

California

1906	3,016	(2,084)	2,433	(1,786)	....		583	(298)
1916	4,029	(1,992)	3,380	(1,992)	....		649	
1926	7,809	(4,091)	6,115	(3,514)	569	(454)	1,125	(123)
1936	10,501	(6,258)	9,871	(5,270)	521	(489)	1,109	(499)

APPENDIX VIII

Five Tables: Statistical Survey of Holiness
and Methodist Church Membership

Table 13. Selected Holiness and Methodist Churches and Average
Membership per Church, by Denomination, 1906-1936 (churches-
members) [NR = no report].

Holiness bodies:	1906	1916	1926	1936
Church of the Nazarene	100-67	866-37	1, 444-44	2, 197-62
Heavenly Recruit Church	27-35	NR	NR	NR
Hephzibah Faith Missionary Association	10-29	12-29	14-35	20-35
Holiness Church	NR	33-28	32-27	15-27
Metropolitan Church Association	6-78	7-101	40-28	14-69
Missionary Bands of the World	16-30	10-22	11-22	6-37
Missionary Church Association	30-42	25-62	34-73	47-78
Peniel Missions	11-64	9-29	NR	NR
Pilgrim Holiness Church	74-37	169-31	441-34	510-39
Pillar of Fire	3-77	21-54	48-51	46-88
Methodist bodies:				
Free Methodist Church	1, 541-21	1, 598-22	1, 375-26	1, 084-35
Wesleyan Methodist Church	591-34	579-36	619-35	565-39
Methodist Episcopal Church	29, 742-100	29, 315-127	26, 130-156	18, 349-191
Methodist Episcopal Church, South	17, 683-93	19, 184-110	18, 096-137	11, 454-180
Methodist Protestant Church	2, 825-63	2, 473-76	2, 239-86	1, 498-99

Table 14.   Total Membership of Selected Holiness and Methodist
Churches, by Denomination, 1906-1936 [NR = no report].

Holiness bodies:	1906	1916	1926	1936
Church of the Nazarene	6, 657	32, 259	63, 558	136, 227
Heavenly Recruit Church	938	NR	NR	NR
Hephzibah Faith Missionary Association	293	352	495	709
Holiness Church	NR	926	861	404
Metropolitan Church Association	466	704	1, 113	961
Missionary Bands of the World	487	218	241	222
Missionary Church Association	1, 256	1, 554	2, 498	3, 648
Peniel Missions	703	257	NR	NR
Pilgrim Holiness Church	2, 774	5, 276	15, 040	20, 124
Pillar of Fire	230	1, 129	2, 442	4, 044
Methodist bodies:				
Free Methodist Church	32, 838	35, 291	36, 374	37, 587
Wesleyan Methodist Church	20, 043	20, 778	21, 910	22, 017
Methodist Episcopal Church	2, 986, 000	3, 717, 000	4, 080, 000	3, 509, 000
Methodist Episcopal Church, South	1, 638, 000	2, 114, 000	2, 487, 000	2, 061, 000
Methodist Protestant Church	178, 000	186, 000	192, 000	148, 000

Table 15.   Holiness Church Membership in Cities of 25, 000 Population and Over, 1906 and 1916.

	1906	1916
Total membership:	13, 804	42, 675
Total, cities 25, 000 & over:	5, 503	9, 401
Membership by city:		
Baltimore, Md.		40 N*
Chicago, Ill.	635 MN*	701 N
Cincinnati, Ohio	28 P*	
Los Angeles, Cal.	1, 768 MN	1, 425 N
Milwaukee, Wis.	70 M	9 N

(Table 15, continued)

	1906	1916
New York, N. Y.	335 N	598 N
Philadelphia, Pa.		92 N
Pittsburgh, Pa.	211 N	110 N
San Francisco, Cal.	256 MN	49 N
Washington, D. C.	166 N	44 N
Birmingham, Ala.		19 N
Cambridge, Mass.	166 N	93 N
Columbus, Ohio		185 N
Dayton, Ohio		122 N
Denver, Colo.	187 M	155 MN
Detroit, Mich.	15 M	
Grand Rapids, Mich.	15 P	155 N
Indianapolis, Ind.	290 M	306 N
Kansas City, Mo.		234 N
Louisville, Ky.		127 N
Lowell, Mass.	129 N	211 N
Nashville, Tenn.		400 N
Oakland, Cal.	60 N	83 N
Portland, Ore.	150 MN	283 N
Providence, R. I.	95 N	130 N
Rochester, N. Y.		21 N
Seattle, Wash.	75 MN	99 N
Spokane, Wash.	146 N	175 N
Syracuse, N. Y.		70 N
Worcester, Mass.		27 N
Akron, Ohio		40 N
Camden, N. J.		25 N
Dallas, Tex.		104 N
Evansville, Ind.	19 P	85 N
Ft. Wayne, Ind.	50 M	94 M
Hartford, Conn.		40 N
Lynn, Mass.	112 N	154 N
Manchester, N. H.	27 N	50 N
New Bedford, Mass.		57 N
Norfolk, Va.		70 N
Oklahoma City, Okla.		52 N
Peoria, Ill.	46 M	
Portland, Me.		23 N
St. Joseph, Mo.		8 N
San Antonio, Tex.		112 N
Somerville, Mass.	45 M	55 N
Tacoma, Wash.		20 N
Wichita, Kans.		65 N

(Table 15, continued)

	1906	1916
Allentown, Pa.	45 N	
Battle Creek Mich.		88 P
Berkeley, Cal.		91 N
Bloomington, Ill.		50 N
Cedar Rapids, Iowa		9 N
Colorado Springs, Colo.		61 N
Council Bluffs, Iowa		21 N
Danville, Ill.		89 N
Decatur, Ill.		102 N
El Paso, Tex.		55 N
Everett, Mass.		80 N
Fitchburg, Mass.		76 N
Haverhill, Mass.	84 N	135 N
Huntington, W. Va.		111 P
Knoxville, Tenn.		12 N
Lansing, Mich.		202 NP
Lincoln, Neb.		75 N
Little Rock, Ark.		76 N
McKeesport, Pa.		25 N
Malden, Mass.	115 N	142 N
Mount Vernon, N. Y.		25 N
Newport, Ky.		36 N
Pasadena, Cal.		297 N
Racine, Wis.		64 N
Roanoke, Va.		98 P
Salem, Mass.	36 N	30 N
San Diego, Cal.		47 N
Shreveport, La.		60 N
Sioux City, Iowa		66 N
Stamford, Conn.		24 N
Terre Haute, Ind.	93 M	
Topeka, Kans.	34 N	56 N
Waco, Tex.		81 N

*N = Church of the Nazarene (Pentecostal Church of the Nazarene)
 P = Pilgrim Holiness Church (International Apostolic Holiness
     Church)
 M = Peniel Missions; Hephzibah Faith Missionary Association;
     Heavenly Recruit Church; Metropolitan Church Association;
     Missionary Church Association; Pentecost Bands of the
     World; and Pentecostal Union.

Table 16.   Number and Type of Places of Worship of Selected Holiness Denominations, and Total Number and Type of Places of Religious Worship in the United States, 1906 and 1916 (churches-halls) [NR = no report].

Holiness bodies:	1906	1916
Church of the Nazarene	69-26	591-122
Heavenly Recruit Church	8-15	NR
Hephzibah Faith Holiness Association	9-1	11-1
Holiness Church	NR	28-1
Metropolitan Church Association	4-2	1-6
Missionary Bands of the World	15-1	10-0
Missionary Church Association	19-12	20-5
Peniel Missions	1-10	2-7
Pilgrim Holiness Church	41-31	116-43
Pillar of Fire Church	3-0	8-11
Free Methodist Church	1, 120-239	1, 198-179
Wesleyan Methodist Church	477-64	515-37
All religious bodies:	185, 000-15, 000	200, 000-14, 000

Table 17.   Founding Dates of Congregations of Selected Holiness Denominations as Reported in 1906.

Holiness bodies:	Total no. of congreg. in 1906	Number reporting	Number formed in 1880- 1889	1890- 1899	1900- 1906
Church of the Nazarene	100	96	3	23	70
Heavenly Recruit Church	27	26	0	16	10
Hephzibah Faith Missionary Association	10	10	1	3	6
Metropolitan Church Association	6	6	0	1	5
Missionary Bands of the World	16	15	0	6	9
Missionary Church Association	32	29	1	8	20
Peniel Missions	11	11	3	5	3
Pilgrim Holiness Church	74	72	0	3	69
Pillar of Fire	3	3	0	0	3
Free Methodist Church Organized before 1880: 225	1, 553	1, 334	289	428	392
Wesleyan Methodist Church Organized before 1880: 197	594	513	74	103	139

INDEX

215